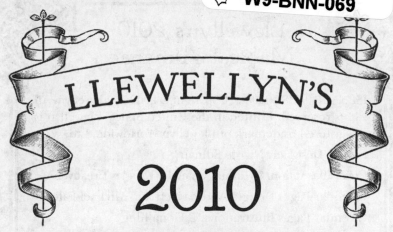

LLEWELLYN'S

2010

Magical Almanac

Featuring
Chandra Alexandre, Elizabeth Barrette, Nancy V. Bennett,
Deborah Blake, Calantirniel, Dallas Jennifer Cobb,
Raven Digitalis, Ellen Dugan, Denise Dumars,
Sybil Fogg, Lily Gardner, Abel Gomez, Magenta Griffith,
Melanie Harris, Elizabeth Hazel, James Kambos, Lupa,
Estha McNevin, Mickie Mueller, Paniteowl,
Diana Rajchel, Janina Renée, Suzanne Ress,
Laurel Reufner, Michelle Skye, Harmony Usher,
Tess Whitehurst, and Gail Wood.

*Including a special twentieth-anniversary introduction
and the original introduction by Raymond Buckland.*

Llewellyn's 2010
Magical Almanac

ISBN 978-0-7387-0690-0. Copyright © 2009 by Llewellyn. All rights reserved. Printed in the United States. Llewellyn is a registered trademark of Llewellyn Worldwide, Ltd.

Editor/Designer: Nicole Edman

Cover Illustration: © Tammy Shanele/Langley Creative.

Calendar Pages Design: Andrea Neff and Michael Fallon

Calendar Pages Illustrations: © Fiona King

Interior Illustrations © Carol Coogan: pages 17, 26, 28, 67, 85, 108, 111, 112, 144, 211, 232, 278, 281, 317, 340, 343, 346; © Kathleen Edwards: pages 20, 57, 63, 125, 128, 213, 214, 262, 302, 327, 328; © Melissa Gay: pages 73, 95, 98, 221, 305, 311; © Paul Hoffman: pages 48, 52, 88, 122, 246, 248, 252, 282, 285, 350; © Wen Hsu: pages 31, 34, 83, 135, 139, 227, 256, 293, 336; © Mickie Mueller: pages 38, 41, 44, 77, 101, 104, 238, 241, 269, 272, 322.

Illustration page 113 by Llewellyn Art Department.

Clip Art Illustrations: Dover Publications

Special thanks to Amber Wolfe for the use of daily color and incense correspondences. For more detailed information, please see *Personal Alchemy* by Amber Wolfe.

You can order Llewellyn annuals and books from *New Worlds*, Llewellyn's catalog. To request a free copy of the catalog, call toll-free 1-877-NEW-WRLD or visit our website at www.llewellyn.com.

Astrological data compiled and programmed by Rique Pottenger. Based on the earlier work of Neil F. Michelsen.

Llewellyn Worldwide
Dept. 0-978-7387-0690-0
2143 Wooddale Drive
Woodbury, MN 55125

Magick

"There are more things in Heaven and Earth, Horatio,
than are dreamt of in your philosophy."

Shakespeare—*Hamlet* (Act I, Scene V)

Science has barely scratched the surface of human knowledge. It is slow and ponderous, being by nature cautious and skeptical. It demands proof one hundred (if not one thousand) times over before any theory is accepted as fact. Any event or occurrence that cannot be immediately explained by previous scientific experiment and conclusive proof, does not fit under the scientific umbrella and is usually immediately discarded out of hand as impossible, as mistaken, or as outright charlatanism. Such questions as "Does *magick* really exist? And if it does, how does it work?" are unlikely to even be addressed.

More questions that get scant attention from the main scientific community are: Is there any real significance to the numerological equivalent of your name? Do you have the power to heal the sick from a distance? Can you create your own reality? Are there "entities" that can be conjured?

Yet there are many people who feel that these, and other similar questions, have already been answered and proven, though others think they never will be. The answers actually lie in our freedom to believe or to disbelieve, as we see fit. Belief is not a sign of gullibility, but a sign of honest inquiry, a desire to expand our horizons and not be limited by what we have been told to believe.

It is generally conceded that there are many as-yet-undiscovered forces of Nature, including those of the human mind. The mind is an incredibly powerful force in and of itself. *Magick* can be looked upon simply as a term for the use of some of these forces; and *Magicians* as people who know how to use these forces but who are not yet "accepted" by the scientific community.

Magick is as old as humankind itself. Martin del Rio, in 1592, said, "Magick is the art and power to produce extraordinary and marvellous effects by resort to an existing natural force." Aleister

3

Crowley said that magick is "a question of employing hitherto unknown forces in Nature."

A further distinction between a scientist and a Magician is that the latter seldom seeks to reveal his discoveries. Magick is traditionally shrouded in secrecy, one of the reasons for scientific skepticism. Paracelsus said that magick is "a great secret wisdom." The Magician frequently works as long and as hard on his theories as does the scientist, but when he gets results he goes to great pains to hide and protect them. In past centuries Magicians have employed secret forms of writing to safeguard their notes. *Theban, Malachim, Passing the River, Angelic, Runic,* were some of the styles used.

In the pages that follow we examine some of the many forms that Magick can take. We try to draw back the veil of secrecy, if only a fraction, to give a glimpse behind it. Egyptian Magick, Enochian, Shamanic, Wiccan . . . they are as varied as any other aspect of Nature. And each is as fascinating and as complex. With this brief introduction to the subject we hope to lead you to the hidden world, the world that science tries so hard to ignore.

The word "almanac" probably comes from an Arabic word meaning "to reckon," though it first appears in popular usage in the thirteenth century as the Latin *almanach.* Almanacs have actually been around since Egyptian times; the British Museum has a fragment of one, dating from three thousand years ago, giving dates for festivals, and lucky and unlucky days. Over two hundred years ago, in France, an *Almanac of the Devil* was very popular and stayed so for most of the eighteenth century.

This present *Magickal Almanac,* as an annual, represents a brief introduction to the magickal world. But, as is the nature of an almanac, it will be back again next year, with additional insights and more tidbits for you. And the year after that. Let us know what you would like to see in the almanac, where *your* interests lie, so that we can address them.

—*Raymond Buckland*

Originally printed in *Llewellyn's 1990 Magickal Almanac*

Twenty Years of Magical Living

Twenty years. Two decades. That's a long time! Now that *Llewellyn's Magical Almanac* is almost old enough to have a drink in any U.S. state, it's a good time to reflect on the past twenty years.

A lot has changed since Raymond Buckland so deftly introduced the *Magickal Almanac* in 1990, both in the mundane world and the magical world. Likely the biggest change is technological: the Internet has thoroughly replaced the old card catalog, and information is only a few clicks away. The amazing World Wide Web has greatly benefited alternative ideas and beliefs—the broom closet isn't nearly so small with the entire Internet in your lap. Articles that once had nowhere to go in mainstream publications have a ready-made home in Pagan websites, e-zines, and chatrooms. Connecting with others who share your ideas, even if they are half a continent away, has never been easier.

The last decades have also seen a great mainstreaming of alternative beliefs. From allowing Wiccan pentacles on grave markers in national cemeteries to permitting Pagan students at some colleges to be absent on holidays, our beliefs have reached a greater acceptance than ever before. Yoga isn't just for young hippies these days, but for business people and elderly people looking to improve fitness and state of mind. The connections between mind, body, and spirit continue to gain momentum in the scientific and popular world, so that ideas like the Law of Attraction are even being taught in once-buttoned-down business settings (although the terminology may vary). The world appears to be paying more and more attention to Mother Earth and Nature in recent years, and environmentalism—or all things "green"—is suddenly in style.

And let's not forget the pop culture wave of magical characters: Buffy, Harry, and the Halliwell sisters among them. Whether we've loved or hated them, these fictional characters brought real attention to the subject of magic. While this integration has been sidetracked by some misguided folks along the way, growing acceptance of all religions and beliefs has had a positive effect. We can embrace those who've been awakened to the magical side of life while practicing patience with those who haven't yet quite "gotten it."

But there are also many things that have not changed over the years. Magic is still a mysterious force that both fascinates and inspires us. Even if you're one of the many who read and collect each year's *Magical Almanac*, there are still unknown facets of magic left to explore. Bringing some of those facets to you continues to be our aim with this annual. Our topics circle the globe and span the centuries. From practical applications, such as travel and budgeting, to introductions to possibly unknown ideas, such as Tantra and Huna, we hope to show you the magical world in all its glory. And although the world of magic is endlessly diverse, it can also bring us together by revealing how alike we really are, such as the connections between Christianity and Santeria.

Today's life is often hectic and nonstop. There often seem to be too few hours in the day! The articles here can offer you a short break—take a few minutes to relax with a practical new idea or transport yourself to another part of the world to learn about their gods and goddesses. We hope you'll find a few ideas that move you to further exploration. And we hope you'll continue to be a reader of Llewellyn's annuals, year after year. As Raymond wrote so long ago, let us know what you'd like to see here. Although the title is *Llewellyn's Magical Almanac*, this book ultimately belongs to you, our readers.

About the Authors

CHANDRA ALEXANDRE is an initiated Tantrika and hereditary Witch whose practice and life are infused with a deep appreciation for the unseen realm, a belief in the importance of our ability to alter consciousness at will, reverence for nature, respect for Spirit in all its forms, and a commitment to doing the work of spirituality. She has worked since 1998 to help create a vehicle in the West for those seeking to embrace the ancient (yet living) embodied and goddess-centered spiritual traditions of India. This has manifested in the creation of SHARANYA (www.sharanya.org), a goddess temple run by a community in the San Francisco Bay Area, and the Sha'can tradition, a syncretism based on Hindu Tantra and witchcraft. Chandra holds a Ph.D. in philosophy and religion, a doctor of ministry degree, and an MBA in sustainable management.

ELIZABETH BARRETTE has been involved with the Pagan community for more than twenty years. She serves as the Dean of Studies at the Grey School of Wizardry (www.greyschool.info). Her book *Composing Magic* explains how to write your own spells and rituals. She lives in central Illinois and enjoys herbal landscaping and gardening for wildlife. Her other writing fields include speculative fiction and gender studies. Visit her LiveJournal "The Wordsmith's Forge" at: http://ysabetwordsmith.livejournal.com/.

NANCY V. BENNETT is a writer of more than 300 articles, essays, and poems. Her work has also been featured in *We'Moon*, *Silver Wheel*, and other Llewellyn publications. She does mainstream articles as well, normally centered around history or animals, two of her passions. She can be reached at nvbennett@shaw.ca. Currently, she is working on a collection of essays, spells, and poems from a Canadian Witch perspective.

DEBORAH BLAKE is a Wiccan High Priestess who has been leading her current group, Blue Moon Circle, for three and a half years. She is the author of *Circle, Coven & Grove: A Year of Magickal Practice* and *Everyday Witch A to Z*, both from Llewellyn. Deborah's short story, "Dead and (Mostly) Gone" was included in Llewellyn's 2008 *The Pagan Anthology of Short Fiction*. When not writing, Deborah runs The Artisans' Guild and works as a jewelry maker, tarot reader, an ordained minister, and an Intuitive Energy Healer. She lives in a 100-year-old farmhouse in rural upstate New York with five cats who supervise all her activities, both magickal and mundane.

CALANTIRNIEL has practiced many forms of natural spirituality since the early 1990s. She lives in western Montana with her husband and teenage daughter, while her older son is in college. She is a professional astrologer, tarot card reader, dowser, flower-essence creator, and practitioner, and she became a certified Master Herbalist in 2007. She has an organic garden, crochets professionally, and is co-creating Tië eldaliéva, the Elven Spiritual Path. www.myspace.com/aartiana

Life is what you make it, and **DALLAS JENNIFER COBB** has made a magical life in a waterfront village on the shores of Lake Ontario. Forever scheming novel ways to pay the bills, she currently teaches pilates, works in a library, and writes to finance long hours spent with her daughter, in nature, and on the water. A regular contributor to Llewellyn annuals, she wrote two novels this year with the support of National Novel Writing Month (www.NaNoWriMo.org). You can contact her at jennifer.cobb@live.com.ca.

RAVEN DIGITALIS (Montana) is the author of *Goth Craft*, *Shadow Magick Compendium*, and a forthcoming book of planetary spells, all from Llewellyn. He is a Neopagan Priest and co-founder of the "disciplined eclectic" shadow magick tradition and training coven

Opus Aima Obscuræ, and is a radio and club deejay. With his Priestess Estha, Raven holds community gatherings, tarot readings, and a variety of ritual services. The two also operate the metaphysical business Twigs and Brews. Raven holds a degree in anthropology from the University of Montana and is also an animal rights activist and black-and-white photographic artist. He has appeared on the cover of *newWitch* magazine, is a regular contributor to *The Ninth Gate* magazine, and has appeared on MTV News and the X-Zone Radio program. www.ravendigitalis.com or www.myspace.com/oakraven

ELLEN DUGAN, the "Garden Witch," is an award-winning author and psychic-clairvoyant. A practicing Witch for more than twenty-five years, she is the author of ten Llewellyn books: *Garden Witchery, Elements of Witchcraft, 7 Days of Magic, Cottage Witchery, Autumn Equinox, The Enchanted Cat, Herb Magic for Beginners, Natural Witchery, How to Enchant a Man,* and her newest book *A Garden Witch's Herbal* (May 2009). Ellen wholeheartedly encourages folks to personalize their spellcraft, to go outside and to get their hands dirty, so they can discover the wonder and magick of the natural world. Ellen and her family live in Missouri. www.ellendugan.com

Rev. **DENISE DUMARS** is a Priestess of Isis, Thoth, and Yemaya in the Fellowship of Isis. She is co-founder of the Iseum of Isis Paedusis, an Isian group that sponsors rituals at Pacific Unitarian Church in Rancho Palos Verdes, California. Denise is a college instructor, a writer, and a literary agent. When not busy with those activities, she lends her hands as a volunteer at Grauman's Egyptian Theatre on Hollywood Boulevard.

SYBIL FOGG has been a practicing Witch for more than twenty years. She's also a wife, mother, teacher, and belly dancer. Her family shares her passion for magic, dance, and all things Bollywood.

She lives in Portland, Maine, with her husband and their plethora of children.

LILY GARDNER continues to pursue and write about her lifelong passion for folklore and myth. In addition to writing for Llewellyn, she has written several short stories, a murder mystery, and is working on a book of saint folklore. Lily is an avid reader, gardener, skier, and hiker. She's been practicing witchcraft in the rainy but magnificent city of Portland, Oregon, for sixteen years.

ABEL R. GOMEZ is committed to walking a path of mystery, ecstasy, and wonder. A freelance writer in his spare time, he performs, sings, leads ritual, attends school, and worships Maa Kali in the San Francisco Bay Area. His magick is aimed at uncovering the beauty of the Earth and using it as a tool of transformation and deep healing. Abel currently studies Shakta Tantra with SHARANYA and is a member of the Reclaiming community of Witches.

MAGENTA GRIFFITH has been a Witch more than thirty years and a High Priestess for twenty years. She is a founding member of the coven Prodea, celebrating rituals since 1980. She presents classes and workshops at events around the Midwest. She shares her home with a small black cat and a large collection of books.

MELANIE HARRIS is the founder of United Witches, a global coven for magical people of all paths. She has written for many esoteric publications including *Pentacle Magazine*, *Circle Magazine*, and *Tarot Reflections*. Passionate about personalized magick, she teaches classes on tarot, witchcraft, and the occult.

ELIZABETH HAZEL is a noted astrologer and tarotist, author of *Tarot Decoded*, and creator of the *Whispering Tarot*. She is the editor of the American Tarot Association's Quarterly Journal, and writes the "Astro-Spell" column for *newWitch* magazine and other horoscope columns. Her nom de broom is Lady Vala Runesinger, and

she has attempted many experimental craft projects, charms, and spells with her coven. Liz has given lectures on tarot, astrology, and practical magic in the United States and Great Britain. www .kozmic-kitchen.com

JAMES KAMBOS was raised in Appalachia. As a boy he learned the folk magic traditions of rural Appalachia, as well as the folk magic of Greece as taught to him by his Greek grandmother. James is also an artist. He writes, paints, and gardens from his home in southern Ohio.

LUPA is a Pagan and neoshaman living in Portland, Oregon, with her husband and fellow author, Taylor Ellwood. She is the author of several books and numerous articles on Pagan and magical topics, primarily for intermediate to advanced practitioners. She is also an environmentalist and sustainability geek, and enjoys spending time in her garden talking to the plants, hiking in the Columbia River Gorge, and volunteering with various local non-profit organizations. www.thegreenwolf.com

ESTHA MCNEVIN (Montana) is a Neopagan priestess, author, and lecturer. She is the oracle of the Opus Aima Obscurae tradition and is passionate about symbolic languages and ancient history. In addition to offering cottage-craft classes and public rituals for the sabbats, Estha hosts personal women's divination rituals each Dark Moon and holds private spiritual consultations and tarot readings. www.myspace.com/twigsandbrews

MICKIE MUELLER is an award-winning Pagan spiritual artist. She is Co-High Priestess of Coven of the Greenwood and an ordained Pagan Minister. In addition she has been a Reiki healing master/ teacher in the Usui Shiki Royoho tradition since 2001. Mickie is the illustrator of the critically acclaimed divination decks, *The Well Worn Path* and *The Hidden Path*. She is also the writer and

illustrator of the upcoming *The Voice of the Trees: A Celtic Ogham Oracle*. Mickie is a regular Llewellyn contributor and her art is published internationally. www.mickiemuellerart.com

PANITEOWL, Jacci Sutton, simply known as "Owl" in the Pagan Community, lives in the foothills of the Appalachians in northeast Pennsylvania. She and her husband, Will, have fifty-six acres of natural woodland and are in the process of developing a Private Retreat for Spiritual Awareness. They host two annual events, and Jacci is co-coordinator of two annual events in Virginia. She is founder and Elder High Priestess of the Mystic Wicca Tradition, with covens throughout New England. Jacci has given workshops at Pagan events on the East Coast and Canada. Her articles and poetry have been published in various Pagan periodicals and Web sites and Llewellyn publications. www.cronespeak.com

DIANA RAJCHEL lives in northeast Minneapolis, well within view of the city skyline. She owns Magickal Realism natural perfumery and writes full time. She has ambitions of converting her balcony to its own city jungle and at any given time she shares her home with a few robots. http://magickalrealism.etsy.com or www.dianarajchel.com

JANINA RENÉE is a scholar of folklore, psychology, medical anthropology, the material culture of magic, ritual studies, history, and literature. Her award-winning books include *Tarot Spells*, *Tarot: Your Everyday Guide*, *Tarot for a New Generation*, and *By Candlelight*. Janina continues to work on book projects, with ongoing research exploring the ways folk magic and medicinal techniques can apply to modern problems, including the modulation of Asperger's Syndrome and other neurosensory processing problems.

SUZANNE RESS has been writing nonfiction and fiction for more than twenty-five years. She is an accomplished self-taught gardener,

beekeeper, silversmith, and mosaicist. She lives in the woods at the foot of the alps in northern Italy with her husband, daughter, two dogs, three horses, and an elusive red stag.

LAUREL REUFNER lives in gorgeous Athens County, Ohio, with her husband and two daughters. Attracted to topics of history and mythology, she is slowly working on her first book. www .spiritrealm.com/laurelreufner

MICHELLE SKYE, a practicing Witch for more than ten years and author of *Goddess Alive!* and *Goddess Afoot!* (both from Llewellyn), has been working with the Fey since she was a child. Although solitary, Michelle presents workshops and classes in southeastern Massachussetts and at Womongathering, a Goddess festival in Pennsylvania. An ordained minister (Universal Life Church), she performs legal handfastings, weddings, and other spiritual rites. Michelle shares her home with elfy husband Michael and the little Witch-in-training Neisa.

HARMONY USHER is a country mouse living in the city who spends her days writing, researching, and practicing social work. She shares her life with two beautiful children and two mischievous animal companions.

TESS WHITEHURST is an eclectic and (mostly) solitary Witch. She lives in the strange and mystical enclave of Los Angeles called Venice Beach with her musical boyfriend and their two feline babies. Her writings—both fiction and nonfiction—reveal and celebrate the inherent magic in the seemingly mundane.

GAIL WOOD has been a Witch and priestess for nearly thirty years. She teaches many topics and is a Wiccan High Priestess in the RavenMyst Circle. She lives near Ithaca, New York, with her partner, Mouse, and their two dogs. www.rowdygoddess.com or darkmoonwitch@earthlink.net

Table of Contents

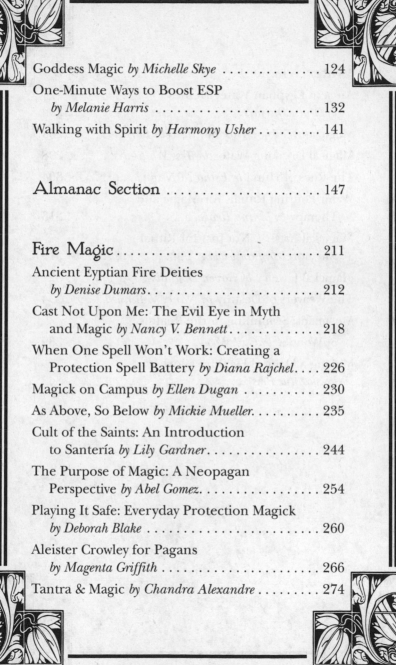

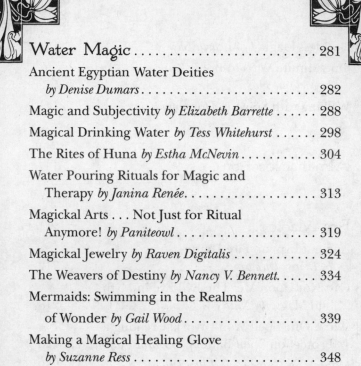

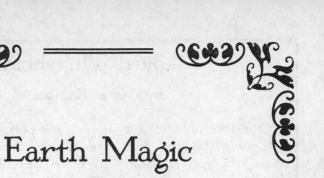

Earth Magic

Magical Thresholds

by James Kambos

The thresholds of our homes are portals for magical energy. Whether it's a window, a porch, or a front door, these architectural features are more than mere necessities; they also serve as entry points for the flow of magical energy.

This belief is very old. In ancient Rome for example, house spirits were thought to dwell in courtyards, and in Eastern Europe, ancestral spirits are sometimes still believed to inhabit dark spaces beneath the front porch.

Today, practitioners of the ancient art of feng shui place a great deal of importance on a home's threshold. Windows, porches, and doors are seen as openings that channel energy into and through the home, affecting all who live there.

You can easily turn a window, porch, or the front door of your home or apartment into a place of beauty, magic, and protection. No matter if you own a large home with a wrap-around porch or live in an apartment with a terrace, you can create a magical threshold that's cozy and protective.

Windows: The Eyes of Your Home

Windows are truly the eyes of your home. They provide us with light and beauty and can also help keep out negativity. Windows have been associated with magic for centuries. If you look closely at Moorish-influenced architecture for example, you'll notice that the windows are frequently made in different sizes and shapes. This is not just an architectural oddity; it was believed that varying the sizes and shapes of the windows would confuse evil spirits so they would not enter.

Windows have also been linked to one of the world's oldest magical beliefs, the evil eye. It was believed that the dreaded curse of the evil eye could pass into a dwelling through a window from the envious glare of a passerby. This belief was especially strong in England during the seventeenth and eighteenth centuries. During that time, reflective glass spheres know as Witch balls were displayed in windows in many homes. It was thought that the shiny reflective surface would return the spell of the evil eye back to the sender. This tradition lives on today in the form of garden gazing globes.

If you are fortunate enough to find an authentic Witch ball today, they can be pricey. Sometimes they still turn up in antique shops. To magically protect your windows using the same idea, but without the expense, try these suggestions.

You could find an inexpensive small gazing ball at a garden center. Magically cleanse and charge the ball with your intent, then display it near a front window. For an attractive look, place the gazing ball among a grouping of houseplants.

Glass ornaments available in gift stores and art galleries can also be used in windows to repel negativity. The best types have a swirl pattern, which is believed to trap any negative energy directed at your home and render it harmless.

Stained-glass pieces and suncatchers can also be used to protect your windows. I once found a suncatcher in the shape of a crescent New Moon; it was a beautiful shade of blue. It hung for many years in my bedroom window keeping out unwanted energy. Suncatchers made with glass or crystal beads also create a magical barrier. Their natural ability to capture and reflect light will help protect your home.

Porches: A Magical Sanctuary

Porches are transitional spaces between the outside world and our private inside living space. Even if you have only a front step instead of a porch, this area can easily become a magical sanctuary. With the right plants and decorative accents, your porch will become a haven for you and inviting for others, attracting positive energy at the same time.

To begin, your porch décor should echo the changing seasons. I've had neighbors tell me they enjoy seeing the seasonal changes I make to my front porch. Here are some ideas to keep you in step with the seasons.

Spring: Give your porch a good magical cleaning. Sprinkle some salt on the porch floor and give it a good sweeping.

Sweep away from your front door toward the street. Pot some pansies or primroses to attract or strengthen love—primroses also are used for protection. If you don't have a garden, buy a pot of daffodils and place them on your porch step—daffodils will draw fertility and love. If you have any wall space, hang a garden plaque in the shape of the Green Man—this nature deity represents spring and growth.

Summer: Nothing says summer like a simple terra-cotta pot planted with red geraniums. They are protective and attract good health. This is also the time to plant a pot of fiery, protective herbs (basil, dill, and rosemary are superb choices). The herbs will super-charge any space with protective energy and add zip to summer recipes. If you have a trellis connected to your porch, plant some morning glory vines, especially in blue. Morning glories will promote peace and provide shade.

Autumn: Now nature takes on the colors of a Persian carpet—gold, red, and rust dominate the landscape. These are colors of strength and protection; they're the colors of the sun. To bring these colors to your porch, plant a pot of chrysanthemums, used to protect against evil spirits. Or plant the flowers in a window-box with some ivy to trail over the sides. The ivy protects against negativity and doesn't mind the cooler temperatures of autumn. To promote fertility and protection, display some pumpkins and Indian corn in a basket. And for a bit of old-fashioned protection magic, hang a dried gourd in a corner of your porch.

Winter: The air may be crisp and icicles may hang from the eaves, but your porch can still be inviting. For good luck and protection, hang a swag of holly on your porch or layer it in a window-box. As a symbol of ever-lasting life, pine is the best choice. Combine it with holly in a window-box, a swag, or a wreath to symbolize eternity and protection. The fragrance of pine will purify your porch and a few pine needles sprinkled by your front steps will repel any negativity. Darkness comes quickly now and the year draws to a close. To symbolize the Divine Spirit and light the way for the coming year, hang a string of tiny white or blue lights on your porch railing. Or, add them to a pine garland for a nice effect.

For a New Year's resolution, promise yourself you'll make time to relax on your front porch during the coming year!

Doors: Your Personal Gateway

Doors stand at the point where the internal and external forces of magical energy meet. Doors are our personal gateway from the past to the future. And they act as a sentry—protecting, guarding, and keeping us safe. There are many magical beliefs associated with doorways. Here are some examples to help you guard your door with protective magic.

Long ago in rural America, if a housewife wanted to protect her home against malevolence, she might have sprinkled a few grains of salt along the door sill. At night, she'd lean her trusty broom across the inside of the front door.

To favor household spirits, small bits of food would be left outside the door at night. This was also done on nights of the Wild Hunt to protect the home against unseen spirits that rode the wind beneath the Full Moon.

In rural Greece years ago, if only one knock was heard at the door after dark, the door wouldn't be answered, because a single knock was believed to be that of a vampire.

One of the most enduring forms of magic associated with the front door is the welcoming shape of a wreath. Whether it's made of pine at Yule or bittersweet berries in the fall, the wreath is the symbol of eternity and the wheel of the year. When a wreath is blessed with your magic, it will protect hearth and home.

Whether your threshold is a simple step or a spacious veranda, your threshold should be warm, inviting, and above all, magical.

Nine Stones Every Witch Should Know

by Laurel Reufner

Gemstones are beautiful to look at, beautiful to have around, and can come in quite handy in the metaphysical sense. I believe that since the minerals found in crystals are often quite elemental, we can tap into those elemental energies to affect our own lives.

I've found that the best way to choose a stone is to let it choose you. Still yourself in front of the selection. Hold your hand out over the stones and wait until one calls to you. Sometimes a stone will shout for attention, sometimes the call is more subtle, and sometimes you won't "hear" anything. Don't force it. Instead, come back for that type of stone another day.

It's my hope that you enjoy learning about the following gemstones and what they can do. And for the Witch not yet out of the broom closet, remember that folks usually don't question a crystal sitting around the home looking pretty.

Amber

Amber is unique in its organic, rather than mineral, nature, possessing no crystalline structure. This beautiful substance has a warm inner glow and is a fully fossilized resin. (Copal, another organic gem, is resin that is partially fossilized.) While amber is found the world over, the best-known deposits come from around the Baltic Sea and from Dominica, whose amber became famous in the Jurassic Park movies.

There are many myths as to amber's origins. Some claim Apollo wept tears of amber after being cast off of Mount Olympus. Another Greek myth concerns the legend of Phaeton, who lost control of his father's sun chariot, coming too close to the Earth's surface, setting it afire. Zeus zapped him with a lightning bolt, plunging him into the Eridanus River, where nymphs buried him upon the shore. Phaeton's three sisters, the Heliades, wept over his grave, wasting away. In sympathy, the gods turned them to trees and their tears to amber.

Symbolizing divinity, amber represents the dividing line between individual and cosmic energy. For me, amber is a universal spark, a representation of future potential. It is a stone of health, healing, and spirituality.

Amethyst

Ancient Mesopotamians were among the first to use amethyst. A quartz, amethyst's royal coloring comes from an interaction between iron and aluminum. One of the interesting things about amethyst is the way its appearance varies from source to source. An expert can tell where a stone came from just by looking at it.

Take care of your amethysts, as prolonged exposure to sunlight will cause their purple colors to fade. Furthermore, low-grade amethysts are often heat-treated and sold as their golden-colored cousins, citrines.

Amethustos, the origin word of amethyst, means "not drunk." The ancient Greeks believed that wearing amethyst would keep one from getting drunk. Legend has it that the maiden Amethyst spurned the advances of Dionysus. To protect the girl, Artemis changed her into a rock crystal. A remorseful Dionysus shed tears over the stone, changing its color to purple.

The Christian church continued the stone's association with sobriety and piety. An amethyst ring is still worn by Catholic bishops. Leonardo da Vinci wrote of the stone: "Amethyst dissipates evil thoughts and quickens the intelligence." Eastern philosophies connect amethyst to the seventh, or crown chakra, where meditation upon it helps connect one to the Universal Consciousness. Buddha considered the stone sacred.

For me, amethyst is very spiritual, a soul stone for exploring past lives and your inner self. It is also a very healing, protective stone. Place it around your home to absorb negativity.

Carnelian

Carnelian is a beautiful, translucent form of chalcedony that is colored by traces of iron oxide, giving it a blood-red to orange-brown color. In many cases, the stones are given a sunbath to make the colors less brown and more intensely red. Major sources for carnelian are in India, although it can be found the world over.

Used through the centuries, carnelian was found in Egyptian tombs, where it was believed to aid the soul into the afterlife. Romans and Greeks were both fond of the stone, using it for jewelry, such as signet rings and intaglios. Hindus, Muslims, and Hebrews have also used the stone. Carnelian was believed to bolster courage and/or endear one to Allah.

I use carnelian to feel strong, courageous, and calm in times of stress. It's also a stone of passion, used to strengthen the first, or root, chakra. Curiously, carnelian also helps create balance. If you need to speak in public, carry carnelian with you for more confidence.

Fluorite

Fluorite has a wide range of industrial uses and is also used in pretty jewelry and carvings. It has one of the widest ranges of colors of any mineral, being found in colors from blue-violet to completely colorless. One of the coolest things about fluorite is the way it can form a near-perfect octahedron (a polyhedron with eight faces). Also, fluorescence—the phenomenon of light-emitting objects—was first noticed in fluorite, which lent its name to the new phenomenon in a paper published in 1852 by George G. Stokes. Fluorite itself comes from the Latin *fluere*, meaning "to flow," referring to its aid as a flux in smelting and refining.

The Egyptians carved scarabs from fluorite's beautiful colors. Carved stones have been found in Pompeii and the Chinese also carved statuettes from it. In the eighteenth century, folks used powdered fluorite to relieve the symptoms of kidney disease and to strengthen bones and teeth.

Said to give the wearer clearing thinking and better concentration, I use fluorite to feel at peace. The stone works to calm the wearer, as well as to aid them in seeing things as they really are.

Hematite

One of the heaviest minerals used for jewelry, hematite is also a primary source of iron ore. Interestingly, this stone as the same crystal structure as the corundums (rubies and sapphires). Hematite is harder than pure iron, but it's also a brittle stone that can be easily damaged. In powdered form, it's used as a red pigment in paint, as well as a polishing powder for jewelry. The Lake Superior area in the United States is the world's largest producer of hematite, although deposits occur in many places around the globe. Hematite even exists on Mars, no doubt helping give the Red Planet its name.

Hematite takes its name from the Greek *haimatitis*, meaning "blood red," although it was used long before the Greeks. There are Neolithic burials showing its use as a pigment. In the tenth millennium BCE, hematite was scattered around burials in Chou-Kou-tien, China (Bonewitz, *Smithsonian Rock and Gem*, 147). The Egyptians inscribed passages from The Book of the Dead on hematite at burials. Romans and Native Americans alike used the stone to protect themselves in battle, believing it could make them invincible. The Victorians used hematite in mourning jewelry. A form of hematite was even used by the Aztecs to make mirrors.

A very powerful grounding stone, hematite is said to promote inner peace and calm, aiding mental clarity. I use it for its grounding effects but need to pair hematite jewelry with another gemstone (soldalite) to counter a draining affect. Worry stones and beads made out of hematite are very calming. It's also a very good general purpose stone for those times you don't have the right stone or aren't sure which stone to use.

Kyanite

Perhaps the most unusual stone on this list, kyanite has, for much of its history, been mistaken for aquamarine or sapphire. The stone is extremely brittle, but its hardness on the Mohs Scale varies depending on whether you're testing along its width (7) or its length (4.5). Its crystals tend to be long and thin, like a blade. In industry, the stone is used in spark plugs, electrical insulators, and heat-resistant ceramics. This background might make kyanite a good stone to reach for when you know the heat is on, literally or figuratively.

The name "kyanite" comes from the Greek *kyanos* meaning "blue." However, the rarest, most colorless stones come from Machakos, Kenya. Kyanite also comes in beautiful deep blue as well as green varieties.

Kyanite is a powerful stone, useful for protection while channeling, altered states, dreamwork, and visualizations. Kyanite is also known to calm mental confusion, which is how I use it.

Labradorite

Labradorite was first identified in the 1770s in Labrador, Newfoundland, Canada. Naturally, then, there are some Inuit legends surrounding the stone. One legend tells that the Northern Lights were trapped within rocks on the Canadian coast. A brave Inuit warrior shattered the rocks with his spear, releasing the beautiful lights back into the northern sky. However, some of the color remained behind, forming the stone we call labradorite. Comparing this stone to the Northern Lights isn't too big of a stretch for anyone who's ever seen it. A property known as shiller reflects light off of surfaces within the stone's crystalline structure. The play of shiller in labradorite is similar to the play of light on the wings of a tropical butterfly or the tail coverts of a peacock.

Labradorite is a stone of the mind, helping clear mental confusion and indecision. It also benefits the aura, keeping it clear and protected. I like to lose myself in the color of labradorite, seeking inspiration.

Tiger's Eye

Believe it or not, tiger's eye is actually part of the quartz group. That beautiful banding is caused by iron oxide replacing crocidolite, which is a blue asbestos. The iron oxide is then replaced with silica, giving tiger's eye its beautiful yellow-brown color. The alternating light and dark bands can do a magic trick. Simply reverse the stone in your hand and the bands switch their orientation, so

that what was once dark is now light and vice versa. Hawk's eye is a blue version of tiger's eye where the silica directly replaces the crocidolite, skipping the iron oxidation. Red tiger's eye results when the iron has oxidized in such a way as to color the stone red.

Tiger's eye is a stone of strength and protection. Because of these properties, Roman soldiers carried tiger's eye into battle, but it didn't become popular for jewelry use until the nineteenth century, when it was expensive as well as popular. Probably the best-known source for the stone is Griqualand West, South Africa. Because of this, tiger's eye was briefly known as griqualandite.

I use tiger's eye for courage, prosperity, and protection. It is also a good stone to ease tension of an intimate nature between partners, bringing them more in tune with each other. Tiger's eye will also help shift you out of a bad mood.

Turquoise

Turquoise has been used in jewelry for at least five thousand years and has been mined for nearly that long as well. It was the de facto official stone of Persia, where a stable, hard variety of the gem was mined for thousands of years and was a source of turquoise for the Western world for centuries. Now only mined by nomads, Persian turquoise is still one of the most preferred varieties.

One of the oldest turquoise mines in Egypt lies at Serabit el-Khadim, sitting just four kilometers from a temple of Hathor. Turquoise objects were found in the tomb of Tutankhamun, including his famous funeral mask.

In pre-Columbian America, turquoise was sacred to the gods and the Aztecs used the stone to decorate ceremonial objects. The Apaches believed turquoise fell from the heavens, a gift from

Father Sky. A turquoise amulet on an archer's bow gave him perfect aim. Navaho and Pueblo people also considered the stone sacred, using it in amulets. The Ancestral Puebloans became quite wealthy from their production of turquoise and turquoise objects for trade.

While the Chinese preferred jade, they've also used turquoise for beads and carvings. In Europe, turquoise finally found favor in the late fourteenth century, becoming very popular during the Victorian era.

Turquoise is truly a stone of spirituality and wholeness, managing to provide a sense of self and yet connect one to their surroundings. It's a comfort stone that can open all of the chakras, particularly the heart chakra.

For me, turquoise deals with matters of spirit and soul, courage, health, healing, protection, and prosperity. It's another good all-around stone.

For Further Study

Bonewitz, Ronald. *Smithsonian Rock and Gem.* New York: Dorling Kindersley Ltd., 2005.

Ether Covening

by Elizabeth Hazel

Ether—sometimes called the fifth element—flows through the fabric of reality and is the natural conduit for magical energy. A ritual or spell done by a group of practitioners simultaneously at remote locations is called ether covening. When it isn't possible to gather at a single location, it is possible to share spellwork through the Etheric Net—similar to the Internet, but free and available exclusively for spiritual work.

Etheric rituals involve a bit of luck. A person may discover that friends at a distance share their needs or concerns of the moment or have specific issues that would benefit from gathered, focused strength. This is when dedicated home altars, personal guides, or special talents can be leveraged to increase the power of a spell. Much like an ensemble cast, etheric rituals and spells encourage each participant to add their own flourishes. Coordinated remote spellcasting packs a wallop and everyone benefits from the unified efforts.

Preparing Etheric Rituals

All participants must agree on a day and time to perform the etheric ritual. Instructions should be circulated in advance so everyone can gather the recommended instruments and supplies. If a chant, charm, or ritual text is involved, everyone will need a copy.

For enhanced effectiveness, work with the principle of similarity resonance. If a group decides to perform a Full Moon ritual, everyone should agree to set up their personal altars with a white candle in a silver candleholder on a white cloth. Uniform tools and candle colors enhance and harmonize the resonance flowing through the ether from person to person. Participants are free to add other elements to the basic ritual or procedure as long as the agreed-upon text, color schemes, ingredients, and tools are consistent.

Having participants begin the ritual at the same time adds a huge boost to the overall effect. This may mean starting at the exact moment (adjusted for various time zones), or at the same event at each person's location, e.g., sunrise or moonrise. People may also start when a planetary hour begins at their locations. The most precise timing mechanism is to begin with the Ascendant (or rising) at a particular degree of the zodiac at each location.

Each person should agree on the format and purpose of the spell before it is performed. If an individual

doesn't need the benefits of a spell, they should not participate—a person with a good job shouldn't participate in a spell for attracting new employment. Furthermore, if some people aren't meant to participate in the spell, even for unknown reasons, something may even prevent them from doing so. In one case, I had calculated precise zodiacal rising times for a talisman construction spell. One of the would-be participants was pulled over by the police for no reason and was unable to perform the spell on time.

At the appointed time, each participant should cast a circle and spend a few moments concentrating on the other participants—by saying the names of each participant aloud, concentrating on group members, or visualizing the other people sitting in the circle. This concentration spins an etheric bond between practitioners and entwines their energies and intentions.

Anticipation generates intense energies, which is why it's important to arrange details well in advance of the ritual. As each person prepares and concentrates on the intentions of the spell, the impact of group purpose becomes more apparent. Group energy can be a remarkable experience, even when participants are separated by great distances.

House-Cleansing Spell

This kind of spell is ideal for ether covening because everyone will want to cleanse their own home of negative energy. Select a day during a fourth-quarter moon. Participants will cast a circle in their kitchen, place a pale-blue candle on their stove, and light it. Each person mops the floors with lavender water, or sprinkles crushed lavender and vacuums it up. All participants say a specific chant or charm, such as, "Lavender clean,

lavender clear; troubles be gone, good luck appear," as they clean.

Vesta Home-Protection Spell

This spell should be performed on the first day of a new month. Preferably in the morning, each participant casts a circle and lights a candle in an area that can be considered the center of the home. If not in the physical center of a building, perhaps the center of activity, like the kitchen or family room. The participants all evoke Vesta (or Hestia), the first-born guardian goddess, and request her protection for the home and family members for the coming month.

Prosperity Spell

Choose a day before the Full Moon when the Moon is in an earth or water sign. On personal altars, participants set up a tray with a green candle and an item that represents a repository of wealth, such as a checkbook or a wallet. As the Moon rises at each person's location, the crafter casts a circle, concentrates on the flow of energy between participants, and visualizes wealth flowing into their hands. Sprinkle cinnamon or a money powder mixture in a circle around the tray, chanting, "All for one and one for all, wealth flows to me at my call / Abundance in plenty for everyone, by rising Moon and setting Sun." Sprinkle cinnamon or money powder in the wallet or checkbook, at the front door, and in the mailbox. This spell can be repeated three nights in a row; group repetitions boost the effectiveness of the spell.

Amulet Charging

Participants choose a necklace or amulet and the desired focus of the charging (protection, attraction, healing, etc.). Compose a suitable charging charm for the spell.

Use the principle of similarity resonance: same color candle, same chant, and identical ingredients in a tray or bowl where the amulet is charged. I organized a protection amulet spell before a series of difficult planetary aspects. Crafters across the country joined the working, each selecting a necklace pendant with a personally meaningful animal image. Throughout the series of difficult aspects, problems and difficulties were averted and minimized by wearing the charged amulets.

When Help Is Needed

In addition to benefiting all members, groups can create spells to direct helpful energies toward one individual with special needs or difficult circumstances.

Justice spells help an individual win a legal dispute. When a woman faced a difficult divorce trial, her group performed a three-day ether covening spell focused on

bringing the man to justice and freeing the woman with favorable terms. The ritual evoked the African loa, Ogun. Participants placed appropriate offerings to Ogun on their personal altars, used the same evocation, and same-colored candles and incense. The case was settled in her favor.

Etheric spells can also generate protection. The group surrounds the person under attack with a protective barrier. Using a figurine, photo, or written name to represent the person, participants visualize an impenetrable cone of light around the person. Reinforce the barrier by sprinkling black sand, consecrated sand, or some other protective powder around the representation. The coordinated intentions form a powerful web of protection around the individual, repelling and discouraging trouble. Barriers can absorb and neutralize negative energies or bounce the trouble back to the perpetrator, depending on the spell's construction and the individual's needs.

Healing prayers and spells are some of the most powerful etheric magic a group can do. In one case, a group of women had become friends through an e-group. When a member needed surgery, the group arranged to offer healing prayers at the exact time she went into surgery. Each participant added her own special touches. One woman placed the woman's name in her charged healing bowl; another called in spirit guides to protect her during surgery; one woman visualized healing light; another performed remote Reiki. This is a good example of how individual embellishments can add to the efficacy of an etheric spell.

Protection for Little People

by Dallas Jennifer Cobb

Whatever you ardently desire,
Sincerely believe in,
Vividly imagine,
and Enthusiastically act upon,
Must inevitably come to pass.
—Sybil Leek, *Diary of a Witch*

Our children are precious to us, whether they are newborn babes, school-aged, or teens. Even when they grow up and move away from home, they are still our children and the maternal and paternal bond is still present, driving us to protect them. We often feel deeply protective of not just our own children, but all the little people in our communities, and we strive to protect them from any perceived harms.

With daily media images of violence in our schools, universities, and colleges, many of us are fearful of everyday dangers and what they might mean for our children, grandchildren, and young friends. When we send our little ones off to school or out into the world, we wish we could go with them to protect them.

But realistically, we can't always be there. At different times, children must go off on their own, away from us and away from our protection.

Without following them throughout their lives, there are ways that we can protect our little people. With some simple tools from the Pagan practice, we can send them off with loving protection. Not just for small children sent off to daycare or school, these protective practices can be used on children of all ages among our friends, family, and community.

Natural Law

The Pagan tradition holds natural law at its core, observing not only the cycles of nature, but the deeper scientific understanding of energy and natural order. Remember, the physical universe is comprised of energy. Energy is magnetic, so like attracts like and opposites repel. Ideas, which are mental energy, can make physical energy manifest in form. And, each action has an equal and opposite reaction, so whatever you send out into the universe will also come back to you.

Knowing the natural laws that govern the universe and allowing them to guide your actions lets you tap into the vast power of natural law, using these principles in a focused and fantastic way. Magic, quite simply put, is the act of consciously using the principles of natural law for the creation of good, for all.

In the Pagan tradition, the Threefold Law states:

Everything you do comes back to you three times, or
What you send out will return to you three-fold.

This notion is sometimes paraphrased as, "What goes around, comes around."

We also know that energy is never destroyed but can change form or transform.

Earth Magic works Threefold:
The Work is stated and performed in the World of Form.
It goes out into the Invisible World,
And comes back to manifest in the World of Form.
—Marion Weinstein, *Earth Magic*

In my circle we often say:

The circle is cast, we are between the worlds.
What happens between the worlds affects all worlds.

Knowledge of natural law reminds us to be magically responsible, knowing that energy finds its way back home, and that ultimately, through natural order, rightness rules.

We are reminded to be careful what we wish for, because our wishes carry power, create energy, and effect change in the world. With recent research documenting the "power of prayer" (See Dosey, "Research suggests . . .", 2002), the scientific and academic communities have tried to quantify what we Pagans already know: that a measurable energy is created from prayer, meditation, thought, intention, visualization, and wishes—proof positive of efficacy and effect of blessings and protective spells.

How to Protect Little People

So how do we harness this energy to the protection of our little people? In the rich Pagan tradition there are many techniques for invoking protection and blessing upon someone, protective energy that will be there even when we can't be. So when they leave home—whether for a few hours to play with a friend, for a day at school, or for months away living on their own—we can send our children out into the world, armed with good sense, a practice of fairness and faith, and surrounded by a protective shield of energy that we have consciously placed around them.

Based upon natural law, the Pagan practices of harnessing natural energy for protection include blessing, charms, magical items such as amulets, visualization, and affirmation.

Blessing comes from the Old English *blestain* or *bleodswean*, meaning "to sanctify with the shedding of blood" (Walker, *Woman's Encyclopedia*, 110). Traditionally, altars were consecrated by sprinkling them with blood, and individuals were blessed by marking them with blood. To be blessed meant to be saved or to be infused with the living energy of the person or animal whose blood "blessed" you. While blood blessings are uncommon these

days, the tradition is carried on using other substances like wine or grape juice. Lots of folks use salt to both bless and purify.

The word *charm* comes from the Old English *cyrm*, a hymn or choral song, which came from Latin *carmen*, a sacred incantation to the goddess Carmenta, inventor of alphabets and "words of power" (Walker, *Woman's Encyclopedia*, 162). Historically, it was believed that we could charm someone by singing to them, lulling them with our voice. When we sing our children off to sleep with a lullaby, we are charming them, invoking safety and peace while they dream.

Magical Items

Never underestimate the value of an everyday item. Many parents will tell you that the most mundane object can become imbued with magical powers, whether it is the favorite fleece blanket that sends your toddler peacefully off to sleep, the tattered teddy bear that calms and soothes a child, or that special jacket a teenager simply must wear. These objects are familiar and soothing to the little one, and they are filled with the power of their wishes, secrets, and dreams.

When small children are sent off to daycare or preschool, they love to take along a familiar, personal item. Talk to the child about the upcoming transition, telling them why the change is necessary. Remind them of all the good things they will enjoy there, and then introduce the idea of taking a symbol of you with them. A transitional object is one that a child can transfer their attachment to and feel safe with. With the object, they can move into a new environment, feeling secure in your love. The object can be whatever works, but realistically, smaller objects are most portable. Stuffed animals, a special toy, or a family picture are favorites. With infants, a piece of the mother's clothing that smells like her is an excellent transitional object.

Spend some time in advance charging the object with your wishes. Put lots of your energy into it. While you handle their transitional object, use your intention to imbue the object with protective energy. Chant your intentions, and fuse them with the object:

> *Little bear, be filled with ease,*
> *Keep my child safe, and at peace.*

While teenagers are more accustomed to being away from us, many of them still like a connection. It is important to offer teens security without offending their growing sense of autonomy. Younger teens love to have hand-me-down clothes, and will wear Mom or Dad's big shirts as an expression of individuality and style, literally wrapping themselves in our protection. Let your teen choose what they want to take with them, allowing them the power of choice. Older teens may opt for the blessing of money from you, or the security of carrying a cell phone so you can stay in touch.

Don't underestimate the power of the mundane. These everyday items can work their special magic in your stead. When you offer your teen money, let them know that it is a blessing you are offering, and that your intention is to help them and keep them safe. It is not "mad money" to be spent on just anything, but money to be used consciously in ways that bring them goodness:

> *With this money, I bless you,*
> *May it bless you and carry you through.*

Cell phones also have their place with teens when they are used as a tool. The technology allows them to call for help if they need it and enables us to find them, wherever they may be roaming. You can also attach a charm that both personalizes the cell phone and imbues it with protective energy. Choose a symbol or material that holds meaning for you. Amethyst is often associated with emotional protection and was historically thought to inspire sobriety (Frazer, *Golden Bough*, 44). Other good talismans include a family photo key fob or a likeness of the goddess.

The phone itself can be charged with protective energy:

> *Phone, as you are charged, I charge thee,*
> *Keep my child happy, safe, and free.*

Visualizing Protection

Protection can be an energy that we visualize surrounding our children, and it can transform, becoming a palpable electromagnetic energy shield.

We can visualize a protective shield surrounding our child. Envision a glowing white light enveloping your child, a vibrant energy that uplifts and protects. Regularly, repeat the visualization to reinforce the strong current of energy surrounding your charge. Like a magic balloon, this bubble will travel with them throughout their journeys. In your mind, draw a circle, oval, or bubble around your child that will protect them from harm.

When you are traveling in a vehicle, bless it and infuse the energy of safety within and upon it. Before you start your vehicle, take a moment to place your hands upon the steering wheel and say, "I bless this car with love and light, that it may carry us in safety and protection." Envision a bubble of energy surrounding the entire vehicle, protecting yourself and your children as you travel to and fro in your daily litany of chores, practices, and appointments.

Teaching Little People How to Protect Themselves

We can also teach our children the practice of self-protection, a skill they can take with them everywhere. Teach your child to draw protective energy from the earth. Tell them to stand with their feet slightly apart, and as they inhale, draw the earth's energy up through their legs, through the torso and to the head, pulling it to the crown. As they exhale, let the energy flow out of the top of the head (the crown chakra), cascading down around their body and to the ground again. Envision this energy as a glowing white light or a luminous golden energy.

Many people feel significant shifts energetically when exercising this visualization, as if the energy were bathing them, restoring and enlivening them. A variation on this visualization is to imagine being a tree that sends its roots down deep into the ground to access Mother Earth's goodness, pulling it up into leaves, which give off oxygen, returning the good energy to the universe.

While there are many practices that encourage the visualization of a safe space, it is better to teach children to be fully present in the moment and aware of their surroundings. Techniques that will help to ground and protect them are preferable to those that may lead to an overabundance of airy energy, a separation from current reality, or a mild dissociation from potential present danger.

Affirmations

An affirmation is a declaration that something is true. Affirmations can be an act of self-blessing that creates a positive outlook, raises self-esteem, and refocuses attention on positive energy and outcomes. Affirmations can come in many forms: phrases repeated to oneself or aloud in the course of a day or mantras used in meditation, in focused intention, or in conjunction with mirror work while looking deep into your own eyes. Affirmations are commonly phrased as though they are already happening, not phrased as something that will occur in the future. "I am safe and at ease," as opposed to, "I will be safe."

Teach your little people to use affirmation to boost their self-image and affirm their reality. "I am protected as I come and go."

For little people going off to school or day camp where they will encounter lots of other little kids, it is good to teach them the responsible way to use their hands. Remind them, "we don't hit people" and show them how to draw their own personal limits. My young daughter will stand sturdily, and with a deep breath, pull her hands up the middle, overhead, and then opening them wide, trace an egg-shaped "personal space" around her body. "This is my personal space," she says, "and I can decide who can enter it and who cannot." Aware of her rights, my daughter is primed to protect herself, and to refuse and rebuff unwanted physical contact.

Ritual Practices

Kids love small rituals, because they are fun, easy, and familiar. While many of us meet in community for sabbats and larger celebrations, it is not necessary to cast a circle and draw in the elements to ritualistically protect your child. Use your everyday rites and rituals as opportunities to consciously bless and protect your children. Make it a habit, continually reinforcing the good energy.

As they head out the door and away from you, give your little people a ritualistic hug that envelopes them in your protective circle, simultaneously envisioning a protective shield around them. As you kiss them goodbye, say a quiet blessing, the vibration of these energies suffusing the child and subtly protecting them throughout the day. I often tell my daughter, "Be safe." But most importantly, children need to hear those magical words, "I love you."

At night, before sleep, use the quiet of bedtime to cultivate peace in your home and reinforce protection. Singing to or with your child, reading, chanting, or talking are wonderful ways to shift the energy within and around them. In my house, bedtime is when we climb into a quiet, safe space together, reading, telling stories, and whispering. It is also a time for processing things that happened during the day, making peace where there might have been conflict, and resolving worries or troubles.

As my daughter prepares for sleep, we exchange blessings. There are a few standards we repeat, for in the repetition is comfort, familiarity, and a sense of rightness, especially for a small child. My daughter and I whisper an ancient European rhyme, left over from the time of the plagues:

> *Night night, sleep tight, don't let the bugs bite,*
> *If they do, take your shoe and beat them 'til they're black and blue.*

My mother whispered this rhyme to me when I was small, and her mother whispered it to her. I find comfort in the familiarity of the rhyme, and my own associations with my mother and childhood. I also feel the power of the three generations of women in my family there with my daughter as she makes the transition to sleep and the dream world. For my daughter, this is a ritual exchange that connects us and makes her feel safe. She knows what is going to happen. She knows the words. She feels in control. She is safe.

Sometimes I sing a blessing to my daughter. My favorite is from a Sufi traditional prayer. Both a blessing and a call for protection, it is uplifting and soothing. And when I sing, I let my voice carry the resonance of love:

May the longtime sun shine upon you,
All love surround you,
And the pure light within you,
Guide your way on.

Another, more modern blessing that I have used many times over the years, including in my handfasting ritual and my daughter's baby blessing ritual, is from *The Fifth Sacred Thing* by Starhawk. Delivered by the character Madrone to a newborn babe, I call it Madrone's Blessing:

44

Be free,
Be strong,
Be yourself,
Be lucky,
Be proud to be a woman,
Be loved and be loving . . .
Know that you are a precious gift to us,
Be blessed.

The four directions can also be ritualistically called upon to travel with our children, their energies guiding and protecting them while they are away from us. However you call in the directions, use your words to cast protection around your own little people.

With the earth that is Her body,
With the air that is Her breath,
With the fire of Her shining spirit,
And the waters of Her living womb,
I bless this child that she may travel and dwell in peace, returning safely to me.

Blessed Be

Whatever techniques you use or teach your little people to use, remember the natural law that guides the Pagan path: whatever you send out will come back to you, usually threefold.

So when energy is spent focused on blessing and protecting the little people in our communities, it is also energy invested in the creation of the greater good: it flows out, around, and through the universe, to return to us at a later date. Subsequently, we not only seek goodness for our little people, but create goodness and protection for ourselves, our communities, and our world.

In this way, the practice of blessing and protecting our little people becomes a practice of blessing ourselves, our lives, and the lives of those who dwell with us on the planet. While we cannot directly challenge the violence, negativity, and evil that exists, we can continue to use our intentions to increase positive practices, subtly shifting the universal balance toward greater good.

"All acts of love and pleasure are my rituals," says the charge of the Goddess, and the acts of protecting our little people are our rituals of love.

May the grace of the Goddess go in your heart,
Merry meet, and
Merry part, and
Merry meet again.

For Further Study

Dossey, Larry, "Research suggests consciousness can change the physical world – Measuring the Power of Prayer." *Whole Earth Magazine*. Spring 2002.

Frazer, J. G. *The Golden Bough*. London: Macmillan and Co., 1960.

Leek, Sybil. *Diary of a Witch*. New York: Signet, 1969.

Starhawk. *The Fifth Sacred Thing*. New York: Bantam Books, 1993.

Walker, Barbara. *The Woman's Encyclopedia of Myths and Secrets*. San Francisco: Harper and Row, 1983.

Weinstein, Marion. *Earth Magic*. Blaine, WA: Phoenix Publishing, 1986.

Budget Witchery

by Melanie Harris

Sure, we know some wealth-bringing charms, but we magical folks still need to watch our cash flow. We want the tools and ingredients we use in magic to enrich our practice, not empty our pockets. Essential oils, robes, candles, incense—the costs of even a simple ritual can really add up. Luckily, the savvy spellcaster can save a bundle of money on witching supplies with just a few simple techniques.

Versatility Equals Big Savings

Knowledge is power, and it's also a key to frugality. The more you know about magic, the more versatile you can be, enabling you to substitute ingredients and adapt spells and formulas so that your witchy work won't break the budget. Can't afford the jasmine or rose oil called for in a love spell? No problem. Just use the basil or rosemary from your spice rack, the Ace of Cups card from your tarot deck, a piece of rose quartz, a wildflower from your yard, or even a heart or another love symbol drawn on a piece of paper. If you don't have any of those things handy, you could wear pink or red, paint the number 2 on your chest, dance a slow dance, sing a love song, or gaze at romantic artwork. Any ingredient called for in a spell can be replaced with a color, herb, tarot card, symbol, stone, number, movement, sound, or image with similar attributes.

Investing in good books will cost some money up front, but it is essential. Spending thirty dollars or so on an extensive herbal dictionary or stone-attribute guide might seem a bit much, but the knowledge you'll gain

can save you hundreds over the years. Armed with information, you will have the versatility and know-how to customize any spell so that it uses the tools and ingredients you have on hand.

Keeping versatility in mind when you do buy new ingredients is another way to save money. Choose multipurpose herbs, such as sage, cinnamon, and rosemary—herbs that are suitable for many types of spellwork. For example, rosemary can be used for love magic, purifying charms, healing rituals, psychic awareness . . . the list goes on. An exotic plant might be nice to use every once in a while, but is it good for the types of magic you do the most? Make the common, multipurpose herbs your old standbys and save the pricey exotics for a special treat. Without having to spend too much money, you can get a stock of versatile herbs that will suffice for most of your witchery. Versatility is a very valuable magical asset; let your imagination build what it will upon the foundation of knowledge.

Use the Free Stuff

Another basic principle of budget witchery is to use what you can get for free. In all those things we cast aside or overlook lies a stockpile of magical supplies. Old wine bottles become containers for potions. Empty jars provide a great place to store loose herbs. An out-of-fashion skirt becomes a witchy cape or a slew of fabric squares for charm bags and herbal sachets. Worn-out sheets become altar covers, and a faded curtain gets new life as a tarot cloth. You can even find a lot of useful items in the food waste that would otherwise be chucked into the compost. Save fruit seeds, nut hulls, orange peels, lemon peels—these things have potent magical properties that can be put to use in your spellwork. It's free, so take advantage. You'll add some great new stuff to your magical bag of tricks without spending anything at all.

Frugal witchy folks know that when it comes to plants for natural magic, nothing beats what you can find growing in your own area. Learn about the magical uses of your native plants or take the time to experiment and get in touch with each plant's mystical attributes. You can also make use of stones, feathers, sticks, and other natural objects that you find. A stroll through the woods can yield some pine needles for a wealth-bringing charm, an acorn to use in a protection spell, mud to turn into magical ink, some vines for a headdress, and a brand-new wand from a fallen branch. Just look around and get creative.

Starting your own little magical garden will also save you money. Grow versatile herbs that you can use for both cooking and witchery and flowers that add both beauty and magic to your space. Nature is the essence of magic, and Mother Earth invites us to embrace her, free of charge.

Make It Last

Another way to save money on witching supplies is to use all the tricks you can to make the magical products you buy last as long as possible. Store potions and oils in dark glass, as sunlight can break down the components of many of these substances. Keep your wand in good shape by putting it away when not in use, and purify and charge it regularly so that it does not lose its magic. Use small amounts of herbs and oils, just enough to get the job done. Think little when using candles, too; choose small candles when working spells that require the candle to burn out completely. You might want to try cooling your candles before use, as they will burn more slowly and last longer. By conserving magical resources, you'll conserve financial resources.

There are certain charms that can be used to help conserve your magical ingredients and ensure that you are really getting the most value from them.

Expansion Charm

To cause something to expand, visualize lines of lavender light going into the object and plumping it up. Think about it growing larger as you say, "Take this light and expand!" Tap the object with a swift flick of your wand if you are using one. Otherwise, tap it three times with the tips of your index, middle, and ring fingers. Now say, "You have grown. Hold your shape! So will it be."

Denser Charm

To cause something to become denser and stronger, first get in tune with the energies of the object. Once you feel familiar with its energetic vibrations, mentally push the energy toward the center of the object. Now draw in some of the energy around you and then release it to wrap around the object and hold it in its new denser form. Tap the item and see it glow with dark-purple light as you say, "Go dense!"

Long-lasting Charm

This charm works especially well for slowing the effects of fire, such as with a candle that you need to make last. Visualize a curved, darkish-blue cap covering the object you wish to conserve. Now curve your hand over the item and say, "This cap is impervious to flame, wind, water, and careless man. The object is protected and will not be used up. It will be long-lasting until my need is fulfilled. So will it be!"

Shop Seasonally

One of the best ways to get magical supplies for less is to shop seasonally. Plan ahead so that you can stock up on what you need when prices are lowest. Look for white, pink, and red candles on sale around or right after Valentine's Day. Near Halloween, buy orange and black candles, spooky goblets, witchy makeup, ritual robes, and accessories. At Christmas, stock up on white, red, green, silver, and gold candles. Stop by Christmas tree lots and pick up scraps of pine to use in purification, protection, and prosperity blends. This time of year, you might want to pick up some jingle bells for your fairy magic, too, as well as some larger bells for casting charms and circles. Whenever you go shopping, just think witchy, and you'll see the many uses that holiday and post-holiday clearance items can serve in magic.

Cooperate!

Just think of the strength that lies in a community of ants! They all work together so well, and we humans can, too. Cooperating with those around us gives us access to more resources for less money or effort. Share rides to your meeting sites. Trade tarot readings for handmade incense or exchange hand-stitched clothes for cleansing rituals. You can also get some money-saving co-op action going in the garden. It's quite simple to coordinate with a group of like-minded gardeners. You grow lavender, a friend grows basil. You grow roses, another friend has an apple tree. Then share and trade your surpluses with one another. You'll strengthen your friendships and lessen your expenses.

If you want to save a lot of money, think big when you buy your magic supplies. It's often cheaper in the long run to buy big stocks of certain herbs and ingredients in bulk. Sage, garlic, cinnamon, rosemary, candles, soaps, incense, charcoal blocks—if it's storable, and if it's something you use frequently or can share, buy as much as you can at once. Bulk purchases are usually sold at a lower per

unit price, saving the planet the waste of overpackaging, and saving you several dollars and cents.

Get Theatrical or Crafty

If you're hosting a bit of group magic and you want the scene to be truly impressive, think theatrics. You don't need a lot of fancy decorations or gourmet food and wine. Instead, go bold with loud music, crazy makeup, wild movements, lavish costumes, a big cauldron of stone soup . . . whatever you already have, mixed with the energy and personalities of the people at your event, will make for a very magical celebration for very little money.

Custom-made magical tools are the best anyway, so why not craft your own? Pentacles can be made by painting the symbol on a flat river rock, or by scratching it on a clay disk. Wands, staffs, and scepters can all be fashioned with stuff found in the woods. A ritual cup can be formed with clay or carved from a coconut shell. It's nice to support artisans who make such tools, but if you can't afford it, just make your tools yourself. All you need is a good book on magic crafts and just a touch of creativity.

Think Power

Mediocre spellwork is a waste of money. The frugal know that the most cost-effective spell is the one that packs the biggest punch. The mystic who is stingy with their power will see their spellwork falter and fail. When you have to repeat the same magic over and over because it isn't working properly, those costs add up quickly. If you make each spell as strong as it can be, you can count on its effectiveness, and you can count the money you save on supplies by not having to try the same spell again. If you want to get the most out of your magical dollars, always rely heavily on spellwork's most powerful ingredient: you. This means investing your full energy in each and every spell. Really go for it, without a trace of wavering faith. Know that whether you've been practicing magic for a day or for a lifetime, you have the ability to manifest change in the universe through your own energy and will. Take your power to its absolute limit, and you won't need to count on, or purchase, the extras.

~

The real secret to budget witchery is to save money and work magic by any means available. Whether it's buying in bulk, freezing your candles, foraging in the woods, or getting down and dirty in the garden, low-cost tricks of the frugal and magical can save money without sacrificing power. By planning ahead, being savvy to a bargain, being smart, and having an eye for treasure, you can keep your magical cupboards—and your wallet—well stocked.

Birthing from Within
by Sybil Fogg

I have given birth five times, and each pregnancy and delivery has changed me, altered me, created a new me. It is as if I have given birth to myself over and over again. Any mother worth her salt will admit that bringing forth life is akin to visiting the underworld. Even with our modern medical inventions and creations, we women still barely cling to a fragment of ourselves while we become incubators. It is frightening to carry a child, to know that something is growing and that we are responsible for how it grows. It is easy to lose ourselves to this process, but if we take a spiritual attitude, we can gain much from this life-changing experience.

My Personal Story

I had my first baby seventeen years ago. At that time, I was a young child myself, barely nineteen, out of school for less than one year, married one month after graduation, pregnant two months past that. Needless to say, I did not know who I was, much less understand that I was about to leave maidenhood behind for the next stage of life.

That first pregnancy was easy physically. I drifted through the first trimester relatively unchanged, but thoroughly confused emotionally. There was so much to learn and prepare for. I read everything I could get my hands on and did my best to educate myself and create a safe and welcoming nursery nook in my bedroom on our limited budget. Still, I would awake in the middle of the night and create lists. I wrote out menus and toy charts, scared that I would starve my baby or break the tiny creature as soon as it was released from my womb.

Before I knew it, winter had given way to spring and the air was clear and whispering. My body had begun to change, making room for the entity growing within it, creating food to nourish it. One morning in March I woke up itchy all over. When I took my daily shower, I noticed that my belly was covered with red welts. In a panic, I called my midwife and was promptly informed that my rash was simply stretch marks indicating that my body had stretched beyond my skin's capacity.

I stood in front of the mirror taking in my expanding waistline, round figure, full face, and realized I was no longer the ninety-eight-pound girl on the brink of womanhood who had begun this journey. My flat shape had given way to the Willendorf Goddess form. My litheness was replaced by a bulk that was difficult to drag around, my femininity was replaced by a Jabba the Hutt impersonator. I realized I no longer knew who I was, and I turned away from my reflection.

Trying to conjure up images of my former self ate away at me for the rest of that pregnancy. Playing Dungeons and Dragons was no longer appealing. Daydreaming about meeting my favorite rock star felt petty and wasteful of the time I needed to prepare for this change. I was going to be a mother. The hour and a half I was accustomed to spending to paint my gothic face was going to have to be left behind (besides, it had become ludicrous in my new condition).

I opened my dresser drawers and closet and pulled outfits free. I threw crochet collars, lace skirts, crushed velvet hats, and granny boots onto my bed. None of it fit anymore. I was certain none of it ever would again. I could not envision myself dressed like Elvira carrying around a baby on my hip. I could not for the life of me picture my old self sipping a cappuccino at a round table in a coffee bistro scribbling depression poetry in my black spiral notebook with a howling tot strapped into a high chair beside me.

I cried as I shoved everything into a lawn bag to be hauled off to the Goodwill. "Goodbye Sybil," I whispered. I was racing toward a life-changing event and I did not know who I was anymore or how to reconcile my old and new selves. Although I was married and my family lived nearby, I felt terribly and utterly alone in my knowledge that I needed to find myself. Now, I am aware that what I went through in my quest to learn about my baby and myself is a normal sensation for women about to embark on the journey of motherhood.

My first labor was long, like most first labors. Contractions began small approximately one week before the actual big day. My body slowly and gently opened up to prepare for the delivery of my first daughter. I had taught myself enough through literature and Lamaze class to know that I needed to let go and welcome the experience and simply flow on the path my body had to take. I spiraled inward toward silence and unwrapped layer after layer of my soul. I delivered my first baby before I reached my core because I was young and unformed myself. I did not know how to use this experience to really dig down deep into my soul.

Five years later, I found myself pregnant again. This time, I welcomed my changing woman persona. I was still young and naïve, but I allowed myself to fully experience my journey.

I was all ready to hit labor as a transcendental learning experience and come away secure in my own self-knowledge and self-worth. But, I still had some developing and work to do on my soul. This second labor was violent and aggressive. It was full of blood and pain that I could not manage. Without focus, I found it difficult to ride the labor and dig deep into myself. I was passionate and warlike in my attempt to fight each contraction as it hit like an enemy. My second daughter was born in a torrent of anguish.

When she was handed to me, I took her greedily, exhausted and defeated. I learned my weaknesses and now know this birth

was part of my growth. Being forced to meet my physical match taught me that I had true fire in the belly.

My third pregnancy challenged my spirit. I was afraid of the pain I had experienced with my second childbirth and, frankly, I was not excited to find myself with child again because I was scared. Birth is physically traumatizing and I was not certain I could handle it again because I was still reeling from the delivery only two years before. I remembered the pain! Throughout my third pregnancy, I grew distressed. My spirit waned until I despised myself for my weakness and my melancholy. I hated my body as it grew, trapping me in flesh that I knew would rip itself from me when the time came.

This emotional turmoil proved unhealthy and I limped into preterm labor and was forced to remain on bed rest for six weeks. This time of retrospection gave me what I needed to understand my inner workings. I had to fight against labor and keep it quiet. I had to soothe my spirit and learn what calmed me. The day I was finally able to stand up again, I gave birth to my third daughter, who slipped into this world pain-free and screaming at the world, showing her strength of spirit.

Five years, a divorce, and a new relationship later, I found I was expecting again. This pregnancy proved to be fleshy. I spent so much time bleeding and clotting that I am now convinced I was carrying twins in the beginning. Digging down deep, I felt every movement, every cramp, every pound gained, until I really knew what my body could and would do to grow life. This pregnancy brought me farther along the path of motherhood and truly allowed me to experience a link with the Mother Earth.

This brings me to my last pregnancy, which was unremarkable until the very last month. I experienced the same preterm labor I had on my previous two pregnancies and was facing bed rest again. During that time, my teenager made an attempt to strike out on her own and made some very poor choices. A body is battered by pregnancy and mine had survived five. I was tired. My maternal feelings were siphoned by struggling to keep my family together. A child lashes out at the parents to disengage and become a Maiden or Youth. In healthy circumstances, this is a normal rite of passage. I would have marked this transition with celebration and love. Unfortunately my daughter fell under the spell of another woman's influence and turned her back on me as a mother while I was in a very vulnerable position. Like the mythological belly of the whale or descent into Hades, I had sunk as deep and dark as my unconscious mind could bring me safely. If I was to ever recover vitality, I would have to make the Night Sea Journey—the dark night of the soul.

As psychologist Carl Jung often interpreted legends symbolically, he theorized that when the hero is swallowed by a dragon, whale, or other large creature/monster, it is analogous to the loss of energy one experiences when they sink into depression. This lack of strength is a necessary prelude to rebirth. This is a solar archetype: think of how the sun disappears into the horizon each evening only to be reborn from the body of Mother Earth the next dawn. One can compare this descent into the belly as a return to the warmth and flow of the womb. It is possible to use this iconography to adapt childbirth to our own journey into the belly of the beast. And that is what I did in my fifth delivery.

My son was facing the wrong way. Because of this, his descent was hindered and his head lodged at my pelvic bone. As is common knowledge, giving birth is primal. I felt my ancestors tugging at me as wave after wave of contractions pounded my being. Together, my son and I were at a plateau. The pain I was experiencing severed my mind briefly from the physical plane and I saw myself linked to my female ancestors throughout history. A flood of them wandered through my mind touching me a bit with each of their own journeys. I became aware that if I did not take action, my son and I would linger in this moment for eternity. With the help of my skilled midwife, I was able to push down deep and move my son over the obstacle my body had put up before him.

On the most basic level, this birth had forced me on a Night Sea Journey. I became aware that birth could be used to find ourselves, develop our strengths, and work over our weaknesses. I am no longer the ninety-eight-pound waif who stumbled into motherhood seventeen years ago. I am stronger, I am woman, I am Mother.

Night Sea Journey Ritual

This ritual is best done as a prelude to labor, as birth itself is a sacred rite that takes on a form of its own and I would never propose to tell any woman how she should behave during labor! That said, calling upon this meditation while laboring can be beneficial. Choose the Full Moon closest to your due date, and prepare your bedroom for the ritual with the following tools:

• Heavy fabrics in earthy tones
• Light gauzy fabrics in water tones
• Rosemary incense
• Five large, fat candles in the corresponding elemental colors, all anointed with the following essential oils: rose for love, frankincense for courage, lavender for happiness, sandalwood for good health, myrrh for protection
• Rose petals and lavender buds
• Athame or black-handled knife for casting the circle
• Gems, beads, seeds, seashells, and trinkets that you have a special affinity with. Some I have used in the past are jasper, amethyst, rose quartz, cowry shells, and charms that represent infancy (booties, baby carriages) and strength of womanhood (Venus symbols, breasts, goddess images).
• Music: Choose something light with a meditative quality (I have had great success with Ravi Shankar, Radiohead, Iron and Wine, and Loreena McKennitt).

Before beginning this ritual, it is important to charge all the items under a Full Moon. To create and maintain the mood, the most appropriate time to do this is to take advantage of the three nights of the Full Moon. Use the night before to charge your items, the actual evening to perform the ritual, and the following night to digest what you have learned.

To fully take advantage of the Great Mother Goddess' blessing, I find it best to charge my items by the ocean. (You may use another water source, depending on your location.) Anything that can be dipped without ruining it, I pass through these primeval waters, focusing my intent on my own ability to make a Night Sea Journey. If it is at all possible (and safe), bathing in the ocean while pregnant does wonders to help make this connection. By "bathing," I do not mean to whip out your bar of soap and shampoo. This is a spiritual cleansing. You are attempting to feel at one with all of the mothers who have gone before you into the realm of Hades and returned changed and at one with themselves.

On the night of the actual Full Moon, set your stage. It is best to have your bed in the center of the room. If you are moving your bed for this ritual, make sure to have someone else do so for you. (I have been guilty in the past of pushing and lifting things that I should not have in the late stages of my pregnancies. I could have avoided at least one preterm labor and many a chastising from my husband by following my midwife's advice.)

1. Decorate by draping the bed and walls with the heavy fabric. Scatter the rose petals and lavender over the bed. Lay out the meaningful items you have gathered. This represents the earth that is the Goddess' body.

2. Hang the gauzy fabrics over the bed and windows. Load the CD player or turn on the music player. This represents the water that is her blood and her womb.

3. Place the candles in their appropriate quarters. These represent the fire that is her passion and her strength.

4. Set up the incense. I find it useful to have a few sticks burning at the same time. These represent the air that is her breath.

Take a moment to sit and gather your thoughts and focus. Try to think of nothing but your body and the rushing fluids within your womb that caress and support your child. When you feel that you are ready, stand and cast your circle as you normally would.

Call the quarters in the manner you are accustomed to and light the candles.

Make your way to the center of your bed and sit or lie down comfortably. I often start in the cross-legged position and as I work through the meditation, I eventually lie on my left side; this position promotes the healthiest flow to the baby and eases you into the journey you are about to take. Gather the items in your hands—these will anchor you to this world once you have entered the spiritual realm.

Breathe deeply and hold the breath for three full seconds. Exhale.

Repeat until you feel your air rushing to each corner of your body, from the tips of your toes to your fingertips. Feel the air that expands your chest and diaphragm. Work it through to the strands of your hair. I can tell that I have reached the point of relaxation necessary to successfully feel a meditation when my skin begins to prickle and my forehead tingles. When you are certain that your third eye is activated, begin to meditate on your pregnancy.

Stage One

Think of the moment your little one was conceived. No, this is not the time to relive the action that created life, but to see that instance as an explosion of light from darkness. Start by imagining that you are in the night. It is pitch black. You do not know what you look like, you do not know what you are. You cannot feel your feet or your hands. Your body is unformed. You are alone with no sight, no hearing, no feeling, no senses. Suddenly, there is a prick or a piercing and you are filling with light. It engulfs you and you are raging with it as it overwhelms and overtakes you. Feel this incident overcoming you, for you are about to be born again. Sit with this thought for as long as you need to.

Stage Two

Think of your baby swimming in a primeval sea. You are swimming fast. Taste the womb waters. They are salty, they are dark, they are warm. Swim with your infant. Stretch your toes, your fingers, roll your head around your neck. Think of all the things that you brought this far in your journey. What attributes would you like to temper? Which of your strengths can be honed? See yourself filling up with what holds you back. This is the time to really let your weaknesses work on you. Do not be afraid to face the shadowed aspects of yourself—they are a part of you. Watch your personality fold into itself as water engulfs you. Keep breathing.

Stage Three

You are growing fast, your limbs shoot out of your body. You feel fuller and stronger. You feel the arms of the Great Mother encircling you and holding you fast. It is suffocating, but you keep growing. You stretch but there is nowhere to go. The Mother's embrace is crushing but loving. Stay here for as long as you need to. Let go of all that hurts and weighs you down. Allow yourself to be comforted by the Mother. Give yourself over. Cry if you need to.

When you are ready, open your eyes and look at the items in your hands. These helped you through this Night Sea Journey. They will also help you through delivery and birth. When you feel it is time, blow out the candles, thank the quarters, and open the circle. You might want to fashion a bracelet or necklace from your treasures to bring back this meditation while you labor. I tucked each bracelet under the mattress of my babies' crib for protection after using it as a focus during delivery; you may find you want to do the same.

Alternative Fertility Magic

by Lupa

I've been Pagan for more than a decade, since the mid-1990s, and I've been to my share of Pagan festivals across the United States. One thing I've noticed for sure is that while for some people Paganism is a fertility religion, there are plenty of us who take that fertility pretty seriously! The growing number of Pagan children is a visible testament to that fact, especially as the wave of teens and twenty-somethings who discovered Paganism about the same time I did are now older and having families of their own.

One of the first things people often learn about Paganism, especially Wicca and its derivatives, is the triad of the Maiden, Mother, and Crone in the mythology of the Goddess. While debate rages on as to how ancient this trinity really is, the fact remains that it has become firmly ensconced in Neopagan imagery. These stages of the Goddess are often encouraged as symbols of life-stages for Pagan women. Unfortunately, they aren't one-size-fits-all. They're based primarily on a woman's fertility, both potential and actual. The Mother in particular is linked to fertility and is very often portrayed in pregnancy.

However, not all Pagans—male or female—are interested in this sort of traditional, literal fertility. I am one of a number of deliberately childfree Pagans; while I won't begrudge Pagans (or anyone else) their right to have children, I don't want any of my own. Additionally, people who are unable to have children may find the emphasis on human fertility to be discomforting, to say the very least. And sometimes there's just a need to find something new to do with fertility magic besides focus on the family.

For those of us who either can't or don't choose to have children, what can we do with all this fertile energy? Plenty!

Safe Sex Magic

Without the act of coitus, most of us wouldn't be here. Certainly there are those who opt for artificial insemination, which is no less an important act. However, fertility magic most often involves sex and sexuality, and for good reason. Sex raises a lot of energy and is very good for keeping participants focused on what they're doing.

However, let's look at the actual definition of "sex." Thankfully, the Pagan community acknowledges (and embraces) relationships beyond heterosexuality, and therefore the concept of "sex" need not be limited to what goes on between a man and a woman. In fact, sex need not ever involve penetration of any sort. There's a wide range of sexual acts out there that won't cause anyone to get pregnant.

All sexual acts, whether vanilla or kinky, are potential fuel for sex magic. While the various systems and styles of sex magic differ, the general concept is the same: sex raises energy, and that energy can be used for magical purposes. (Or, if you're coming from a more psychological viewpoint, sex creates altered states of consciousness that may then be used in magical practice.) The fact that erotic actions often lead to physical fertility just adds to the power (actual and/ or perceived) of sex magic.

My husband and I, while childfree, have used sex magic to birth other "children." In one case, we worked together to create a servitor, or magical thoughtform, to help us with a specific set of magical workings. We built up and shaped the energy from a sex magic ritual to form this being, and at the peak of the rite I "gave birth" to it. We've also used the energy from sex magic to charge sigils (magical inscriptions that are abstracted representations of a particular desire we want to manifest) and various magical objects.

Fertility Magic and Artwork

Fertility is linked intimately to creation. The most basic form, of course, is the creation of the next generation. However, fertility need not be taken so literally. Many Pagans are artists of one sort or another—we may paint, draw, sculpt, sing, play music, or otherwise produce any of a number of artistic acts. And those of us who are artists are quite aware of the energy that goes into our creations.

Have you ever experienced (or watched someone experience) intense focus during the creation of artwork of any sort? Your attention narrows down to whatever you're working on, and you may experience what feels like a complete alignment with the process of creation. You may even feel you are channeling a piece of yourself into your work. This is very similar (or, in some cases, identical) to the mindset you may experience at the height of a successful magical ritual or other working.

If you haven't ever used artwork in magic, you're definitely missing out. The state of consciousness where you are immersed in your artwork is perfect for magical practice. All that's missing is the specific magical intent. This can be achieved in a number of ways:

• Make the subject of your artwork a magical act. This is the most direct manner of creating magical artwork. Not only does it link the act of creation to the desire you wish to manifest, making each brushstroke (or note, or movement) a ritual action, it also makes the artwork a shrine or offering to your magical intent. While you are creating the artwork, keep yourself focused on exactly what it is you are doing. For example, if you are painting a picture of a spirit that you would like to help you with a particular desire, act as though each brush of paint brings that spirit more fully into the world. Even better, portray the spirit as successfully bringing about whatever task you have asked it to complete. Let the energy of your creation be an aid to that spirit.

• Use magical items, specifically charged, in your artwork. Mixed-media art in particular lends itself to this tactic. Instead of making a mojo pouch, make your magical components into something nifty to hang on the wall or a unique sculpture. Jewelry is also a really good choice—you can choose various stones and other materials for their innate qualities or charge them for specific reasons. The way you arrange the components may help, too. I once created a wolf necklace with gray, white, tan, and black stone beads. I arranged them so that they followed the same general color patterning of a gray wolf—black near the pendant for the nose, then white, tan, and gray for the face, gray and black for the shoulders, and so on.

• Use something you previously charged/created in a ritual. Sometimes a magician gets hold of a neat-looking

pendant or other object that they know needs to be used for a particular purpose, but they're not completely sure how it will be executed, so they add an initial charge to it until they figure out what to do with it. Other times a magical object may simply lend itself to an art project at the right time. Either way, you can enhance an art project with a magical item, whether you create the artwork in a formal ritual setting or not.

Opinions vary as to what should be done with the artwork once the magic has been completed. Some magicians, particularly some chaos magicians, advocate destroying a piece of magical artwork (such as a sigil) once it has been successfully charged, so as to not taint the working with doubt and other interferences. Others prefer to make the artwork an offering to whatever being(s) may have helped with it, and may even make it a permanent part of an altar setup. My thought is that if you can't keep it around, at least find a good use for it (though make sure that whoever receives it is aware of its properties). Give your art piece away or sell it as a fundraiser for a good cause, especially if that cause benefits whoever may have helped you with your magic. For example, I create a lot of totemic artwork and a portion of the proceeds goes to various nonprofit organizations that help wildlife and protect their habitats.

Fertility and Activist Magic

Humans are incredibly fertile, and we're good at staying alive despite disease and injury. Other species aren't so fortunate. Some are negatively impacted by our actions, others simply don't reproduce all that quickly. So focusing fertility energy can be an environmental act as well as a personal one.

This is a more indirect form of fertility magic than the others. The point is essentially to promote and support the fertility of other living beings and of the Earth itself. There are several ways in which this can be accomplished:

• Send fertility energy to an endangered species of animal or plant to promote their reproduction. I work frequently with animal totems, and some of the best offerings I've made to them have been magical workings designed to aid their physical children (often along with donations or volunteering for more material efforts). These rituals not only give the animal a boost in raising its young, but they also can help raise other people's awareness of beings that need our help.

• Use the creativity of fertility magic to help promote healthier attitudes toward sustainability and environmental issues. Sustainability is focused on creation, not destruction. Use fertility magic to add extra oomph to a letter sent to a public official who has a hand in an important environmental policy. Place a blessing on a wild place that needs protection from development or that is recovering from damage. Work magic before and during a demonstration or workshop designed to raise awareness of environmental issues.

• Let fertility happen in your own backyard. One of the best lessons in fertility is a garden. This need not be a huge piece of land tilled and sown. In fact, a window-box with some herbs or a few lettuce plants may suffice. By observing the miracles of growth and reproduction, as well as the process by which food is grown, you can gain a greater appreciation for the fertility inherent in all of nature. Show other people your garden and they may very well be inspired to start their own. In a time when much of our food is shipped thousands of miles, using countless amounts of resources, keeping some of your food local is a step toward preserving the fertility of the Earth. Corporate agribusinesses most often use chemical pesticides and fertilizers, wear out soil by not rotating crops or letting fields lay fallow every few years, and engage in other destructive patterns that reduce the Earth's fertility. By lessening your dependence on them and by gardening in a sustainable manner, you add to the fertility of the land.

The main issue with activist magic in general is that it isn't always easy to tell whether your work has been successful, at least not in a detailed manner. If you send energy to an endangered species, and a few years down the line the species begins to recover in a major way, you can't really tell for sure whether your magic had anything to do with it. In the end, none of us can be sure if magical acts that are done in conjunction with mundane activities have made a difference. However, that's no reason not to try. I've done a good bit of activist magic, and I've determined some success through divination, as well as speaking with the totems of species I've worked to help. This is reason enough for me to continue.

So When Fertility Rituals Occur...

. . . you don't have to think of the children. You don't even have to think about sex of any sort (though you're more than welcome to). Just take that creative, fertile energy and channel it toward another endeavor that you feel it fits. What I've discussed here are just a few ideas—take them as inspiration, and elaborate however much you like. Fertility energy is creative energy! Go out and create!

Lucky Coins

by Janina Renée

The practice of keeping a lucky coin is found the world over. People may carry such coins in their pockets or wallets, or they may attach them to charm bracelets, necklaces, anklets, and watch fobs, or stick them in shoes or hatbands. Because they are so rich in symbolism, the coins of the world have attracted a wealth of folk beliefs and practices.

The most obvious use of lucky coins is to attract more money, on the principle that like attracts like. This idea is utilized in Chinese charms, where coins may be hung on a red string (for yang energy) to activate money luck and combined with other auspicious symbols. However, when we look into the magical uses of coins, we see that they are also protective and promote overall well-being. As most coins are round, they share the circle's symbolism of soul and self, unity and wholeness, and they also serve as emblems of the Sun, world, and cosmos. Again, old Chinese coins illustrate this principle: being round with a square hole in the center, they serve as cosmograms that harmonize the energies of Heaven and Earth. Singapore's octagonal dollars in the shape of a pa-kua charm—another image of cosmic harmony—were consciously designed to promote the entire country's well-being.

Because of their luck-amplifying qualities, coins are a part of celebration customs. Thus, it is a common practice to bring a coin into the house first thing New Year's morning. In a local version of this practice, Sicilians place a shiny coin, heads up, on the windowsill at the stroke of midnight on New Year's Eve. Coins are also given as New Year's presents to wish luck to the recipients. When the Chinese make presents of coins, they may give them in groups of three, because as a creative yang number, three generates wealth. Chinese charms may feature coins in groups of nine, for as three times three, nine perpetuates wealth. Coins are traditional presents for newborns—especially upon a first visit, as in North Yorkshire, where a silver coin is placed in the baby's hand, or in Germany, where a visitor slips money under the infant's pillow. There is also a general practice of keeping a coin in the baby's buggy or crib.

Weddings are another event calling for amulet coins, as in the custom of a bride wearing one in her shoe. The tradition of the lucky sixpence is well known, though the type of coin varies in different countries. In Spain and Sweden, the bride wears a gold coin from her mother in the right shoe and a silver coin from her father in the left shoe. When they move into their new home, some Scottish couples nail the bride's coin to the doorframe.

The practice of nailing a coin to the doorframe is also used by Scottish businesses, and in the old South, coins were nailed to the threshold to attract trade to serve as protection. As a practice both for luck and protection that goes back at least as far as Roman times, coins were nailed to the masts or placed under the masts of ships. In Herman Melville's novel *Moby Dick*, the gold doubloon that Captain Ahab nails to the mast is described as the ship's navel.

Some other customs emphasize coins' more protective qualities. To ward off evil Witches, some Irish put a silver dime under the fireplace, while some Germans put silver under their pillows. And some French Canadians carry a gold coin to keep mischievous fairies away. Gold coins were a favorite charm among British fighting men in World War I, believed to put an individual in communication with his lucky star. Silver coins protected against Hoodoo and were especially worn around the ankle (often on a string tied with nine knots), to protect against cramps, sprains, and heart trouble, and to prevent poisonous magical influences from coming up from the ground and through the feet.

In the 1930s, folklore collector Harry M. Hyatt observed that wearing a protective silver coin was "almost exclusively a Negro practice," and Sam Jordan, a man born into slavery, commented that in his youth, "All of them wore a silver dime on a raw cotton thread around their ankles . . ." This hearkens back to the African custom of wearing some kind of disc to keep the circle of the soul

complete. One of Hyatt's North Carolina informants suggested fastening a silver coin to a baby so he won't "blink himself" if too many people admire him (this is a variation of the evil eye belief, though that term was not used).

Beliefs about lucky coins also concern the fortuitous ways they may come to you and the special features of the coins. Found coins (especially if found face up), or those given as gifts are particularly lucky, as is a coin featuring one's year of birth. In Austria, coins found during a rainstorm are poetically viewed as having fallen from heaven. A coin may be kept as lucky if you were carrying it when you experienced some stroke of great good fortune. Crooked coins are also lucky, and bent coins are supposed to provide protection against Witches, perhaps because disrupted patterns baffle malevolent supernatural forces.

The inspirational images on many coins enhance their powers as amulets. Ancient coins often featured images of gods and goddesses, who might be appealed to for help and protection, while modern coins may use figures such as leaders, heroes, and other achievers. In France, an angel design on different issues of gold francs was considered lucky: such a coin was reputed to have been carried by Napoleon, and also to have saved its designer from the guillotine. The coin most widely used as a luck charm has been the Maria Theresa silver dollar, which was prized by gypsies and others throughout Europe, and even into parts of Africa and Asia—having been especially popular in the Ottoman Empire, perhaps because the Austrian Empress's buxom figure represented luxury and sensuality. The coin favored as a bodyguard by Hoodoo believers seems to be the Mercury Head Dime (actually a representation of Winged Liberty), which is also a standard ingredient in mojo bags. The Indian Head Penny has been used as a "look-out" to keep the law away, as well as for luck; however, practices vary as to whether you nail one, two, or four Indian Head Pennies across the door, sill, or frame. The Seated Liberty was part of a recipe to expel bad magic from the body (this pertains to the Hoodoo belief that sorcerers can magically insert living things into victims' bodies).

Although I haven't encountered any superstitions along these lines, it would seem that a Mercury Head Dime could express a wish for fleetness of mind, and a Walking Liberty (deemed America's most beautiful coin) could convey hope for people ranging from prisoners to persons suffering from bad feet or general ill health. Although the Indian heads on older coins may have originally had some derogatory associations, Native Americans could now appropriate them as symbols of economic strength. Many other inspirational associations could be made with the images on coins—and of course, when we consider the coins of other lands, the selection is very great indeed. Examine some foreign and domestic coins to find if one speaks to you. You may wish to carry such a coin for luck, protection, or inspiration.

Leaf Magic

by Michelle Skye

No matter where you are, there's probably a leaf somewhere nearby. Tree, herb, flower, weed . . . it doesn't matter from whence the leaf blooms, as long as it is (or was) alive. Leaf magic is wonderfully accessible, both on a mundane and a magical level. Mundanely, leaves are easy to find in a world that has become increasingly industrial. Dandelions burst through city sidewalks; cacti bloom in the desert. The power of Mother Nature is mind-boggling! At the same time, the magic of leaves is rather simple in construct. So uncomplicated at its very core, children can perform leaf magic effortlessly. Join me in connecting with your inner, leaf-loving, tree-hugging child.

Not only accessible but truly utilitarian, leaves can be used for just about any kind of magical purpose. Wishing to manifest a specific goal in your life? Moving to a new location? Looking to attract the attention of your neighbor? Use leaves! Burn them, bury them, wrap them, tear them, write on them, dry them, float them, wave them. You can do just about anything with a leaf. There's no need for fancy candles and expensive ingredients if you've got a couple of trees and a plant or two nearby.

Leaves cover a wide variety of issues. However, due to their essential nature, leaves are naturally powerful in certain magical areas. Leaves manifest food out of thin air. Through photosynthesis, leaves create sugars and starches for the tree to eat. Therefore, leaves are especially useful when casting creation or manifestation spells. They also resonate well with any kind of movement magic because of their wind-driven existence on the tops of trees. Leaves are also helpful in attracting attention. They

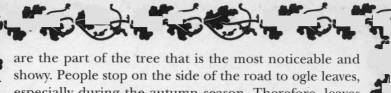

are the part of the tree that is the most noticeable and showy. People stop on the side of the road to ogle leaves, especially during the autumn season. Therefore, leaves are great to use when trying to attract someone's attention. As the "hair" of the tree, leaves can also be useful when casting self-esteem and beauty spells. They practically ooze beauty, grace, and elegance. Powerful, accessible, and simple, leaf magic can help you transform your life for the better.

Creation Magic and Manifestation

Since leaves take the intangible, elusive element of light and transmute it into the tangible, substantial product of food, it only makes sense that they would serve as a fabulous metaphor for your own personal creations and manifestations. Leaf manifestation works best when you want to bring a concept out of the idea phase into the material phase. Perhaps you've wanted to own a yoga studio, write a book, or design your own fashion line. Make a decision to consciously work toward your goal, as deciding to work toward its accomplishment is the first step. Once you've made the commitment, it's time to grab a leaf and cast a spell to manifest your goal in this reality. A leaf needs rain or ground water, carbon dioxide, and sunlight to transform light into food. It also must have chlorophyll, a green pigment that gives the plant its color, which is stored in the photosynthetic cells. Therefore, we need representations of all four elements: water (rain), air (carbon dioxide), fire (sunlight), and earth (chlorophyll). The following spell combines the four elements with the power of the leaf to manifest your idea in your world.

Leaf Manifestation Spell

Items needed: a green leaf, rainwater, a charcoal pencil, a small spade (optional).

Before performing your spell, collect rainwater in a bucket or bowl. If you live in a dry area, use some of your drinking water. On a sunny day, gather your spell materials and go outside. Set up your ritual altar near a tree, preferably the tree from which you took the leaf. (Remember to ask the tree before taking a leaf and always give an offering back to the tree, such as cornmeal, a cup of water, or a pretty ribbon.)

Next, ground and center as you normally do, then, grasping the leaf in your hands, visualize your goal. See it completed with as much detail as you can imagine. Once your idea has fully formed in your mind, anoint your leaf with the rainwater. Set it in the sunlight and allow the water to dry naturally. (This might take some time, so continue to meditate, visualizing your completed goal.) Once the water has evaporated, write your goal on the leaf with the charcoal pencil and blow on it with your

breath. Take a few more moments to fully visualize your goal and then thank the leaf and bury it under the tree. Your spell is complete! Now it's time to take the necessary mundane steps in realizing your goal.

Movement Magic

High atop the tree, the leaves flutter and dance to the rhythm of the air while still remaining connected to the earth through the sturdy trunk of the tree. If you want change in your life while still remaining grounded in everyday reality, try leaf magic. Leaf movement magic allows you to transform some aspects of your life while keeping others that are helpful and useful to you. So leaf magic will not destroy your orderly life; rather, it will shift those aspects that are out of sync with the whole. You probably won't lose your job, but you might stop biting your nails. Leaf magic will gently shimmy your world instead of turning it upside down. Since leaf movement magic is intrinsically connected to the element of air, it is especially useful with air-like activities, such as education, intelligence, inspiration, writing, and speaking. However, you can use the following spell for any kind of change you want in your life.

Leaf Movement Spell

Items needed: a leaf, a windy day (or night), a place above the ground (such as a second-story building, a tree, or a tall mountain).

With your leaf in hand, carefully climb to your high place. As you do, concentrate on the aspect of your life you want to change. Maybe you want to open up to love or lose weight or work fewer hours (while still getting the same pay). It's best not to send away an annoying co-worker or cranky boss. Remember, their lives and will are their own.

At the top of your climb, hold the leaf above your head and allow the wind to caress it. (Obviously, you'll need to open the window if you're inside.) Bring the leaf down and state your desire three times, getting louder and louder as you do. With the last statement, which can be a shout if you'd like, release the leaf into the air and turn away from its flight. You want to send the energy out, away from you, and not hamper your thoughts with your perceptions of the leaf's flight. It is flying up to the realm of the gods, whether or not it flies in reality. Leave your release point with the knowledge that your leaf carries your wish and is working with you to manifest your heart's desires.

Attracting Attention Magic

Sometimes you just want to be noticed, and leaves are especially good for attracting attention. After all, we don't wax poetic about the roots of the tree, do we? No! It's the leaves that draw us in so we can appreciate a tree's subtle beauty. The following spell can be used for attracting the attention of a specific person or for boosting your own self-esteem. This will help you to feel more attractive internally, thus projecting your winning ways in a positive, outward manner. Utilizing the Law of Reciprocity, what you feel within will be projected without, altering your life in a positive manner.

Leaf Attention and Self-Esteem Magic

Items needed: a dried, beautiful, blemish-free leaf (preferably one that is in the peak of fall color); a charcoal disc; lighter; charcoal incense burner or bowl of sand; various herbs of your choosing; mortar and pestle.

Set up the items on your ritual altar. This spell can be done at any time, but I think it works best when performed at night. Beforehand, decide which herbs you wish to combine with your leaf. The herbs should

correspond to your specific goal. Pick herbs that remind you of the person whose attention you wish to attract or choose herbs related to love or beauty. There are numerous herbal correspondence charts on the Internet, or you can check out Scott Cunningham's *Encyclopedia of Magical Herbs*. Make sure you have no more than four herbs total, including your tree leaf, otherwise your desire might become muddied and confused.

State out loud each herb's name and what it represents to you. You might say, "This is cinnamon. It represents love flowing into my life." Place the herb in the mortar and grind it with the pestle. Add the tree leaf last, as it is the activating force of the spell. When all the herbs and leaf are ground together into a fine powder, light your charcoal on the incense burner or bowl of sand. Sprinkle the herb and leaf mixture on the charcoal. Breathe in a bit of the fragrance, being careful not to inhale too much smoke. Watch the smoke carry your wish up to the ethers. Burn as much incense as you wish, allowing the smoke to infuse your body and drift up to the heavens. The smoke connects you to the world of spirit, where anything and everything is possible. When you are ready, dispose of the charcoal in a reasonable manner and store the extra incense in an airtight container. Be sure to label the container!

∼

Subtle, gentle, and grounding, leaf magic can help with all your inner wishes and desires. By connecting and uniting to the world around you, leaf magic forms the conduit through which the spirits of earth, air, fire, and water can enter your life. Leaves are delicate, easily torn apart, yet hardy enough to withstand the strongest storms. They are a wonderful symbol of the persistence and grace needed to succeed on this planet. Open your life to the blessing of leaves and watch your goals manifest!

Everyday Children's Rituals

by Laurel Reufner

No doubt about it, childhood is a magical time. Why not tap into that natural inquisitiveness and sense of wonder using rituals created just for them? We're sure to learn a few things in the process as well.

Working rituals with children can be so much fun, but there are a few things to consider before you get started. These key points may seem familiar; if so, just consider them to be gentle reminders.

• Keep in mind the ages of the children involved. A ritual designed for a five-year-old usually doesn't appeal to a teen. There are also different safety concerns for different ages. For example, an older child would be safer around fire than a younger one.

• Keep it short, or at least be able to shorten it if needed. Kids tend to get bored easily.

• Keep it fun. Needless to say, this is the most important point for the little ones!

Children's rituals are a great time to introduce kids to how adult rituals are performed. If they're interested, help them learn the parts of a ritual and let them help you with the planning. Kids like helping create sacred space. Let them cast the circle, help call the quarters, or do any of the other tasks you use when performing a ritual.

The following ideas are for you to use as you will with your kids. You can take the basic frame and adjust it to your family, location, or hobbies.

Protecting Your Pet

You'll need paper, clear contact paper and pens/markers/crayons, a large jump ring (or other means of attaching the charm to the pet's collar), scissors, and a hole punch. After creating your sacred space, cut a triangle or circle out of the paper and decorate it with a protective design. Let your child use their imagination for this, creating an image they feel is protective for their pet. Carefully seal the image front and back with the contact paper and cut out the finished charm. Punch a hole in the top and attach the jump ring. Show your child how to hold the charm in their hands and focus protective energy into it. Talk to them about visualizing their pet being surrounded by a protective sphere.

Next, attach the charm to your pet's collar. This can either be done during or after the ritual. This ritual can easily be adapted for pets that don't wear collars by placing the charm somewhere safe near the pet.

Mirror, Mirror

This ritual can be useful for a variety of needs: low self-esteem or self-confidence, negative self-image, trying to make friends at school. The finished mirror can also be used to give an ego boost before tests or public performances. To perform the ritual, you'll need either a small hand mirror or a small mirror to hang on the wall as well as items with which to decorate it. Use your imagination for the decorations, creating things to hang from the mirror, such as beads or feathers, or keep it simple with stickers or paint pens. If you feel your child is old enough and you're feeling brave, you could even try glass etching the mirrors using glass etching cream.

Together, create your sacred space and then get down to the business of decorating the mirrors. Create designs that make you feel good and that confirm you are a worthwhile individual.

After the ritual, the mirror should be kept handy near the owner's dressing area. Kids should make a habit out of looking in the mirror often and visualizing or reminding themselves that they are confident, outgoing, and worthy of love.

Chasing Bad Dreams

Traditionally used to trap bad dreams, a dreamcatcher hung over where your child sleeps can also help protect them from those monsters under the bed. The materials for this project can be gathered together so they'll have more meaning to your child. Either use a small embroidery hoop or a branch tied into

a circle for the base. Red thread is traditional among the Ojibwa people for forming the web. Small beads and charms with meaning can be strung on at regular intervals and feathers or other dangles can be added after the web is made. While helping your child spin their web, the two of you can talk about what scares them at night and maybe brainstorm ways of dealing with those fears. After the dreamcatcher is ready, the two of you can take it out into the moonlight to charge it for the child's nighttime protection.

Keep 'em Safe

You and your child can make a protection amulet for them to carry in their backpack. You'll need a small bag or pouch. Beforehand, help your child decide what will go into the amulet. Suggested attributes to include are protection, courage, luck, blessings, peace, and balance. Have your child hold each item in their hands and charge it with the chosen attribute before placing the item in the bag or pouch. If working with young children, you may wish to demonstrate the process with each item, which allows you to charge it as well. After the ritual is over, the amulet can be tucked safely into a backpack.

Just Because

This is a great ritual that can performed anywhere and at anytime, just because. Celebrate life, childhood, and playfulness! Make creating your sacred space fun, letting your child skip or hop while casting the circle. Set a blanket in the middle of it all, eat cupcakes and juice or tea, and share what makes life special at that moment. Use this ritual to simply enjoy your children, just because.

～

Remember to enjoy your children and let them enjoy the power of magic in their young lives. Some of these rituals concern serious issues, making us find that fine line between keeping our kids safe and showing them the pleasure, power, and satisfaction of helping take matters into their own hands and shaping their own lives.

Air Magic

Planes, Trains, and Magical Spells

by Harmony Usher

The very nature of travel is magical. When we plan to travel, we experience a shift in our desires, a clarification of our intentions, and the unfolding of a journey. The traveler is an archetype found in myths, traditional tales, and spiritual texts and has long been associated with growth and wisdom. It is a time of being between the worlds, a state of mind in which new experiences and insight are invited.

As a traveler, you voluntarily give up the comforts of home for the unknown. You fly from your nest, venture from your cave, swim from your inlet. You enter into a labyrinth—a set course on your mind. You take the journey, reach your destination, and at some point, find your way back home. How do you prepare for this journey? How do you work with spiritual forces to invite safety, security, and pleasant adventure along the way?

When ancient Greeks got the traveling bug, they threw a knapsack on their back and called on the god Hermes to guide them through craggy hills and across treacherous seas. When early Christians had to get away from it all, they called on St. Christopher to bless them with safe passage and protect them from highway robbers. Although modern-day travel isn't fraught with the same dangers that existed in days of old, there are certainly things we fret about when we need to make a voyage from our home. Here are some ideas for magical traveler wanting to experience safe passage from "here" to "there" and back again.

Although spiritual pilgrimages continue to be an important ritual for some people, most of us will never become a pilgrim in the strict sense of the word. For the most part, travel is something we do for practical purposes on a daily basis and something we take for granted as more of us live farther away from our places of work and families. We may travel a specific highway each day in our car to work, take a particular bus every Wednesday to reach an art class, or board an airplane every summer to visit our parents in a distant city. Because travel is so commonplace, and because trains, planes, and automobiles allow us to cover many miles in a short time, we are not conscious of travel in the same way our ancestors were. Typically, preparations are hurried and we have come to begrudge travel time as wasted time away from more important things.

Commuter Magic

Routine car travel doesn't need to be wasted time. The daily commute offers a wonderful opportunity to create a new sacred space in your mind and in your vehicle. A quick ritual as you approach your car is a good way to start. Walk once or twice around your vehicle, taking note of the things that you appreciate about it. Be thankful for its well-inflated tires and track record getting you to and from your destination. Some might employ a banishing ritual at this time, but I prefer a clockwise ritual, full of appreciation and an expectation of a safe journey.

Some find giving their car a name reminds them of the spiritual nature of travel. If this is your style, choose a name that invokes an image or idea you wish to cultivate for your travel time. My first car was a little gray Mazda I christened "Pegasus," after the immortal winged horse

of Greek mythology. I employed a simple ritual with Peggy—always greeting her when I got in and buckled up, and thanking her for safe passage when I returned home. Just saying the name "Pegasus" evoked a sense of journey in my spirit and opened my mind and heart to new adventures.

As you begin to see your vehicle as an extension of your spiritual practice space, you will find yourself wanting to take extra care of it. Many people practicing travel magic become more intolerant of clutter and garbage inside their car and take extra time to regularly clean and tidy this space. Not only does this help to keep your spiritual space free of physical and psychic clutter, but it's good practice not to have too many unsecured items in the vehicle should you need to make a quick stop!

You might also use a little essential oil in your vehicle to encourage states of mind conducive to a safe trip.

Jasmine is linked to alertness and quick thinking, lavender can be used to relieve anxiety, and citrus is good for keeping you awake on long trips. All of these scents can be helpful in thick traffic or when traveling on unknown highways. They are also much more pleasant than some of the odors associated with large city driving.

Commuter Incantations

Once you have attended to the environment in your vehicle, you will want to think about rituals to invoke safety. Do make sure you choose rituals that don't distract you from concentrating while you drive, which would be counterproductive to say the least!

The use of a travel amulet or pendant has long been a tradition associated with safety. Choose an object that has personal meaning to you. This object should not obstruct your view of the road in any way or cause any safety hazards—I would suggest staying away from crystals or other highly reflective materials that may cause distracting light reflection for yourself or other drivers. You might want to hang your special object from your rearview mirror, place it under your seat, or put it in the glove box. Some people like to tuck amulets right under the car's hood, close to the engine.

If you have a feline companion that doesn't mind you using a couple of her whiskers, you might consider gently snipping a couple from her cheek and placing them in a small amulet bag. This bag can be hung from your rearview mirror. Just as cats use their whiskers to navigate in the dark, you can invoke your companion's feline abilities to guide your own vehicle at night, or along an unknown highway.

When you arrive in your vehicle, it is good practice to take a moment to notice your emotional state. If you feel tense or worried, take a deep breath and attend to your state of mind. Most traffic incidents occur when people are agitated or angry. Breathe in deeply and as you allow your breath to release, say, "I travel through life with ease," or, "I travel the path of peace and harmony." These meditations will help you see traffic situations as they arise and be able to respond to them with clarity.

If you commute on heavily traveled highways, take a moment to offer blessings to all those fellow travelers on the road each day, sending them peace and contentment for their drive. Such a state of mind and spirit will keep traffic flowing around you and help avoid unfortunate and unnecessary incidents.

Traffic Tangles and Parking Woes

Despite mindfulness, invocation, and magical attention to travel, sometimes things do not go our way. My grandmother, who is ninety-four and whose earliest memories of travel involve a horse and cart, continues to delight and bless me with words of wisdom. On a recent occasion, I arrived at her home two hours late for a special dinner due to a traffic accident that caused a long delay on the highway. When I finally arrived, my mood was less than cheery. "Dear," she said, "don't be cross. Take a moment to be thankful for those things you were spared today. Who knows what was farther along the other path?" I often remember her words when I find myself becoming agitated at congested traffic and detours.

Car travel in a large city has its own set of challenges, often including a lack of parking! It is good practice to use public transportation whenever you are going into the heart of a city, but in the event you are faced with needing a parking spot, an invocation might be helpful. A dear friend taught me a lovely little invocation I now say whenever I enter a lot: "Loving Mother, full of grace, show to me, my parking space!"

The Magical Car Kit

Just as you may travel with an emergency kit that includes a flare, flashlight, and a bit of food, you might consider putting together a magical kit for other kinds of emergencies! Use a small box with a lid, a special fabric bag, or a sandwich baggie and tuck it into your glove box. Some people like to include a small notebook with incantations and spells to handle things like soothing strong emotions after a close call or finding your way when you are lost. Magical maps can be helpful as well. Before your journey, invite the universe to provide safe passage while tracing the route of your journey onto the map. Then use a yellow, white, or orange crayon to lightly color over the route and envision a protective light enveloping you as you travel this path. Fold up the map, wrap it in ribbon, and place in the glove box with your other tools.

The Pilgrim's Nudge

Occasionally we are called to take a journey—something quite different from our daily commute or our occasional trip to a nearby city. The journey is quite different in nature from routine travel, and many people experience a shift in consciousness before it happens. Keep attuned to any feelings of "itchy feet" or restlessness that may be characterized by lack of sleep or increased gazing at the horizon. Pacing can also be a sign that travel is in your cards. These "symptoms" are normal, and when you become attuned to them, you will begin to recognize them as signs that it is time to pack a suitcase. You have been nudged—it's time to go!

Perhaps you need to visit your birthplace or a specific lake, mountain, or monument. Perhaps there is a relationship you need to attend to, which involves traveling to see your loved one. Once you realize you have been called to take a journey, spend time in meditation and reflection, contemplating what you want to experience, achieve, resolve, or gain by making the trip. A successful voyage begins with clear intention and purpose. That is not to say that wandering is not also a perfectly valid form of travel! If you have been called to wander, your intention is simply to be moved along by the wind, to let go of agenda and become attuned to trust and abundance.

When the time comes, you stand at your door, suitcase in hand. The taxi is in the driveway, engine running. You glance back into your darkened home, and your mind races through a list: Do I have my tickets? Is the key available so my neighbor can water the plants? Are the windows closed? Will I make it to the airport in time? You take that bold first step onto the front step, and in that moment have become a traveler, a pilgrim. You turn, lock the door, and dash to the taxi. Rest easy, there is magic to be found all along the path.

Safe Passage

Whether you travel as part of your daily routine or are about to set off on the journey of a lifetime, using magical wisdom and meditation will help you find your way. Each moment "between the worlds" will offer insight and blessings. Share these with all you meet on the path.

Safe passage to you all!

A Short and Sweet Guide to Pendulums

by Gail Wood

*The pendulum of the mind alternates between sense
and nonsense, not between right and wrong.*
—Carl Jung

Pendulums are used in science to measure gravitational pull; in practical ways, such as the old grandfather clocks to tell time; and in magical matters to gauge our inner wisdom. We've seen Witches on a popular television show use a wildly swinging pendulum to reveal or locate the information they needed. Most of us are aware of the superstitious practice of determining the sex of an unborn child by using a wedding ring suspended on a string. It swings one way for a boy and another for a girl. The swinging pendulum reminds us of the universal balance and harmony as it swings back and forth and then rests at center. Deceptively simple, pendulums can be profoundly revealing of our inner connections with our highest self and to the Divine.

A pendulum is usually a weighted symmetrical object suspended from 2 to 3 inches of cord, chain, or string. The object can be a specially made pendulum, a ring, a necklace, a charm, a stone, a shell, or any object that weights the string. Anything that calls to you and is special to you can be used as a pendulum. You may choose to buy a specially made pendulum, use a piece of jewelry you love, or find an object in nature and fashion one yourself. Practical items like plumb bobs and fishing weights are also pendulums in disguise.

The skills used in pendulum work are simple and, as is so often the case in divination work, it is practice and persistence that makes pendulum divination an effective magical skill. Through continued application, the pendulum becomes an effective tool for the magical worker. Becoming skillful with the pendulum takes a combination of trust and patience. This is a very personal divination system, answering questions about both our outer and inner lives.

Preparing yourself to use the pendulum is part of the process. You can be formal, fussy, casual, relaxed, or ritualistic, but you should never be flippant. You are consulting the deep powers of yourself and the universe, so an attitude of respect is absolutley required. Find within you that quiet, still point—your center—before you begin. You might want to wash your hands in cold water, ground, and smudge yourself and the pendulum. Do those things that help you focus and be firm in that place where you know magic happens and you are the Goddess, you are the God.

After you have found your pendulum, practice finding a good position for holding it. In general, people use their dominant hand between the thumb and forefinger, but practice with both until you determine which hand works best for you and then use that one consistently. Many people draw a circle with a dot in the middle on a piece of cardboard to use as a target and hold the pendulum perpendicular to the surface. You may wish to rest your elbow on your other hand or on a surface. Like so many magical skills, finding what works for you and practicing consistently is key.

The first part of using a pendulum is being able to move it and understand how the pendulum communicates. Hold the pendulum above the target card until it becomes still. You can either say aloud or silently words such as "quiet" or "still." Once you have quiet, determine the positive or yes pattern. I say, "Show me YES." The pendulum will swing in a circle one way or the other, or back and forth. Once the positive pattern is found, determine the negative pattern. I say, "Show me NO." Again the pendulum will swing a different way, either circular or back and forth. Then determine the neutral pattern. I say, "Show me I DON'T KNOW." You will need to determine these patterns each time you use the pendulum, and you will probably find that your patterns are amazingly consistent.

After you are comfortable holding the pendulum and determining the positive, negative, and neutral positions, take some time to try moving the pendulum. A useful exercise is to still your pendulum, close your eyes and ask it to move clockwise. After you sense it moving, open your eyes and look. Then repeat the exercise asking it to move counterclockwise, and then a third time, asking it to move back and forth. The pendulum works in harmony with the vibrations of your thoughts and desires.

Take some time to connect with your pendulum and understand how your energy and the energy of the pendulum harmonize and connect you to the rhythms of the universe. Most people add ceremony to their pendulum work. Ask your guides to assist as you ask questions and find answers.

People use a pendulum for a wide variety of magical reasons, and it is part of a series of techniques called dowsing. Dowsing is a way of uniting opposite ways of thinking—the intuitive and the rational. Pendulum work requires that we trust our intuition and that we use our conscious mind and intellect to analyze what we want to know. Then we can develop a series of questions to get to the heart of the matter. The pendulum helps us bypass the critical, judging part of our conscious mind. Even though it helps us survive, our conscious mind can also be a barrier to the part of us that understands without words, the intuitive part. The intuitive part of our nature understands and uses what our rational brain tells us is nonsense. The pendulum combines both ways of knowing, the intellectual and intuitive, so we can use our brains more fully.

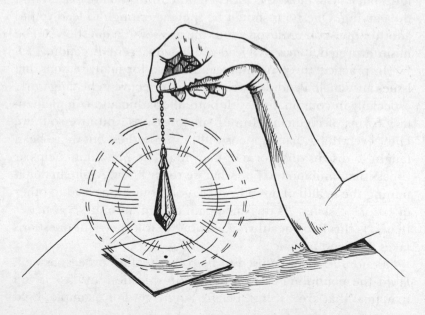

Pendulums use our body as a conduit and channel to our intuitive inner selves and to our inner divinity, which spark within us that connects us to the transcendent Divine Universe. Because we are powerful beings and that power within often goes unacknowledged and unexplored, it is possible to override our inner wisdom and overpower the messages with our own wishful thinking. Your will is often stronger than you know, and desire is a powerful energy. That's why it's important, when using the pendulum, to be sure you are connected to the life-force energies of the universe, that which we call the God and Goddess, in authentic ways. Be true to yourself. Sometimes when we ask a question, we have to let go of what we want to hear in order to hear what we need to know. Our desires can create limitations. If we ask for our highest good, we may get unexpected blessings.

As you question the pendulum, you will realize that a good, well-phrased question is part of the art of this kind of dowsing. Usually, one question leads to another, so the game of "twenty questions" is good practice! In this way, a good question leads us through a chain of reasoning until we come to an understanding. For example, if you are asking the pendulum to help you find a lost earring, you start with, "Is it in the house?" Continue with, "Is it upstairs?" Get more specific each time until you are able to find the earring. Questions should be specific enough to lead you to another question until you get to the answer. If a question can be misinterpreted, it may well lead you in a different direction.

In practice, the pendulum can be used for many reasons, big issues and small. Pendulums can be very effective in healing work, especially in combination with both allopathic and complementary forms of medicine. In our subconscious, intuitive soul, we know everything that happens within our bodies, but we've been taught to distrust that form of knowing. The pendulum helps us bypass that inhibition to find what we really know. Again, in determining the health of an individual, good questions lead to other questions. Asking, "Is this knee pain due to an injury?" is better than, "Is this knee healthy?" Learning to ask the right questions takes time and patience.

Pendulums can be used to help the healing process as well. Hold the pendulum above the area in question and ask if you may heal that area, using specific language. For example, hold the pendulum above a joint, and ask, "May I heal this area of the arthritis pain?" If the answer is yes, hold the pendulum over the area until it stops moving and goes to stillness. That has cleared the area of the pain. Often, frequent applications of this as a healing modality (in addition to more traditional medical applications) will alleviate many symptoms and aid in overall health.

Many people use pendulums to determine if the food they eat is good for them before purchasing, during preparation, or before eating. Questions such as, "Will this serve my health?" or "Will this serve my highest good?" are excellent questions to ask before purchasing or eating food. Determining the effectiveness of vitamins and supplements is another good way to use the pendulum.

Any situation that needs clarification or requires making a choice is suitable for pendulum divination. Job searches, moving, and major purchases are all areas where the pendulum can help you make a better decision. As with all magical practices, you still need to do the work on a practical, everyday level. Affirmative answers to questions such as, "Will this be a good job for me?" imply that you should send in your résumé and do your best at the interview. The pendulum can help you to put your best foot forward, but you still have to do the walking yourself! A pendulum won't get you the job, but it will help you develop the best, most effective ways to be successful.

A pendulum is very effective in helping you understand how you feel about situations, people, or ideas. Questions of emotion and the heart are often clarified through use of the pendulum. This is a tender area that can easily override your desires and wishes, so it's best to approach the situation with your strong connection to your spirit guides and Divine being. Ceremony, focused intent, letting go of expected outcomes, and asking your guides to assist you is especially important here, though these practices are important anytime you ask questions of the pendulum. Once you are grounded and centered in the Divine, you can ask your questions. Avoid questions like, "Should I divorce him because he cheated on me?" If you find yourself asking negatively charged questions, you are probably too emotionally overwrought, and either need to consult the pendulum at another time or spend some time centering and grounding. When you feel centered in your own inner divinity and power, ask the pendulum the best

way to handle emotional situations focusing on how you feel about them rather than what you should do about them.

In all cases, the pendulum is a powerful and responsive tool to your magical work. It can aid you in your everyday life and help you make good choices. It's simplicity itself and the wisdom and complexity it brings to your life are revealed as you practice with it. Using the pendulum wisely and well takes time, patience, and active use. As a magical tool, it should be treasured as much as your other divinatory tools and magical materials. Regularly cleanse your pendulum with sage or other incense, set it out in the moonlight or sunlight, and store it in special places wrapped in special cloths. Your tools are your magical partners and treating them with honor will enhance their connection to you. Through your pendulum's use, you connect with your ageless, wise, highest self and simultaneously dance in harmony with the universe and the divine energies that surround you and reside in you.

The Mysteries of Rhiannon

by Mickie Mueller

A song by Fleetwood Mac inspired merely by Rhiannon's name has been part of popular culture for years, and many of us heard our first snippets of her legend through the medium of music. But who is this mysterious lady who fills our heads with magical visions of the otherworld? She is the goddess Rhiannon, a Welsh deity who appears as a classic Mare goddess as well as a goddess of birds, both very ancient associations. This lunar goddess hails from the underworld known as Anwynn and is often connected to the Fey. Her stories are told in the medieval manuscript of Celtic mythology known as *The Mabinogion* (ma-bin-OG-yon). The tale leads the reader through her courtship, during which she displays her intellectual prowess and ability to get exactly what she wants. Her wedding tells us of her great generosity. Later in her story, she meets with tragedy and suffers humiliation, which she bears with great dignity and grace. Rhiannon eventually overcomes her tragedy with great triumph. As she ages, her birds have power over the living and the dead and she makes a final trip to the underworld to retrieve a loved one and is then released.

From the mythology of Rhiannon, the clever researcher will discover that she is represented in the classic forms of Maiden, Mother, and Crone. She is a powerful energy to work with magically and will offer guidance to bring wisdom, fertility, abundance, strength, and transformation to the lives of those who simply ask. Let's explore her legends, associations, and mysteries to further understand and work with the ancient Great Queen.

Rhiannon the Maiden

Rhiannon (hree-AHN-nohn) was a being from the underworld of Anwynn (an-NOON) who was betrothed to a man she didn't love. Interested in a mortal man named Pwyll (poo-UL), a lord of the land of Dyved (DIV-ed), she appeared to him riding her enchanted white mare past a faerie mound. Smitten at seeing her racing by upon her horse, gold brocade dress flowing about her, Pwyll naturally followed her. However, no matter how hard he rode he couldn't catch Rhiannon, although her horse didn't seem to be running faster than his. Bewildered, he finally called out and asked her to stop, which she did, teasingly telling him that it would have been better for his horse if he had only asked sooner! She really knew how to grab a guy's attention, and they fell in love and planned to marry.

There was a great feast in honor of the couple at her father's great halls in Anwynn and during the festivities, a man approached Pwyll asking him for a favor. Feeling rather full of himself at his wedding feast, and before Rhiannon could shut him up, he hastily replied, "Whatever you ask, so long as it is within my power, you shall have it." The man was Rhiannon's ex-suitor Gwawl (gwoul), who told Pwyll that he had come to claim her and the wedding feast for himself! Rhiannon whispered to Pwyll that he better let her do the talking at this point, and that he had now given his word in front of all in attendance and could not back out. But Rhiannon had a plan. Rhiannon explained to Gwawl that the feast was not Pwyll's to give, it was already given to the guests, but that they would plan another feast, and she would belong to Gwawl at that feast.

The night of the next feast, Rhiannon's plan unfolded. Pwyll showed up disguised as a beggar, and asked Gwawl for a favor, to which he replied, "Your request is welcomed, and if it is reasonable, I will gladly grant it." Pwyll presented him with a small bag and asked that Gwawl fill it with food. Gwawl ordered the bag to be filled, but the bag had been enchanted by Rhiannon and no matter how much was put into the bag, it could not be filled. Pwyll then explained that the only way the bag would ever be full was if a nobleman put both feet in the bag and declared that it was full. Rhiannon suggested that he better do it quickly before the feast was gone, so Gwawl

put both feet into the bag. Pwyll then quickly pulled the bag up over his head and tied it shut! He called in all his men (who had been waiting outside), and they proceeded to hit the bag with staff or foot calling out, "What is this? A badger!" And they wouldn't let Gwawl out until he agreed to leave and make no further claims or seek revenge. And so Rhiannon and Pwyll, her chosen husband, were married. It was a great celebration, and no one left without being given a gift of fine jewelry or precious stone.

From this story of Rhiannon, we learn many things about how to work with her in the Maiden aspect. She will be glad to assist us, but we must ask her first, for if we chase her with no courtesy, we will never catch her. We can work with her when we need to be eloquent and wise in negotiating dealings, and she reminds us to be careful of our words. She also teaches us that no matter how bad things seem, there is a way out if you use your head and your magic. In the end of the story, we can learn from her to share our blessings and good fortune with others.

Rhiannon the Mother

The first two years of Rhiannon and Pwyll's marriage were wonderful, and the people of Dyved were happy. The third year, as the people were becoming anxious to see an heir to the kingdom, Rhiannon finally bore a son. That night the infant mysteriously vanished as the women charged with watching him fell asleep on the job. Fearing retribution, they committed a gruesome act. They killed a deerhound pup and smeared Rhiannon with the blood while she slept, leaving the bones as evidence that she had murdered her child in the night. Horrified, Rhiannon told the women that if they would tell the truth, she would offer them mercy and protect them from punishment, but they stuck to their false story.

Once word of the supposed murder got out, the other nobles in the land were furious and demanded that Pwyll split from his wife for committing such an atrocity. But Pwyll remained true to Rhiannon and refused to leave her, so she had to be punished for the crime she didn't commit. She had to remain at the court of Arberth and sit at the gate, telling her story to everyone who passed. In addition she had to offer to carry the guests to the court on her back, like a mare. She held her head up and did what was required of her with grace and dignity. Rhiannon was well loved and respected by her people, and as the years passed there were fewer and fewer takers on the offer to be carried.

Meanwhile, a lord named Teirnon (TEER-nan) had a mare that gave birth to a colt every May Eve, but every foal always mysteriously disappeared in the night. He decided to camp out and see what was happening and managed to hack off the arm of some great beast that tried to take off with the colt. He then discovered an infant boy wrapped in brocade nearby. He and his wife decided to raise the child as their own and named him Gwri Golden Hair. He grew unnaturally fast and was raised in a happy home. After several years, they heard the news of Rhiannon's misfortune and punishment and looked at the boy they had been raising with new eyes. Seeing the resemblance to Pwyll and realizing that this must be Rhiannon's son, Teirnon rode to meet with Rhiannon and return her son to her, thus freeing her from her unjust punishment. Upon his return, Rhiannon expressed her relief over all the anxiety she had experienced since his loss, and they renamed their son Pryderi (pruh-DARE-ee), which means "care." The boy's return brought all the nobles in the land together. Pryderi grew up with much love from both his parents and foster parents, and eventually grew to be beloved by his countrymen and ruled his father's lands with prosperity and success.

The story of Rhiannon as Mother shows us a woman's strength, mercy, and grace in the face of adversity. Rhiannon is a benevolent goddess who understands all too well the worry that a mother goes through over her children. Work with her Mother aspect when you have worries about your children or family and wish to restore harmony. Also ask for her help when you are in a situation where you need to remain graceful under pressure. Rhiannon is also a great deity to enlist if you have been wronged and are looking for the truth to come out and justice to be served.

Rhiannon the Crone

Years went by and Rhiannon's son Pryderi took over the duties of a lord of Dyved when his father Pwyll died. Pryderi ended up fighting alongside the hero Bran the Blessed. When Bran was wounded by a poisoned arrow in battle, it was the magical birds of Rhiannon whose song kept his head alive as an oracle and guardian of his people. Her birds also soothed the souls of the remaining warriors after the battle. Pryderi returned to his home in Dyved with his companion and brother of the fallen Bran, Manawydan (man-u-WA-dan), son of Llyr. He had lost his family and home in the battle. Pryderi introduced his mother Rhiannon to Manawydan and suggested the two marry. Rhiannon was one of those women who had aged gracefully, and she was clever, bold, and kind. She agreed to the marriage to the brave and talented Manawydan. It turned out that she made a wise choice, as Manawydan eventually released the lands of Dyved, herself, and her son from a curse. (The land had become wasted, and Rhiannon and her son ended up trapped in the otherworld with their hands fixed upon a golden cauldronlike bowl suspended by chains. It turned out that Gwawl—her spurned suitor from years ago—had a friend cast the enchantments against Rhiannon, Pryderi, and the lands of Dyved. Manawydan returns to the wasted land and captures a mouse. When Manawydan plans to kill the mouse for destroying the fields, a mysterious stranger trades the mouse's life for the freedom of Dyved, Rhiannon, and Pryderi.)

Though there are not as many mentions or as in-depth legends of Rhiannon in her Crone aspect, her story and associations clearly encompass her as a Crone. Her magical birds are one of the oldest representations of the spirit realm. Birds were believed to be the go-betweens from the realms of the living and the next world. Rhiannon's birds had the power to bring the dead to life and lull the living to sleep. Rhiannon is also a gatekeeper who originally comes from Anwynn,

the Celtic underworld. She returns there for a time in her tough-as-nails Crone aspect to attempt her son's rescue.

Call upon Rhiannon in her Crone aspect by asking her to send birds to soothe anxiety and end insomnia or nightmares, especially after a trauma. This aspect of Rhiannon is also a goddess of transformation. If you wish to do Celtic shamanic work, she would be an excellent protective guide on a journey to Anwynn. Rhiannon in her Crone aspect is a loving and protective usher of souls into the next world.

Now that we know Rhiannon's story and have explored her aspects of Maiden, Mother, and Crone, we can look into her other magical associations to help us further connect with this Welsh goddess.

Element: air

Feast Day: March 4

Animals: birds, horses, dogs

Associations with other goddesses: Epona, Macha, Rigatona, Vivianne, Lady of the Lake

Oil or incense: sandalwood, bergamot, lavender, rosemary

Gemstones: moonstone, garnet, amethyst

Colors: gold, deep green, maroon, white

Plants: rosemary, lavender, sweet clover, dandelions, roses, apples

Goddess of Horses and Birds

One of Rhiannon's most recognizable forms is that of the Mare Goddess. The White Mare Goddess is a very old representation. A fine example is the stylized horse scoured into the chalk on a hill known as The White Horse of Uffington, thought to be the oldest hill figure in England. The horse was important to the Celtic people for transportation, agriculture, commerce, and warfare, and with the horse's use by the upper classes, it became a symbol of the kingship.

The Celts close relationship with the horse forged their history. They built wicker chariots for use in warfare and the Mare Goddess was very protective of both calvary and chariots as they went into battle. Mystically the White Mare

Goddess is also linked with death, as evidenced by Horse Goddess figures appearing upon grave steles or markers, as well as figures found within funerary barrows themselves. In addition, there are also examples of horse tack, harnesses, and entire chariots being found as grave goods, further showing the importance of the horse to these cultures as well as the connection with the underworld.

Rhiannon's bird associations probably have foundations in the bird goddesses of Neolithic times. Small carved bird goddess statues have been found as grave goods and guardian figures. These ornithomorphic female figurines have aspects of both bird and woman, carved gracefully with chevrons. These small hybrid statues are among some of our earliest representations of Rhiannon, along with other ancient goddesses like the famed Willendorf goddess. Birds would have been considered messengers of the gods, as they nested and lived close to the sky, in the tops of the sacred trees.

Rhiannon's links to both horses and birds speak of her mystical connection to the Celtic underworld and sovereignty. The Rhiannon that we learn about in the Mabinogion is likely a form of a more ancient goddess archetype, kept alive through legend and lore and written down in the medieval text with several modern translations in publication today. She is alive today in the hearts of those who work with her, and she will continue to inspire generosity, strength, and wisdom in anyone who simply asks.

Astral Projection for the Ultra-Earthbound

by Calantirniel

Astral projection can be defined as our astral selves being consciously activated at the same time as our physical selves; the astral self can usually navigate, leaving the space where the physical self is located, and the experience is remembered. Some people do this naturally without difficulty. However, many of us with a strong earth "imprint" in our energetic signature find it very difficult for our astral bodies to leave our physical bodies while conscious.

How can we tell if we have a lot of earth energy? One way is to examine your astrological birth chart to see how many points are in the earth signs of Taurus, Virgo, and Capricorn. The Sun, which represents our inner core, in an earth sign is a large indicator. Also, having Saturn, the planet of matter and material denseness, prominent in your chart (i.e. on your Ascendant, or conjunct the Sun) can make one feel more Earthbound.

If you want other methods to measure the amount of earth in your constitution, observe yourself and how you operate in the mundane world. Are you practical, skeptical, realistic? Are you attentive, tenacious, mindful, focused, and *grounded* nearly all the time? Do you always have a well-thought-out plan, do things step-by-step, and remain calm when others are hysterical? Do people count on you? Do you rarely remember your dreams? Is it difficult for you to actually feel energetic healing methods (like flower essences or Reiki) working? Do you sometimes, without proof, "know" things, yet doubt your interpretations because you want to see proof? Do you feel pain more intensely physically than emotionally? Does it take a lot for you to get sick, but then when you finally do get sick, it can take a longer time to recover? The more of these that are answered in the positive, the more you likely possess earth in your makeup.

All of us naturally astral project when we sleep. Our attentions during those times easily go into our dream-state astral selves, and in all healthy cases, there are many protective mechanisms so our astral and physical bodies are protected. Earth-signature types likely have even stronger protective mechanisms and more clearly defined boundaries between existence in the astral realms and physical existence. In other words, we are wholly in one, or wholly in the other—not in between, and not in both. This is why we often do not remember what transpires in dreams. In many ways, this allows us to concentrate and have more energy available for whichever world we are in. However, when we consciously astral project, we attempt to combine the two worlds and we can have less energy to be productive.

But there are advantages to being able to traverse the astral and consciously remember it. One advantage is creating

in the astral realms what one desires to manifest on the physical plane, which could be defined as "magic." You can learn these techniques from a variety of sources beyond this article.

An astral-adept friend of mine tells me that the easiest time for this work is past the New Moon after Samhain (November 1 in Northern Hemisphere, May 1 in Southern Hemisphere) and during the winter. Not only do we notice more darkness and more stillness, there is indeed less "busy" activity on the astral level as well. The Full Moons (maximum lunar energy) and the New Moons (maximum stellar energy) also seem to work well, especially if they are in water signs (Cancer, Scorpio, Pisces). If you keep records of your progress, you will soon see a pattern of when astral projection is easiest for you.

If someone with a heavy earth signature wishes to consciously astral project, the following list provides helpful methods that are not usually addressed in other sources.

1. Do not eat dairy, meat, coffee, non-herbal tea, chocolate, chemical/processed foods or salt—possibly for quite a long time, but definitely not right before attempting projection. The dense vibrations may keep you on the ground and in your body, and also inhibit your dream-recall ability. Instead, eat high vibration foods: fruits, vegetables (especially greens and lots of sprouted grains and legumes), nuts, and seeds. Aim for half of your foods to be raw and alive. Roasted dandelion or chicory root with soy, rice, almond, or oat milk and agave juice is a delicious substitute for coffee; start slowly changing the proportions of your beverage until there is no coffee. Omega-3's and 6's can come by thoroughly chewing raw unhulled flax or hemp seeds, or use evening primrose, borage, or black currant seed oil supplements.

2. To facilitate cleansing, try adding some herbs. *Cascara sagrada* is the shaman's "sacred bark" for a reason: it allowed shamans to internally clean and physically prepare themselves for their otherworldly work. But it is strong when used alone. Mix *Cascara sagrada* with gentler turmeric, burdock, and

yellow dock. Herbal colon cleansing supplements/systems are also available at any health foods store; check the labels to see if they are all natural/herbal. Gentle cleansing over a longer time is preferable to detoxing too quickly.

3. Drink lots of distilled water (or at least spring/ozonated/oxygenated water). Work toward two quarts to one gallon a day. Distilled water is a "hungry" water and is excellent at drawing out and washing away toxins and inorganic minerals, but it will not wash away any minerals that are absorbed in your body, because your body is smart! If you are afraid of mineral loss, make a vinegar tincture of raw apple cider vinegar with herbs like horsetail, oatstraw, alfalfa, and lobelia (just plop lots of the herbs into the vinegar and allow them to soak for two weeks during a waxing moon); filter; and take tablespoons periodically. Sometimes, a change of the type of water consumed is all that is needed to successfully project.

4. As much as you can, try to go natural with your external body products (shampoos, deodorants, etc.). Make your own by seeking natural body-care recipes online. Change gradually, one item at a time; as you run out of something, find a better, more natural alternative.

5. Because many of us live in busy cities with lots of human conscious energy around, create an area that is quiet, preferably dark, and attempt to keep it clean/uncluttered and with soothing colors (warm or cool) and—most of all—comfortable. If you have a fresh air source, smudge your area with sage, then perhaps incense that is lunar or helps with astral work. If not, salt the whole room, vacuum, and get a spritzer bottle with some distilled water, and place a few drops of purifying aromatherapy oils in it, such as eucalyptus, pine, cypress, juniper, lavender, rosemary, hyssop, and/or many others. Ylang-ylang loosens nervous tension and helps you relax and feel safe; geranium and citrus oils like grapefruit have an uplifting quality. Many spiritual workers like cedar, dragon's blood, frankincense, and myrrh. You can also add your choice

of flower essences (see below). If you plan on storing it and using as needed, add just enough vodka or brandy to keep the mixture from going sour (you don't need much), and store in a cool, dark place. If you can, use natural aromatherapy or fragrance-free candles (preferably long-burning soy) for lighting, and no heavy lingering chemical perfumes. To purify the room with sound, Tibetan bells can be rung several times to break up the stagnant energy, or even clapping with intention works. Play a CD of crystal singing bowls, or if you have such a bowl, use it!

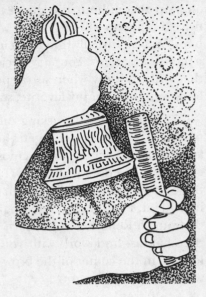

6. Flower essences are not only fun to explore, but very effective at furthering our high vibrations. Flower essences are unlike herbal tinctures, aromatherapy, or homeopathics, which all work on the physical plane. Flower essences work on the emotional plane, and they do so directly by bypassing the mental plane and the ego. For each dysfunction, there exists a flower with a specific message to correct it, thereby gently yet effectively reeducating us—and doing so quite economically. There is absolutely no harm with using flower essences. However, using the wrong one(s) may not work because you didn't need the message of that flower. To save your time and money, learn to "dowse" or have someone knowledgeable dowse or muscle-test for you. If you decide to make a blend, try not to use more than three or four flowers at a time. You only need two to three drops, two to three times a day to re-train your emotional plane. If you carry a water bottle, add a few drops

and sip throughout the day. Even if you take the essences twice a day, you will see results when you are taking the right ones. You can usually find them in the homeopathic section in health food stores. You may decide to also purchase essences that you use only when astral projecting. Good choices are lotus, mugwort, or my favorite, star tulip.

7. Since you are working on raising your vibration, you may want to look into energetic healing. There are many kinds around: acupuncture, Reiki, chios, shamballa, DNA activation, emotional freedom technique (EFT), and many others. Study these and choose what feels right for you. If you decide to look into Reiki, I recommend getting a Level I attunement rather than just a Reiki healing. Learn all you can about balancing the chakras, and work with your third eye or Ajna chakra, located in the center of the brow area, for astral travel to help with otherworldly sight.

8. When you are ready, try an herbal relaxation tea consisting of kitchen sage, mugwort, wormwood, wild lettuce, yarrow, and lobelia. This is obviously a stronger tea than chamomile. Some people have good luck with hops as well, but experiment and see what works for you. I strongly advise against working with legal vision-inducing

Eeftchay symbol

plants/fungi without guidance or extensive research unless you just wish to call upon the energies of those plants without actually consuming them (you may be lucky to find "flower essences" made with these!). Add two to three drops of star tulip or other flower essence(s) after brewing, and drink fifteen minutes prior to astral work. Prepare your space and your body by bathing in epsom salts, baking soda, vinegar, flower essences (optional), and/or more of those purifying and relaxing essential oils (see above). Right before you start, draw the Eeftchay symbol, the Seichim Reiki symbol that opens your astral sight, onto your third eye chakra. You can also use a drop of star tulip or other flower essence, or place a crystal like sodalite or kyanite on the brow.

9. Lie down, close your eyes, and just know you are safe and protected. First, visualize indigo as a color and say, "I see perfectly in this world and the other world, and I know the difference between them." Then, when ready, affirm, "I now easily leave my body for conscious astral projection," and then visualize yourself doing it. "Pretend" your eyes are open and that you are getting up, while placing your sensory attention to your visualized astral body that is getting up. Actually "feel" the sensations of the ground under your feet, "feel" your neck turning to look out the window, etc. Don't look back at your physical body until you have had more practice. Just pretend you are getting up and really feel it in your astral self. Go into the next room or walk outside, but concentrate on your senses that are utterly tuned-in with the astral body.

If you end up back in your physical body (common for earth types), just start over and go easy on yourself—your focus and tenacity will eventually take over. Observe your sensations, even around your astral self, and trust they are right; don't worry if you cannot see, as that may come later. Build up the amount of time of each session. You can start with as little as five minutes, and add five minutes each time. It is important to repeat this over and over until it works. Keep a detailed journal of your progress, with dates/times and phases/signs of the Moon. You may also wish to begin a dream journal, separately or with your astral projection journal, as there is much overlap between astral projection and dream recall. The astral world is often full of symbols, both personal and archetypal, and learning how to interpret them will greatly enhance both practices.

Be happy for what you do accomplish, rather than comparing yourself with someone else. They likely do not share some talents you have, which can be focus, tenacity, interpretation, discernment, and the ability to ground easily after astral work (if anyone has trouble with grounding, keep some salt to put on the tip of your tongue, or grab a grounding crystal like obsidian). Do not doubt your abilities or your sensations just because you cannot "see" the astral realm concretely the way that others can. Some non-earth types who easily astral project and possess excellent clairvoyance have no idea how to interpret their experiences and end up more confused than before they started. Some of these people can also experience a huge inundation of emotional energy (water or empathic types) or mental energy (air or thinking types) and literally feel like they are drowning in negativity and cannot escape. These things rarely happen to well-boundaried earth types.

As an example, I have a classic earth signature. I am not clairvoyant, but I have a great talent of focus, visualization, and manifestation. For me, it seems like I don't really "leave" my body, but it is more of a remote-viewing sensation. I learned that we earth-types are more often clairsentient (that is, we "sense" or feel things), and some of us are also clairaudient ("hearing" things). I later learned that I am clairaudient but do not hear voices. It feels like I just *know* something, as though a thought gets pushed into my head and I felt like I made it up, but I now know better. I can visualize what I learn, and for me, this is almost always as good as actually being clairvoyant.

After years of practicing on and off, I finally had an experience between sleep and waking wherein I sort of "remembered" my astral travels, and it is nothing like I have ever read about. I experienced the entire thing as now-unmemorable, unrecognizable patterns of light that I navigated expertly at the time. Whatever I intended, it instantly happened. I also felt very protected, used empathy properly and was extremely discerning and able to handle everything and be very productive. Though I have no memory of the light patterns themselves, I remember being able to precisely interpret them. A good analogy is in the movie *The Matrix*, when there were only ones and zeros viewable on a screen by the audience, and yet all that was "seen" by the actor working with that screen was blondes and brunettes!

I was very happy with my small success, yet I realized that I function much better when my energy is devoted in one place or the other. At this time, I have much I want to accomplish on the physical plane, and there is very likely just as much work waiting on the astral plane. I noticed my energy management works better during the times I am fully devoted to the designated plane at hand (i.e. physical when awake, astral when asleep).

In order to not entirely lose my new and non-adept ability, I have decided to create within myself a physical-astral intercommunications system. When I wake up in the morning, I lie still and consciously relax my mind and am receptive to my impressions, feelings, and messages that have been left by my astral self. If I had a dream, I analyze and interpret it right then; if I can't figure it out, I write it down to digest and perhaps research while I am awake in the physical. When I go to bed at night, I mentally make a strong intention, much like a To Do list, that I feel my astral self can accomplish more easily than my physical self, and provide any "news" in the physical for my astral self to examine. Often, new information arrives when I awake. I don't remember doing a To Do list while in the astral plane, but I do like knowing what I managed to do in the astral plane while asleep. It can be compared to e-mailing memos back and forth between my physical self and astral self, but without a computer!

For Further Study

Bruce, Robert, and Brian Mercer. *Mastering Astral Projection: 90-Day Guide to Out-of-Body Experience.* St. Paul, MN: Llewellyn Worldwide, 2004.

González-Wippler, Migene. *Dreams and What They Mean to You.* St. Paul, MN: Llewellyn Worldwide, 2002.

Halpern, Steven. *Crystal Bowl Healing* (Audio CD). San Anselmo, CA: Inner Peace Music, 2003.

Penczak, Christopher. *Magick of Reiki.* St. Paul, MN: Llewellyn Worldwide, 2004.

Internet

Astral Society. Message boards. www.astralsociety.us

AstroDienst. "Astrology and Horoscope Homepage." www.astro.com (Free astrological birth charts, as well as many other detailed astrological charts.)

Goldman, Jonathan. Temple of Sacred Sound. www.templeofsacredsound.org

Vibration Magazine. www.floweressencemagazine.com

Woods, Walt. "Letter to Robin: A Mini-Course in Pendulum Dowsing." www.lettertorobin.org

World Center for EFT®. www.emofree.com

How to Contact Ancestral Spirits

by James Kambos

Our deceased loved ones are never really gone. Their spirits remain close to us and we may still communicate with them. In most cases, our ancestors who have passed over to the otherworld are eager to keep in touch with us and miss us just as much as we miss them. There may even be times when a departed ancestor will try to initiate contact with us. But we must be sensitive to these manifestations. For example, you may hear a whisper or catch their reflection in a mirror. Or perhaps their favorite song will come on the radio while you're thinking of them. A good friend of mine knew her late husband was near when she'd see a flicker of light in a stairway. My grandmother would make her presence known after her death by leaving the scent of one of her favorite flowers, jasmine, in the air.

There are many other ways a departed family member may try to contact us—a dream, a touch, or a feeling are just a few. The problem is that when an ancestral spirit tries to contact us, their method of contact may be so subtle we could miss it. That is why many people I've met over the years are eager to learn how they can effectively contact the spirits of their ancestors. The reason someone may wish to contact a deceased ancestor usually varies. In some cases, the living wish to bring closure to a relationship and take care of any unresolved issues, or the living may seek guidance from the deceased. If for no other reason, spirit contact will comfort us and let us know that our deceased loved one is settling into a new existence in the spirit realm. If the deceased is a long-ago ancestor you never knew, contact may still be desired because it will enable you to reach into your past, and in doing so, you'll learn more about yourself, your culture, and traditions. No matter what the reason, to call upon our ancestors for guidance or support is a loving way to connect with them. All spirit contact should be done with respect. Never command your ancestor to communicate with you, always ask—the contact should be desired by both of you.

Preparation

Before attempting to get in touch with a deceased loved one, you should have a few things on hand. If possible, have available a few personal items that belonged to the deceased. These may include clothing, jewelry, eyeglasses, or a key. A photograph of your loved one, especially if you're also in it, would be another good item. Food, perfumes, or anything else the departed enjoyed in life are also good choices.

To set the mood, candles in white or yellow may be used. Herbs associated with spirit contact, such as sweetgrass and wormwood, are sometimes burned during a spirit ritual. Not only do they help spirit contact, their scents are also cleansing and protective. If you plan on using your altar or table, these should be draped in a plain black cloth.

Methods of Contacting Ancestral Spirits

The first things that come to mind when we speak of contacting our deceased loved ones are ouija boards, psychics, and séances. Under the right conditions, and with the guidance of a valid spiritualist, these methods of spirit contact are fine. But, when seeking intimate communication with a loved one in the spirit realm, you may wish to use a more private method, one that you can perform alone. The techniques that follow utilize traditional magical methods to help you contact the spirits of your ancestors safely and respectfully. Let's begin.

Using a Letter to Contact the Deceased

Special verses or letters used as charms to contact the deceased date back to the early days of German magic. These letters are known as *Himmels-brief*, which means "a letter to heaven," or "heaven letter." Few people outside the Pennsylvania Dutch community have heard of them, but Himmels-briefs were frequently used to contact a deceased family member. Some of these charms, if written by a powerful magician, could cost hundreds of dollars.

Here is one way to use a Himmels-brief to contact an ancestral spirit. Select a sheet of clean white paper and a special pen. Light a yellow candle, and place before you a photo of the deceased or a personal item they once owned. Begin writing your letter as you would any letter. You may request help for a particular situation or ask a question. The letter doesn't need to be long. Take your time; you needn't write everything in one letter. End by thanking the spirit and wishing them peace. Finish by folding the letter as if you're sending it and burn it in a ritual fire. The smoke will "send" your letter to the deceased.

Your letter may be answered in a dream, or you may visualize your ancestor actually speaking to you. Another way to seek your answer is to scry into the candle flame of the candle you've just used. A letter is a very personal, loving way to contact a deceased relative.

Contacting with a Magic Mirror

Magic mirrors are an ideal way to contact an ancestral spirit. Before using a mirror for any spirit contact, speak Words of Power to surround yourself with positive energy, and trace a holy symbol (such as a pentagram or cross) over the mirror to prevent any unwelcome spirit from entering your space.

Once again, place a personal item belonging to the deceased near the mirror, or hold the item. Darken the room and light a white candle; set it off to one side.

Concentrate on your ancestor and ask if they wish to communicate with you. Gazing at the mirror, visualize your ancestor and ask a question if you'd like. A misty or sharp image of your relative may begin to form. Be aware that the face may look younger or healthier than you remember. Your question may be answered with a symbol, or an actual scene could appear in your mirror.

Keep your mirror sessions short to avoid fatigue. Thank the spirit; let yourself slowly return to reality and snuff out the candle. If contact isn't made, simply try again in a few days.

Channeling with a Pendulum

Pendulums are usually used to give a yes or no answer to divine the future, but I've found them to be an effective tool to contact a family member on the other side because you have intimate contact with the pendulum, and, in a way, you are helping to channel the communication.

You may use the pendulum for spirit contact in two ways. First, you could ask the ancestral spirit if they are present. Then continue with simple questions that can be answered yes or no.

If you wish to receive more detailed answers, try this: First, I'm assuming that you already know the direction your pendulum will swing for a yes or no answer. If you haven't already established that, do

so now. Next, write all the letters of the alphabet on a piece of paper. Ask the spirit a question and pass the pendulum over each letter. When the pendulum says yes to a letter, record it. A message will begin to form. You may wish to have someone else write the message down as you work the pendulum. You'll be surprised at the answers you'll receive.

When done, thank the spirit and the pendulum for their guidance. Using a pendulum in this manner can be time consuming but rewarding.

These are only a few ideas on how to contact ancestral spirits. Other interesting methods you might want to explore on your own include dream work, meditation, and automatic writing.

However you choose to contact family members and loved ones who've left the physical world, it's important for our ancestral spirits to know that they're welcome to communicate with us. Even when we aren't actively seeking to contact them, let your loved ones know you're thinking of them. Leave a bit of their favorite food on your altar, outside your door, or on their grave if possible. Leaving a gift is an especially loving gesture if you do this on their birthday, or any special day you both shared. Or, you may honor your ancestor by planting a flower in their memory in your garden.

These acts of love and kindness will make your ancestral spirits feel welcomed, and will improve future contact.

For Further Study

Campanelli, Pauline. *Ancient Ways*. St. Paul, MN: Llewellyn, 1991.

Goddess Magic

by Michelle Skye

A long time ago, in a land far, far away . . . Okay, all you sci-fi nerds know where I'm going with this line of thought. But, seriously, as a lover of magic and myth (and George Lucas), why should the movies get all the fun? Spirituality is supposed to enlighten. Notice the root of that word: *light*. Most religions don't seek to *endarken* their followers. A whole host of concepts are connected to the idea of light. There's the obvious brilliance and "source of light," the sun; an illuminating lightness of the soul and of the being that is you; and a light, floaty feeling we experience when a helium balloon is transported through the skies. But all of these examples mirror the meaning of light and all of them have relevance to Goddess magic, a new way to connect with the Divine, which is the source of all this lightness.

Magic can be done by anyone with enough willpower, self-confidence, and knowledge to implement a spell correctly and with intent. You do not need to belong to a particular spiritual path to practice magic. The power resides within yourself and within the knowledge that you possess. Some would say it is necessary to possess wisdom in order to cast magic, but I think wisdom is a discretionary idea, separate from magic. Wisdom lets you know when and how to perform magic, but it doesn't necessarily boost your magical power. In fact, some of the least-learned people have the most natural inclination for magic. For example, teenagers teeter on the cusp of childhood and adulthood, being neither and both at the same time. This insubstantial, transformational time does not give them wisdom, but it does allow them to magically manifest with the best.

Goddess magic is a particular type of magic that connects directly to the female essence of divinity. Like all kinds of magic, it can be performed by anyone from any religious persuasion. It works equally well when attuned to Mother Mary, Mary Magdalene, Kuan Yin, Shekinah, or any other divine female entity. Goddess magic works by combining three major aspects of spirituality—identifying and honoring divinity, strengthening a relationship with divinity, and manifesting transformation in your

life—and anchoring them to your particular dream or vision of reality. As with all magic, the essence of yourself is of primary importance in Goddess magic; however, your relationship to the Divine and your ability to witness and experience the Divine are of equal importance.

The Source of Light: Honoring the Divine Feminine

The first aspect of Goddess magic is expressed in the ancient practice of honoring and worshipping divinity. You've seen the movies where the temple initiates give gifts of honor and praise to a particular deity. Whether it's building temples (like King Solomon of the Bible), burning incense (like Hindus around the world), or offering sacrifice (like the ancients of old), Goddess magic hinges on recognizing and honoring a being greater than ourselves. Technically, the principles of Goddess magic can be applied to any divine figure, whether male or female, negative or positive. However, because of the intimate nature of Goddess magic and the aspect of healing that often occurs as an offshoot of this magical practice, it is most closely aligned to the yin or female element residing within each of us.

In order to honor the Divine Feminine, it is necessary to know about her. The temple initiates of old lived and breathed their spirituality and the path of their chosen deity. Most of us in the modern world cannot be so devoted but we can find out about the goddess that most calls to us, the role of the goddess throughout time, or types of goddesses (such as earth goddesses or space goddesses) around the globe. In short, as with all magic, you have to possess some amount of knowledge. If you don't, it's rather like writing a letter in the dark; you have your tools and thoughts, but your letter usually comes out unreadable because you couldn't see what you were really doing. The knowledge that you gain in relation to the Divine Feminine helps to focus your ideas. It narrows down your perspective so you can begin to form a relationship with your goddess. Think of it this way: instead of having twenty or thirty acquaintances, you are working toward acquiring one best friend.

The best way to become knowledgeable about your particular aspect of the Feminine Divine is to do some research. As you research, look for a goddess that resonates with you. Learn all you can about your particular goddess, type of goddess, or about goddess spirituality in general. Look at pictures. Read stories. Find old manuscripts, and peruse new ones. And don't take everything you read as the absolute truth. The ancient stories were often recorded by Christian monks who threw out concepts that didn't fit in with their spiritual ideals of womankind. Modern writers have twisted the stories to correspond to their particular issues or ways of thinking. Take these writings and think about them for yourself. What do they mean to you personally? How do they reflect your life or the place you find yourself in right here and right now? Come to a personal conclusion about your aspect of the Feminine Divine. Find your own truth in relation to her.

Once you have some knowledge about the Feminine Divine, put it to use on the physical plane. Make a scrapbook of the pictures of the goddess that most calls to you and write captions that express your personal thoughts. Set up a shrine area for your goddess. It doesn't have to be very large or very fancy; maybe you place a candle on a pretty scarf or surround an incense holder with crystals that remind you of your aspect of the Feminine Divine. Create or find an evocation to your goddess and say it every morning when you get up or every evening before you go to bed. In short, begin to focus some of your free time around the Divine Feminine to honor her and form a closer relationship in order to begin seeing her hand in the world around you, in all its lightness and darkness.

The Lightness of Floating: Gaining Intimacy with the Otherworld

Having gained knowledge of your goddess and applied it to your everyday life, the time has arrived to journey beyond the narrow confines of the mundane world for the realm of the Divine Feminine. Depending upon your viewpoint and particular religious affiliation, you may visualize the home of the Feminine Divine in any number of ways. In traditional monotheistic religions, a glance upward would be the most common reaction to this statement. "Mother in Heaven above" is a familiar phrase at church services. A Hellenistic person may glance downward toward Tartarus or the Elysium Fields or upward toward Mount Olympus or even outward at local fields and forests, depending on their goddess of choice. In short, whatever perspective corresponds with your spiritual philosophy is fine, as long as you feel comfortable.

Luckily for us, in our world of fleet-footed information, we do not need to experience death in order to visit with our concept of the Feminine Divine. We simply need to take a shamanic journey to visit with her. I use the term "simply" in a rather loose context. Shamans are people with one foot in the otherworld and one foot in the mundane world at all times. They are intimately connected to the otherworld and work tirelessly to heal our world and the individuals in it in order to bring about the best and highest possibilities for all involved. One cannot be a shaman just on the weekends—it is a full-time commitment. It is a calling, not unlike Catholic priesthood or the life of a Buddhist monk.

However, one need not be a shaman to engage in a shamanic journey. As drums are the instrument most often used around the world for journeying, I recommend finding a drumming CD that you like. Grab a bandana, scarf, or blindfold and your journal and get ready to travel to the otherworld. You might want to hold a talisman in your hand to connect you with your body and to help protect you from any "weirdness" in the otherworld. A rose quartz crystal would be perfect, especially as it is a wonderful stone for opening up and experiencing love. Hold the stone in your hand and tie the bandana around your eyes so you can truly focus within. Also, keep outside distractions to a minimum by turning off the ringer on your phones and making sure you're not disturbed for an hour or so.

Begin to meditate as you normally do, either by grounding and centering, connecting with the angels, or aligning the chakras in your body. Once you feel relaxed, grip the stone and state your intent to visit with your particular image of the Feminine Divine. Traditional shamanism states that you should find a "portal" that is anchored here in this world that you can use to travel to the other worlds—either upper world, lower world, or middle world. You might use a tree in your yard to climb to heaven or a well in the woods to descend to Elysium. I have found that it is best to trust whatever method presents itself to you. If you climb out a window to your middle world meeting place, then so be it, as long as you are safe!

Once you have traveled to the otherworld to meet with your goddess, observe her, hang out with her, ask her questions. In

short, don't be afraid of interacting with the Divine Feminine. This is your time to deepen your relationship with her. Also, be prepared to receive information from her in numerous ways—through sight, sound, touch (both physical and emotional), and intuition. Everyone experiences the otherworld in their own way, as fits their learning style and personality. No one way is the "right" way. After you have visited with your goddess and returned home (by way of the same path you arrived), be sure to write your experience in your journal. This will help you to continue growing in your relationship with your goddess. And, of course, visit the Divine Feminine as often as you would like, but aim for at least once a week.

The Light of the Self: Reflecting Your Transformation

If you consciously and honestly work on forming a connection with the Feminine Divine, you will begin to notice subtle shifts in yourself. You may be happier. You may choose to confront situations instead of running from them. Your communication skills may improve. In short, some of the attributes and activities that hold you back from achieving your whole self may alter and change. The power of the goddess will already be manifest in your life. Now the time comes to harness the power of the Divine Feminine and marry it to your own innate power in order to manifest one of your goals on earth. This is where the magic comes in!

If you have strengthened your relationship with your goddess for a while (at least three weeks), you are ready to perform a magic spell to enhance and better your life. The spell should connect to your understanding and knowledge of the Divine Feminine, as you perceive it. So, for instance, if you have been working with Artemis and believe her to be a strong, independent goddess in relation to feminine power, you probably wouldn't perform a love spell. Ideally, at the beginning of this process, you considered all aspects of the Divine Feminine and chose to connect with an aspect that closely aligned with your personal goals and desires.

Once you understand the reason for your spell and can state it in a simple phrase or sentence, the time has come to create your spellwork. The best way to create a Goddess magic spell is by allowing the feminine spirit to flow through you and guide you. You can do this through divination, shamanic journeywork, dreamwork, or personal intuition. Pay attention to any messages or signs that might be sent by the Feminine Divine. Listen to her voice. And, of course, continue in your personal devotions to her. Before long, the spell will shape itself through your ideas, which were guided by the goddess.

After gathering all the items for your spell, you should schedule a time when you can be alone to focus on your magic. Perhaps you choose to cast your spell at the Full or New Moon. Or maybe you set aside a day that is special to you (such as your birthday) or holy to your goddess (such as her birthday). You will also want to factor in the actual place you cast your spell. If you have a ritual or meditation space in your house, you can always use that area. However, you might consider working outside, especially if your aspect of the Divine Feminine is involved with nature or animals. No matter what time or place you decide on, keep the Divine Feminine in mind throughout.

Although spellwork can be rather mundane (especially as portrayed in the movies or on television), Goddess magic hinges on the spiritual aspect of magic. Therefore, it is important to perform the spell in a sacred manner, setting aside time to honor the Divine Feminine before and after the actual spellwork. You don't need to create an elaborate ritual, but you should include elements of your devotional practice in your spell. Begin by stating your evocation to the Divine Feminine out loud. If you generally light a candle, bang a drum, or include incense in your evocation, you can do that as well. After evoking the goddess, take a few minutes to journey to her. You don't have to spend all day in the otherworld, just enough time to feel the essence of your aspect of the Feminine Divine. When you return from your journey, perform your spell. And, at the completion of your spell, thank your goddess and offer her a gift. Your gift can be something tangible, such as food or drink, or it can be intangible, like a dance, an impromptu poem, or (quite simply) your love.

At the close of your spell, you can choose to continue the daily devotionals to your goddess, take a break to cherish some time to rest, or begin working with a new aspect of the Goddess magic. The choice is yours. Only you can know how to proceed in your relationship with the Feminine Divine.

~

Goddess magic bridges the gap between this world and the otherworld. It calls upon the power of a particular aspect of the Divine Feminine and connects it to your own unique power in order to manifest your goals in this world. It works by enlightening the individual magic practitioner through knowledge and honoring of the Divine, experience and understanding of the otherworld, and the creation and transforming of the self. Goddess magic allows us all to become our most complete selves, both within and without, through connection with the Divine Feminine.

One-Minute Ways to Boost ESP

by Melanie Harris

Psychic awareness is a very important magical skill, as it allows us to locate and communicate with the energies that we direct in magic. It is a perception of the living energy on levels both above and beneath what we usually experience, a view of what lies beyond the illusory boundaries favored by our egos. It is the ability to sense the other side of all, to see the mundane as energetic vibrations and patterns of energy, to recognize the everlasting light and love that is found throughout the creation. Psychic awareness, or ESP, puts us in touch with the spiritual plane. As we develop our ESP (extra sensory perception), we become more aware of the forces around us, and as a result, our magical abilities grow stronger.

But what if you don't feel very psychic? Although psychic awareness is often hereditary, nearly everyone has some measure of aptitude, if not the highly developed ability. Even for naturally gifted seers, honing the craft is necessary if it is to be utilized to its full potential. The more you exercise your psychic faculty, the stronger and more cooperative it will become. Practice stepping out of your identity and simply observing. After letting go of the ego, vibrations and patterns of energy become apparent. The trick is to let your subconscious take the lead. By practicing this on a regular basis, we become more sensitive to the underlying forces of reality. Through frequent use, your psychic sense is awakened. Here are some quick exercises that will sharpen, maintain, and increase your ESP.

Affecting Flame

Candles are a learning tool, a way to exercise and enhance magical power and psychic awareness. Looking at even the smallest candle flame awakens our deepest, primordial essence, the place where our intuition and instinct still rule. It reminds us to be aware of what we habitually shut our eyes to. Here is an excellent way to train one's psychic powers. For this activity, focus on a candle flame and visualize it growing larger, brighter, smaller, or dimmer. See if you can affect the flame with the power of your thoughts. With practice, you can make the flame grow, shrink, and flicker at will.

Psychic Exercises with Tarot

Another effective way to increase your awareness of energetic vibrations and psychic impulses is to practice with tarot cards. Put the cards face down and mix them up freely, swirling the pile and feeling the distinct vibrations of each card you touch. Now close your eyes and see if you can pick certain cards from the pile. You could try to select major arcana cards, cards of one of the four suits, or a card representing a specific person. Don't get discouraged if your attempt is initially unsuccessful. Try again later, and in the meantime, look through your tarot deck and open your heart to the feeling that each card gives you. In this way, you can gain awareness of energetic vibrations exuded by the cards, increasing your psychic perception and also sharpening your tarot-reading skills.

ESP Games

Playing ESP games to test your psychic ability is another great way to boost this faculty. If you have a friend to practice with, the drawing game is a fun choice. Each person has a pad of paper on which to draw. Keeping your work concealed, take turns attempting to psychically determine what the other person is drawing, and try to create the same image on your own paper. When the drawings are finished, compare to see if there are any similarities. You may see similarities in size, shape, form, or theme. Sometimes the drawings are very much alike, alerting you that at the moment, your ESP is dead on.

Another good ESP game is to see if you can guess who's calling when your phone rings. You could likewise see if you know in which direction a bird will fly, what color shirt a friend will be wearing, or who you will run into while you're out on the town. You could even do a small-scale version of the Grateful Dead's ESP shows. The band projected images of paintings throughout the show, asking the large audience to psychically transmit the image to the receiver who was dreaming far away. A similar exercise could be conducted by asking a friend to look at an image and call you on the phone. See if you can use your ESP to determine what the image is. Likewise, you could listen to a song, then attempt to convey that song to a faraway friend. Any variation on this format will do. The point is to open your psychic perception through frequent and varied practice. The magical practitioner who stays in touch with this side of reality will find the relationship to be mutually beneficial, and playing simple ESP games is a quick way to forge this connection.

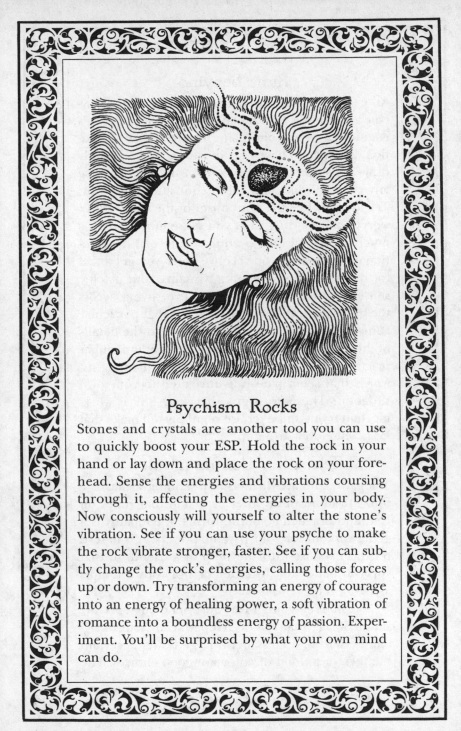

Psychism Rocks

Stones and crystals are another tool you can use to quickly boost your ESP. Hold the rock in your hand or lay down and place the rock on your forehead. Sense the energies and vibrations coursing through it, affecting the energies in your body. Now consciously will yourself to alter the stone's vibration. See if you can use your psyche to make the rock vibrate stronger, faster. See if you can subtly change the rock's energies, calling those forces up or down. Try transforming an energy of courage into an energy of healing power, a soft vibration of romance into a boundless energy of passion. Experiment. You'll be surprised by what your own mind can do.

Rune Scrying

An easy way to expand the boundaries of your psychic awareness is to practice scrying with runes. This is quite different than using the runes for divination. If you don't have a set of runes, you can simply draw the symbols on paper or in the dirt. Choose any rune you like and focus your attention on it. Try to really feel the symbolism of the rune. Don't worry about putting what you sense into words; it's much more helpful to concentrate on the emotional impressions you receive. Once you get a feel for the rune's true meaning, visualize your psychic sense reaching out, your third eye roving across the globe. See who else is gazing at that particular rune right now and open your mind to the details of the scene. Are you receiving visions of unfamiliar places? Are strange words flooding your thoughts, words that seem true but unrelated to your own situation? These are signs that your ESP is working, and trying this exercise regularly will make that extra sense ever stronger.

Telepathic Communication

Telepathy, the act of mentally sending a message into the mind of another, is a skill that relies on ESP, and practicing simple forms of telepathy is a great workout for your psychic powers. It is best to try this exercise with the help of a friend, so that you can better tell whether or not your attempts are successful.

Begin by agreeing with your friend on a specific, simple image that will be telepathically sent to signal the start of a message. A large flower, a certain number, or a flood of color are good choices. The image will act as a telephone ring of sorts, alerting you that your friend is trying to establish communication with you.

To send a message telepathically, simply envision yourself face to face with the person and focus intently on your thoughts, psychically willing the person to receive your message. You can amplify the thought as if you are magnifying energy during spellwork, and then release the energy of the thought into the person's mind. The message must be delivered with great intensity if it is to penetrate through the person's own thoughts. In order to receive a telepathic communication, you must quiet your inner voice and listen to what remains.

As your understanding of the psychic plane expands, so too will your ability to communicate telepathically. ESP will help you develop telepathy, and telepathy will help you develop ESP.

Divination Games

You can also hone your psychic ability by practicing quick divination games. Divination requires you to open that sixth sense, to let go of inhibitions and become aware of psychic sensations. It's an effective way to enhance psychism because it allows you to use these skills through different mediums and in different circumstances. Try tarot, try an oracle, try palmistry, try runes. Get even more benefit out of practicing unusual forms of divination. Doing so will get your ESP in touch with rarely visited aspects of reality.

One such method involves divining by fire. Next time you find yourself at a campfire, find a small piece of wood and try this technique to really turn on your ESP. Hold the wood in your hands and concentrate your thoughts on the matter in question. Transfer this energy into the wood, converting it into a symbol of the subject of your inquiry. Place the wood near the core of the fire, and gaze into the flames to receive psychic visions. Once you are entranced, you can pose questions to the fire and read the movement of the flames to ascertain the answer. Flames growing higher indicate an affirmative response; diminishing flames signify a negative response. For an even quicker ESP-strengthening session, you can omit the piece of wood entirely and employ a candle flame with this same divinatory technique.

Weather Magic

You want results fast, and practicing weather magic will quickly get your ESP in shape. While weather magic can be safely performed for frivolous reasons as well as in matters of necessity, it's best to perform such work only occasionally, as frequent attempts to manipulate the weather can lead to disastrous results. Nature knows the needs of an ecosystem better than anyone, so don't neglect to use your better judgment. If your town has been suffering a serious drought, don't try to stop a needed rainstorm just because you'd like to go on a picnic. If, on the other hand, there hasn't been a lack of rain, it would be perfectly acceptable to ask the rain to hold off for just a bit while you enjoy your special outing. Weather magic increases ESP a lot, but it is an intense form of magic and should be used with a humble, respectful attitude. Beware of conceit, and keep in mind that it is ultimately up to the elemental forces whether or not to comply with your weather request.

To bring rain, visualize gathering clouds. If you like, drip water on a rock, or burn a fresh plant leaf outdoors. See the rain coming in, smell it and feel it. As it starts to sprinkle, close your eyes and feel the rain increase.

To end or decrease rain, visualize golden sunlight streaming out of your fingertips. Feel the warmth of the light as you project it skyward, visualizing the clouds parting and the rain steadily slowing. Say, "I ask wind and sun to help this water on its way to where it is presently needed." Visualize yourself looking up into a dry blue sky. The rain will decrease or end unless there is a worthy and pressing reason for it to continue.

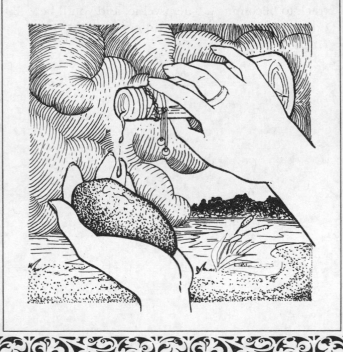

Now, the wind will blow where it wants to, but it doesn't hurt to ask. To invite a breeze your way, inhale slowly and deeply, drawing in winds from afar as you do so. Communicate to the wind that you would like to feel it, and that you would love a visit. If you wish for strong winds to subside, simply blow out slowly, then harder, visualizing the winds being blown onto a different course.

～

ESP is one of our greatest magical investments. It takes dedication and practice to bring our psychic ability to its full potential, but with these easy one-minute exercises, all that dedication and practice doesn't have to take a lot of time. If you exercise your ESP just a few minutes every day, in a few different ways, you will soon find yourself on a fast track to becoming a true psychic, and you'll be well on your way to truly masterful magic.

Walking with Spirit

by Harmony Usher

The longest journey begins with a single step.
—Lao Tsu, Tao Te Ching

Walking is both a physical and symbolic activity that connects our bodies and spirits and a universal metaphor for moving forward. Walking is a whole-body experience that helps us reach our spiritual potential. As we move our body, our mind becomes quiet. When we have a quiet mind, our spirit blossoms. Moving forward changes our scenery and invites new experiences. It enlivens our senses and gets our respiratory and circulatory systems going. When we approach walking from a spiritual perspective, it helps us embrace new opportunities and discover our potential.

It doesn't matter how physically fit we are or what ability we have, there is a form of spiritual walking for everyone. It doesn't matter if we walk with Olympic speed, amble along with the assistance of a walker, or roll in a chair—walking is about moving forward, and it is available to us all.

Walkabouts

Native Australians have practiced the walkabout for centuries. This involves going into the desert with only hunting tools and the clothes on one's back for an extended period of time to push one's physical limits, commune with nature, and connect with the spiritual realm. This walking tradition is based on the belief that we are spiritually linked to our landscape and can experience spiritual growth by becoming closer to it. During this solitary period in the desert, the walker enters a meditative state and connects with a personal spiritual guide, who eventually aids in their return home.

The Pilgrimage

Another spiritual walking tradition is the pilgrimage, which involves traveling on foot to reach a temple, monument, gravesite, or particular geographical landmark. Some pilgrimages involve only short distances, but many pilgrimages last days or even weeks.

Pilgrimages appear in most cultures and religions. Regardless of religious association, pilgrimages share certain characteristics. Almost all involve a specific path or route, a destination, a ritual or activity done at the destination, a belief the journey will provide a spiritual or practical benefit, and a return home.

These journeys are both concrete and metaphoric, representing not only the pilgrim's arrival at a particular location, but their internal spiritual journey as well. The tradition of going on a pilgrimage is often handed down from generation to generation, and it becomes an important subject in some family histories. In some religious traditions, a pilgrimage is an expected practice for all followers.

Walking Inward

While walkabouts and pilgrimages involve considerable time and energy commitments, other forms of spiritual walking focus on the internal journey and are easily enjoyed by most people in their everyday lives.

Buddhists around the world undertake a practice called walking meditation. Unlike a pilgrimage, which is focused on the arrival at a destination, meditative walking is about consciousness and awareness. It requires that we get in touch with each breath we take and each movement of our bodies. It doesn't matter where we go, but how we experience the journey.

There are no right or wrong places to practice walking meditation, and you certainly don't have be Buddhist. This form of walking is becoming a valued spiritual practice across many religions and is becoming increasingly popular in the secular world as well. You can walk along a quiet roadside, at a park, or in your backyard. You can walk on a straight path, in a circle, or just wander as you wish. While you walk, concentrate on your breath and the individual movements that make up each footstep. Through this practice we become conscious of our *intention* to walk, and we begin to pay attention to the motion of lifting each foot, moving it forward through the air, and then replacing it upon the ground.

If you are able, try to walk in this manner for fifteen to thirty minutes in order to allow your mind time to quiet. Of course, if you are only able to walk for shorter times, there will still be benefits! You might walk as long as you are able, and then spend the remaining time sitting quietly, breathing deeply, and envisioning yourself walking. This too will induce relaxation.

Walking the Labyrinth

Another form of spiritual walking involves a labyrinth. The labyrinth is sometimes confused with a maze, which has a number of possible routes and only one "correct" path leading to a destination. A labyrinth, on the other hand, has only one path and it is always the right one!

The labyrinth is a circular pathway winding clockwise from its entrance to the center of the circle. You begin by entering the pathway, leaving behind the worries of the day. You then follow the path to the center of the circle, where you might pray, meditate, or sing. Finally, you return to the original entrance along the same path you traveled. There are no tricks or hidden pathways. The shape of the true labyrinth—a large circle divided into quarters—symbolizes archetypes such as the four elements or directions. Labyrinths can be very elaborate or beautifully simple.

Committed labyrinth walkers often create a backyard labyrinth using garden stones or greenery to define the circular path. This gives them easy, daily access to a healthy and spiritually rewarding activity.

One of the lovely things about a labyrinth is that one only needs to trust the path, allowing it to show you along the way. Although an ancient tradition, labyrinths are still found today in churches, playgrounds, parks, prisons, and school grounds. Labyrinth walking is growing in popularity and is being offered as a part of many spa or meditative retreats. Because it does not require any special skill or fitness level, and because many are wheelchair accessible, this reflective and refreshing activity appeals to a wide range of individuals.

Mindful Walking

Regardless of what kind of spiritual walking you choose, all you need to begin is a pair of comfortable shoes and the intention to walk with spirit. Being mindful can help you in becoming conscious of all of your senses and surroundings. Notice how your feet feel as you slip your shoes on, and how they sound as you place them on the ground. Be conscious of how much tension

you like when you tie your shoes. Be conscious of your thoughts
as they jump around like an excited monkey; acknowledge them
and then let them go. When you begin to move, your thoughts
will begin to quiet.

It doesn't matter if you plan to circle your backyard, walk
around the block, or take a three-week holiday to pilgrimage to
a special place. What matters is your intention, your desire. As
you walk, you may wish to use words, aloud or silently, to become
conscious of the physicality of walking. As you lift your foot, say
"lifting," as you move it forward, say "moving," and as you bring
it back to the ground, say "placing." Breaking the act of walking
into smaller individual acts in this way allows our consciousness
to expand.

Walk at your normal pace and only walk as far as you feel
comfortable going. The focus is not fitness (although that will be
a natural benefit if you continue your practice for some time).
The focus is on consciousness. As you move forward, notice the
air that passes over your face, blows through your hair, or carries
the smells of the season to you. As you notice these things, say
them to yourself: "As I walk, I feel the wind," or, "As I walk, I hear
the rustling of leaves."

Pay attention to your breathing, too. Notice the way air is first pulled into your lungs and then released. You may say, "As I walk I breathe in, as I walk I breathe out," as you move along your path. You may notice your walk has a rhythm and sometimes a familiar song or tune will come into your head as you walk, to keep the rhythm. If this happens, say, "As I walk, there is music in each step," and simply allow yourself to enjoy the song!

This kind of mindfulness while walking is a wonderful bridge between meditation and daily life, a way of bringing spirituality and awareness into the ordinary moments of your day.

Ritualistic Walking

For those who enjoy spiritual practices that use ritual, there are many ways to incorporate them into walking. Ritual walking can add richness and meaning to your day.

You might choose to routinely walk at a particular time. This is an important part of my current walking practice. I wake each morning just as the sun rises in the east. I walk westward, so that the sun rises behind me. I imagine the sun nudging me forward, helping me along the path. I walk to the end of my country road, turn, face the sun, bow, and thank the universe for this new day. As I walk back into the sun, I give thanks for all that is coming into my life, whether it is health, wellness, friendship, good food, or peace. I feel the sunlight on my body and face and feel an infusion of goodness and peace. This ritual offers me a wonderful beginning to each day.

In the evening, I go through the same ritual, except I walk toward the setting sun, giving thanks for all that has transpired through the day, sending worries down with the sinking sun. I begin to imagine my body coming to rest just as the day is, and ask the universe for a good night's rest.

You may use direction as a way of infusing meaning into your walking practice as well. For instance, you might walk toward the north to become more in touch with things associated with earth, to the south to become more attune to passion and energy, to the east to connect with the intellect, and to the west to connect with the psyche and emotions. You might walk in different directions when particular relationships or personal issues are on your mind.

In keeping with banishment and abundance rituals, you might take a counterclockwise path to rid yourself of something, or a clockwise path to manifest something. For example, if you want to attract new friends, walk in a clockwise fashion around your home by way of the town or city blocks, and while you walk, repeat, "My home welcomes new friends." Envision friends driving up your driveway or walking through your front and back doors. The energy you generate walking clockwise will pull these in. Similarly, if you are having an ongoing disagreement with a family member, you may wish to walk counterclockwise around your home, imagining resentment and stubbornness being pulled away from you.

Gratitude Walks and Personal Pilgrimages

Gratitude walks open our hearts to the simple pleasures around us and allow us to receive abundance. As we walk we simply note and express thanks for those things we see that bring us pleasure. "I am thankful for the large trees that line my street," "I am thankful for these feet that carry me forward through my day and through my life." Sometimes I find my shorter walks are perfect for simply noting those things I am most thankful for. I always return home feeling refreshed.

Who says pilgrimages have to be sanctioned by the masses or recognized by a church? I have been known to go on pilgrimages for ice cream, to seek wisdom from an elder up the road, or to find knowledge at the library. Again, it's the intent our attention pays to our innermost desires that truly matters.

~

Whether you enter into walking with the intention to arrive somewhere or you walk to discover some special place inside of yourself, just walk. Along with a nourished spirit, the sunshine, fresh air, and physical activity will do you good! And remember, in the words of comedian Steven Wright, "Everywhere is walking distance, if you have the time."

Almanac Section

Calendar

Time Changes

Lunar Phases

Moon Signs

Full Moons

Sabbats

World Holidays

Incense of the Day

Color of the Day

Almanac Listings

In these listings you will find the date, day, lunar phase, Moon sign, color and incense for the day, and festivals from around the world.

The Date

The date is used in numerological calculations that govern magical rites.

The Day

Each day is ruled by a planet that possesses specific magical influences:

MONDAY (MOON): Peace, sleep, healing, compassion, friends, psychic awareness, purification, and fertility.

TUESDAY (MARS): Passion, sex, courage, aggression, and protection.

WEDNESDAY (MERCURY): The conscious mind, study, travel, divination, and wisdom.

THURSDAY (JUPITER): Expansion, money, prosperity, and generosity.

FRIDAY (VENUS): Love, friendship, reconciliation, and beauty.

SATURDAY (SATURN): Longevity, exorcism, endings, homes, and houses.

SUNDAY (SUN): Healing, spirituality, success, strength, and protection.

The Lunar Phase

The lunar phase is important in determining the best times for magic.

THE WAXING MOON (from the New Moon to the Full) is the ideal time for magic to draw things toward you.

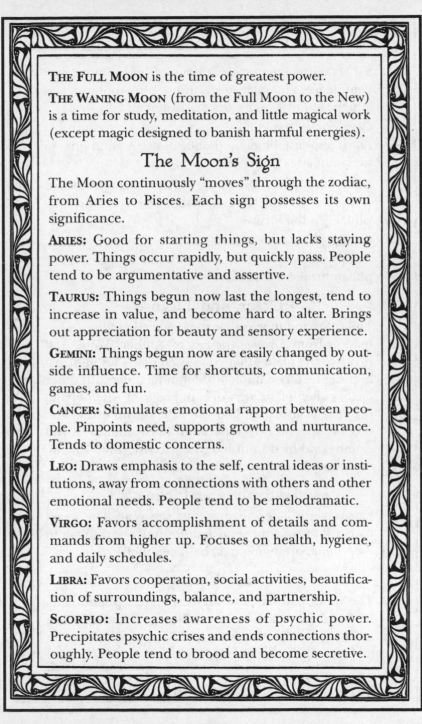

THE FULL MOON is the time of greatest power.

THE WANING MOON (from the Full Moon to the New) is a time for study, meditation, and little magical work (except magic designed to banish harmful energies).

The Moon's Sign

The Moon continuously "moves" through the zodiac, from Aries to Pisces. Each sign possesses its own significance.

ARIES: Good for starting things, but lacks staying power. Things occur rapidly, but quickly pass. People tend to be argumentative and assertive.

TAURUS: Things begun now last the longest, tend to increase in value, and become hard to alter. Brings out appreciation for beauty and sensory experience.

GEMINI: Things begun now are easily changed by outside influence. Time for shortcuts, communication, games, and fun.

CANCER: Stimulates emotional rapport between people. Pinpoints need, supports growth and nurturance. Tends to domestic concerns.

LEO: Draws emphasis to the self, central ideas or institutions, away from connections with others and other emotional needs. People tend to be melodramatic.

VIRGO: Favors accomplishment of details and commands from higher up. Focuses on health, hygiene, and daily schedules.

LIBRA: Favors cooperation, social activities, beautification of surroundings, balance, and partnership.

SCORPIO: Increases awareness of psychic power. Precipitates psychic crises and ends connections thoroughly. People tend to brood and become secretive.

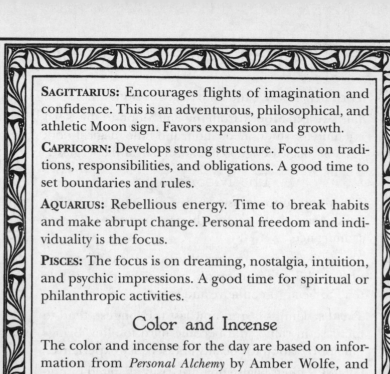

SAGITTARIUS: Encourages flights of imagination and confidence. This is an adventurous, philosophical, and athletic Moon sign. Favors expansion and growth.

CAPRICORN: Develops strong structure. Focus on traditions, responsibilities, and obligations. A good time to set boundaries and rules.

AQUARIUS: Rebellious energy. Time to break habits and make abrupt change. Personal freedom and individuality is the focus.

PISCES: The focus is on dreaming, nostalgia, intuition, and psychic impressions. A good time for spiritual or philanthropic activities.

Color and Incense

The color and incense for the day are based on information from *Personal Alchemy* by Amber Wolfe, and relate to the planet that rules each day. This information can be taken into consideration along with other factors when planning works of magic or when blending magic into mundane life. Please note that the incense selections listed are not hard-and-fast. If you cannot find or do not like the incense listed for the day, choose a similar scent that appeals to you.

Festivals and Holidays

Festivals are listed throughout the year. The exact dates of many of these ancient festivals are difficult to determine; prevailing data has been used.

Time Changes

The times and dates of all astrological phenomena in this almanac are based on **Eastern Standard Time (EST)**. If you live outside of EST, you will need to make the following changes:

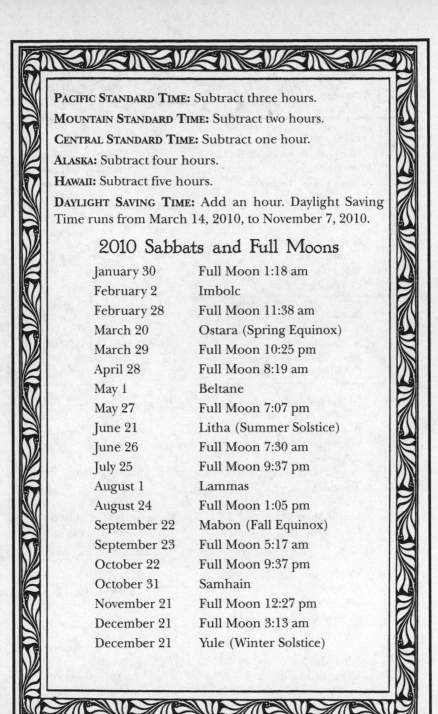

PACIFIC STANDARD TIME: Subtract three hours.

MOUNTAIN STANDARD TIME: Subtract two hours.

CENTRAL STANDARD TIME: Subtract one hour.

ALASKA: Subtract four hours.

HAWAII: Subtract five hours.

DAYLIGHT SAVING TIME: Add an hour. Daylight Saving Time runs from March 14, 2010, to November 7, 2010.

2010 Sabbats and Full Moons

January 30	Full Moon 1:18 am
February 2	Imbolc
February 28	Full Moon 11:38 am
March 20	Ostara (Spring Equinox)
March 29	Full Moon 10:25 pm
April 28	Full Moon 8:19 am
May 1	Beltane
May 27	Full Moon 7:07 pm
June 21	Litha (Summer Solstice)
June 26	Full Moon 7:30 am
July 25	Full Moon 9:37 pm
August 1	Lammas
August 24	Full Moon 1:05 pm
September 22	Mabon (Fall Equinox)
September 23	Full Moon 5:17 am
October 22	Full Moon 9:37 pm
October 31	Samhain
November 21	Full Moon 12:27 pm
December 21	Full Moon 3:13 am
December 21	Yule (Winter Solstice)

January

1 **Friday**
New Year's Day • Kwanzaa ends
Waning Moon
Moon phase: Third Quarter
Color: Coral

Moon sign: Cancer
Moon enters Leo 9:41 pm
Incense: Yarrow

2 **Saturday**
First Writing (Japanese)
Waning Moon
Moon phase: Third Quarter
Color: Gray

Moon sign: Leo
Incense: Magnolia

3 **Sunday**
St. Genevieve's Day
Waning Moon
Moon phase: Third Quarter
Color: Orange

Moon sign: Leo
Moon enters Virgo 9:52 pm
Incense: Hyacinth

4 **Monday**
Frost Fairs on the Thames
Waning Moon
Moon phase: Third Quarter
Color: White

Moon sign: Virgo
Incense: Lily

5 **Tuesday**
Epiphany Eve
Waning Moon
Moon phase: Third Quarter
Color: Red

Moon sign: Virgo
Moon enters Libra 11:58 pm
Incense: Bayberry

6 **Wednesday**
Epiphany
Waning Moon
Moon phase: Third Quarter
Color: White

Moon sign: Libra
Incense: Lilac

☽ **Thursday**
Rizdvo (Ukrainian)
Waning Moon
Moon phase: Fourth Quarter 5:40 am
Color: Crimson

Moon sign: Libra
Incense: Myrrh

8 Friday
Midwives' Day
Waning Moon
Moon phase: Fourth Quarter
Color: Purple

Moon sign: Libra
Moon enters Scorpio 5:00 am
Incense: Alder

---

9 Saturday
Feast of the Black Nazarene (Filipino)
Waning Moon
Moon phase: Fourth Quarter
Color: Brown

Moon sign: Scorpio
Incense: Sage

---

10 Sunday
Business God's Day (Japanese)
Waning Moon
Moon phase: Fourth Quarter
Color: Amber

Moon sign: Scorpio
Moon enters Sagittarius 1:10 pm
Incense: Juniper

---

11 Monday
Carmentalia (Roman)
Waning Moon
Moon phase: Fourth Quarter
Color: Ivory

Moon sign: Sagittarius
Incense: Clary sage

---

12 Tuesday
Revolution Day (Tanzanian)
Waning Moon
Moon phase: Fourth Quarter
Color: Black

Moon sign: Sagittarius
Moon enters Capricorn 11:54 pm
Incense: Geranium

---

13 Wednesday
Twentieth Day (Norwegian)
Waning Moon
Moon phase: Fourth Quarter
Color: Brown

Moon sign: Capricorn
Incense: Bay laurel

---

14 Thursday
Feast of the Ass (French)
Waning Moon
Moon phase: Fourth Quarter
Color: Green

Moon sign: Capricorn
Incense: Clove

☽ **Friday**
Birthday of Martin Luther King, Jr. (actual)   Moon sign: Capricorn
Waning Moon   Moon enters Aquarius 12:17 pm
Moon phase: New Moon 2:11 am   Incense: Vanilla
Color: Rose

16 **Saturday**
Apprentices Day   Moon sign: Aquarius
Waxing Moon   Incense: Patchouli
Moon phase: First Quarter
Color: Blue

17 **Sunday**
St. Anthony's Day (Mexican)   Moon sign: Aquarius
Waxing Moon   Incense: Frankincense
Moon phase: First Quarter
Color: Gold

18 **Monday**
Birthday of Martin Luther King, Jr. (observed)   Moon sign: Aquarius
Waxing Moon   Moon enters Pisces 1:17 am
Moon phase: First Quarter   Incense: Hyssop
Color: Silver

19 **Tuesday**
St. Anthony's Day (Mexican)   Moon sign: Pisces
Waxing Moon   Sun enters Aquarius 11:28 pm
Moon phase: First Quarter   Incense: Ylang-ylang
Color: White

20 **Wednesday**
Breadbasket Festival (Portuguese)   Moon sign: Pisces
Waxing Moon   Moon enters Aries 1:36 pm
Moon phase: First Quarter   Incense: Lavender
Color: Topaz

21 **Thursday**
St. Agnes Day   Moon sign: Aries
Waxing Moon   Incense: Nutmeg
Moon phase: First Quarter
Color: Purple

22 Friday
St. Vincent's Day (French)   Moon sign: Aries
Waxing Moon   Moon enters Taurus 11:39 pm
Moon phase: First Quarter   Incense: Thyme
Color: Pink

☾ Saturday
St. Ildefonso's Day   Moon sign: Taurus
Waxing Moon   Incense: Pine
Moon phase: Second Quarter 5:53 am
Color: Black

24 Sunday
Alasitas Fair (Bolivian)   Moon sign: Taurus
Waxing Moon   Incense: Almond
Moon phase: Second Quarter
Color: Orange

25 Monday
Burns' Night (Scottish)   Moon sign: Taurus
Waxing Moon   Moon enters Gemini 6:11 am
Moon phase: Second Quarter   Incense: Neroli
Color: Gray

26 Tuesday
Republic Day (Indian)   Moon sign: Gemini
Waxing Moon   Incense: Cinnamon
Moon phase: Second Quarter
Color: Maroon

27 Wednesday
Vogelgruff (Swiss)   Moon sign: Gemini
Waxing Moon   Moon enters Cancer 9:01 am
Moon phase: Second Quarter   Incense: Honeysuckle
Color: Brown

28 Thursday
St. Charlemagne's Day   Moon sign: Cancer
Waxing Moon   Incense: Apricot
Moon phase: Second Quarter
Color: White

29 **Friday**
Australia Day
Waxing Moon
Moon phase: Second Quarter
Color: Purple

Moon sign: Cancer
Moon enters Leo 9:10 am
Incense: Orchid

Saturday
Three Hierarchs' Day (Eastern Orthodox)
Waxing Moon
Moon phase: Full Moon 1:18 am
Color: Indigo

Moon sign: Leo
Incense: Ivy

31 **Sunday**
Independence Day (Nauru)
Waning Moon
Moon phase: Third Quarter
Color: Yellow

Moon sign: Leo
Moon enters Virgo 8:23 am
Incense: Heliotrope

Sabbats in the Southern Hemisphere

Because the Earth's Northern and Southern Hemispheres experience opposite seasons at any given time, the season-based sabbat dates listed in this almanac are not correct for those residing south of the equator. Listed here are the Southern Hemisphere sabbat dates for 2010:

February 2	Lammas
March 20	Mabon
April 30	Samhain
June 21	Yule
August 2	Imbolc
September 22	Ostara
November 1	Beltane
December 21	Litha

1   Monday
St. Brigid's Day (Irish)
Waning Moon
Moon phase: Third Quarter
Color: Gray

Moon sign: Virgo
Incense: Narcissus

2   Tuesday
Imbolc • Groundhog Day
Waning Moon
Moon phase: Third Quarter
Color: Black

Moon sign: Virgo
Moon enters Libra 8:42 am
Incense: Bayberry

3   Wednesday
St. Blaise's Day
Waning Moon
Moon phase: Third Quarter
Color: Yellow

Moon sign: Libra
Incense: Bay laurel

4   Thursday
Independence Day (Sri Lankan)
Waning Moon
Moon phase: Third Quarter
Color: Green

Moon sign: Libra
Moon enters Scorpio 11:56 am
Incense: Mulberry

☽   Friday
Festival de la Alcaldesa (Italian)
Waning Moon
Moon phase: Fourth Quarter 6:48 pm
Color: White

Moon sign: Scorpio
Incense: Thyme

6   Saturday
Bob Marley's Birthday (Jamaican)
Waning Moon
Moon phase: Fourth Quarter
Color: Black

Moon sign: Scorpio
Moon enters Sagittarius 7:04 pm
Incense: Patchouli

7   Sunday
Full Moon Poya (Sri Lankan)
Waning Moon
Moon phase: Fourth Quarter
Color: Orange

Moon sign: Sagittarius
Incense: Eucalyptus

February

8 Monday
Mass for Broken Needles (Japanese)
Waning Moon
Moon phase: Fourth Quarter
Color: Lavender

Moon sign: Sagittarius
Incense: Rosemary

9 Tuesday
St. Marion's Day (Lebanese)
Waning Moon
Moon phase: Fourth Quarter
Color: Red

Moon sign: Sagittarius
Moon enters Capricorn 5:43 am
Incense: Ginger

10 Wednesday
Gasparilla Day (Florida)
Waning Moon
Moon phase: Fourth Quarter
Color: Brown

Moon sign: Capricorn
Incense: Marjoram

11 Thursday
Foundation Day (Japanese)
Waning Moon
Moon phase: Fourth Quarter
Color: Turquoise

Moon sign: Capricorn
Moon enters Aquarius 6:24 pm
Incense: Jasmine

12 Friday
Lincoln's Birthday (actual)
Waning Moon
Moon phase: Fourth Quarter
Color: Rose

Moon sign: Aquarius
Incense: Rose

Saturday
Parentalia (Roman)
Waning Moon
Moon phase: New Moon 9:51 pm
Color: Blue

Moon sign: Aquarius
Incense: Magnolia

14 Sunday
Chinese New Year (tiger) • *Valentine's Day*
Waxing Moon
Moon phase: First Quarter
Color: Gold

Moon sign: Aquarius
Moon enters Pisces 7:23 am
Incense: Juniper

February ♓

15 **Monday**
Presidents' Day (observed)
Waxing Moon
Moon phase: First Quarter
Color: Silver

Moon sign: Pisces
Incense: Hyssop

16 **Tuesday**
Mardi Gras (Fat Tuesday)
Waxing Moon
Moon phase: First Quarter
Color: Scarlet

Moon sign: Pisces
Moon enters Aries 7:30 pm
Incense: Cedar

17 **Wednesday**
Ash Wednesday
Waxing Moon
Moon phase: First Quarter
Color: Topaz

Moon sign: Aries
Incense: Lilac

18 **Thursday**
Saint Bernadette's Second Vision
Waxing Moon
Moon phase: First Quarter
Color: White

Moon sign: Aries
Sun enters Pisces 1:36 pm
Incense: Clover

19 **Friday**
Pero Palo's Trial (Spanish)
Waxing Moon
Moon phase: First Quarter
Color: Purple

Moon sign: Aries
Moon enters Taurus 5:55 am
Incense: Vanilla

20 **Saturday**
Installation of the new Lama (Tibetan)
Waxing Moon
Moon phase: First Quarter
Color: Gray

Moon sign: Taurus
Incense: Rue

◑ **Sunday**
Feast of Lanterns (Chinese)
Waxing Moon
Moon phase: Second Quarter 7:42 pm
Color: Amber

Moon sign: Taurus
Moon enters Gemini 1:47 pm
Incense: Hyacinth

February

22 **Monday**
Caristia (Roman)
Waxing Moon
Moon phase: Second Quarter
Color: White

Moon sign: Gemini
Incense: Neroli

23 **Tuesday**
Terminalia (Roman)
Waxing Moon
Moon phase: Second Quarter
Color: Gray

Moon sign: Gemini
Moon enters Cancer 6:29 pm
Incense: Geranium

24 **Wednesday**
Regifugium (Roman)
Waxing Moon
Moon phase: Second Quarter
Color: Yellow

Moon sign: Cancer
Incense: Lavender

25 **Thursday**
Saint Walburga's Day (German)
Waxing Moon
Moon phase: Second Quarter
Color: Crimson

Moon sign: Cancer
Moon enters Leo 8:08 pm
Incense: Carnation

26 **Friday**
Zamboanga Festival (Filipino)
Waxing Moon
Moon phase: Second Quarter
Color: Pink

Moon sign: Leo
Incense: Yarrow

27 **Saturday**
Threepenny Day
Waxing Moon
Moon phase: Second Quarter
Color: Black

Moon sign: Leo
Moon enteres Virgo 7:52 pm
Incense: Sandalwood

☺ **Sunday**
Purim
Waxing Moon
Moon phase: Full Moon 11:38 am
Color: Gold

Moon sign: Virgo
Incense: Marigold

March

1 Monday
Matronalia (Roman)
Waning Moon
Moon phase: Third Quarter
Color: Silver

Moon sign: Virgo
Moon enters Libra 7:31 pm
Incense: Narcissus

---

2 Tuesday
St. Chad's Day (English)
Waning Moon
Moon phase: Third Quarter
Color: Gray

Moon sign: Libra
Incense: Basil

---

3 Wednesday
Doll Festival (Japanese)
Waning Moon
Moon phase: Third Quarter
Color: Topaz

Moon sign: Libra
Moon enters Scorpio 9:11 pm
Incense: Marjoram

---

4 Thursday
St. Casimir's Day (Polish)
Waning Moon
Moon phase: Third Quarter
Color: White

Moon sign: Scorpio
Incense: Apricot

---

5 Friday
Isis Festival (Roman)
Waning Moon
Moon phase: Third Quarter
Color: Coral

Moon sign: Scorpio
Incense: Mint

---

6 Saturday
Alamo Day
Waning Moon
Moon phase: Third Quarter
Color: Indigo

Moon sign: Scorpio
Moon enters Sagittarius 2:36 am
Incense: Patchouli

◐ Sunday
Bird and Arbor Day
Waning Moon
Moon phase: Fourth Quarter 10:42 am
Color: Yellow

Moon sign: Sagittarius
Incense: Juniper

March

8 Monday
International Women's Day
Waning Moon
Moon phase: Fourth Quarter
Color: White

Moon sign: Sagittarius
Moon enters Capricorn 12:13 pm
Incense: Lily

9 Tuesday
Forty Saints' Day
Waning Moon
Moon phase: Fourth Quarter
Color: Black

Moon sign: Capricorn
Incense: Cedar

10 Wednesday
Tibet Day
Waning Moon
Moon phase: Fourth Quarter
Color: Brown

Moon sign: Capricorn
Incense: Lavender

11 Thursday
Feast of the Gauri (Hindu)
Waning Moon
Moon phase: Fourth Quarter
Color: Crimson

Moon sign: Capricorn
Moon enters Aquarius 12:42 am
Incense: Jasmine

12 Friday
Receiving the Water (Buddhist)
Waning Moon
Moon phase: Fourth Quarter
Color: Purple

Moon sign: Aquarius
Incense: Cypress

13 Saturday
Purification Feast (Balinese)
Waning Moon
Moon phase: Fourth Quarter
Color: Black

Moon sign: Aquarius
Moon enters Pisces 1:44 pm
Incense: Pine

14 Sunday
Daylight Saving Time begins
Waning Moon
Moon phase: Fourth Quarter
Color: Yellow

Moon sign: Pisces
Incense: Almond

March ♈

♉ **Monday**
Phallus Festival (Japanese)
Waning Moon
Moon phase: New Moon 5:01 pm
Color: Gray

Moon sign: Pisces
Incense: Rosemary

16 **Tuesday**
St. Urho's Day (Finnish)
Waxing Moon
Moon phase: First Quarter
Color: Maroon

Moon sign: Pisces
Moon enters Aries 2:32 am
Incense: Ylang-ylang

17 **Wednesday**
St. Patrick's Day
Waxing Moon
Moon phase: First Quarter
Color: White

Moon sign: Aries
Incense: Lilac

18 **Thursday**
Sheelah's Day (Irish)
Waxing Moon
Moon phase: First Quarter
Color: Purple

Moon sign: Aries
Moon enters Taurus 12:29 pm
Incense: Myrrh

19 **Friday**
St. Joseph's Day (Sicilian)
Waxing Moon
Moon phase: First Quarter
Color: Pink

Moon sign: Taurus
Incense: Violet

20 **Saturday**
Ostara • Spring Equinox • Int'l Astrology Day
Waxing Moon
Moon phase: First Quarter
Color: Gray

Moon sign: Taurus
Sun enters Aries 1:32 pm
Moon enters Gemini 8:28 pm
Incense: Sage

21 **Sunday**
Juarez Day (Mexican)
Waxing Moon
Moon phase: First Quarter
Color: Amber

Moon sign: Gemini
Incense: Marigold

22 Monday
Hilaria (Roman)
Waxing Moon
Moon phase: First Quarter
Color: Lavender

Moon sign: Gemini
Incense: Clary sage

Tuesday
Pakistan Day
Waxing Moon
Moon phase: Second Quarter 7:00 am
Color: Red

Moon sign: Gemini
Moon enters Cancer 2:16 am
Incense: Bayberry

---

24 Wednesday
Day of Blood (Roman)
Waxing Moon
Moon phase: Second Quarter
Color: Brown

Moon sign: Cancer
Incense: Bay laurel

---

25 Thursday
Tichborne Dole (English)
Waxing Moon
Moon phase: Second Quarter
Color: Green

Moon sign: Cancer
Moon enters Leo 5:39 am
Incense: Nutmeg

---

26 Friday
Prince Kuhio Day (Hawaiian)
Waxing Moon
Moon phase: Second Quarter
Color: Coral

Moon sign: Leo
Incense: Thyme

---

27 Saturday
Smell the Breezes Day (Egyptian)
Waxing Moon
Moon phase: Second Quarter
Color: Blue

Moon sign: Leo
Moon enters Virgo 6:57 am
Incense: Magnolia

---

28 Sunday
Palm Sunday
Waxing Moon
Moon phase: Second Quarter
Color: Orange

Moon sign: Virgo
Incense: Eucalyptus

March

♈

☺ **Monday**
Feast of St. Eustace's of Luxeuil
Waxing Moon
Moon phase: Full Moon 10:25 pm
Color: Gray

Moon sign: Virgo
Moon enters Libra 7:21 am
Incense: Hyssop

30 Tuesday
Passover begins
Waning Moon
Moon phase: Third Quarter
Color: White

Moon sign: Libra
Incense: Geranium

31 Wednesday
The Borrowed Days (Ethiopian)
Waning Moon
Moon phase: Third Quarter
Color: Yellow

Moon sign: Libra
Moon enters Scorpio 8:41 am
Incense: Honeysuckle

Ostara
O'Blessin' Eggs (*Leprechauns*)

Sure and you'll enjoy boonful blessings between Saint Paddy's and Ostara! Crack eggs in half, empty, rinse, and dry overnight. Write tiny Leprechaun blessing notes, such as "pot o'gold," "wish comes true," "full pockets," "spring love," and the like on green paper. Cut them into small strips. Fill the eggs with these blessing notes, and paste the shells shut with colored tissue paper splints. Let them dry. Break an O'Blessin' Egg over a person's head to give them good luck in the spring season. Have the person cup their hands to catch some of the blessings. The ones that are caught will come true!

–Elizabeth Hazel

1 **Thursday**
April Fools' Day
Waning Moon
Moon phase: Third Quarter
Color: Green

Moon sign: Scorpio
Incense: Mulberry

---

2 **Friday**
Good Friday • Orthodox Good Friday
Waning Moon
Moon phase: Third Quarter
Color: Purple

Moon sign: Scorpio
Moon enters Sagittarius 12:53 pm
Incense: Orchid

---

3 **Saturday**
Thirteenth Day (Iranian)
Waning Moon
Moon phase: Third Quarter
Color: Brown

Moon sign: Sagittarius
Incense: Sage

---

4 **Sunday**
Easter • Orthodox Easter
Waning Moon
Moon phase: Third Quarter
Color: Amber

Moon sign: Sagittarius
Moon enters Capricorn 9:07 pm
Incense: Eucalyptus

---

5 **Monday**
Tomb-Sweeping Day (Chinese)
Waning Moon
Moon phase: Third Quarter
Color: Lavender

Moon sign: Capricorn
Incense: Hyssop

◖ **Tuesday**
Passover ends
Waning Moon
Moon phase: Fourth Quarter 5:37 am
Color: Red

Moon sign: Capricorn
Incense: Ginger

---

7 **Wednesday**
Festival of Pure Brightness (Chinese)
Waning Moon
Moon phase: Fourth Quarter
Color: White

Moon sign: Capricorn
Moon enters Aquarius 8:51 am
Incense: Bay laurel

April

8   **Thursday**
Buddha's Birthday
Waning Moon
Moon phase: Fourth Quarter
Color: Turquoise

Moon sign: Aquarius
Incense: Balsam

---

9   **Friday**
Valour Day (Filipino)
Waning Moon
Moon phase: Fourth Quarter
Color: Pink

Moon sign: Aquarius
Moon enters Pisces 9:48 pm
Incense: Mint

---

10   **Saturday**
The Tenth of April (English)
Waning Moon
Moon phase: Fourth Quarter
Color: Gray

Moon sign: Pisces
Incense: Ivy

---

11   **Sunday**
Heroes Day (Costa Rican)
Waning Moon
Moon phase: Fourth Quarter
Color: Orange

Moon sign: Pisces
Incense: Hyacinth

---

12   **Monday**
Cerealia (Roman)
Waning Moon
Moon phase: Fourth Quarter
Color: Silver

Moon sign: Pisces
Moon enters Aries 9:31 am
Incense: Neroli

---

13   **Tuesday**
Thai New Year
Waning Moon
Moon phase: Fourth Quarter
Color: Black

Moon sign: Aries
Incense: Cedar

☽   **Wednesday**
Sanno Festival (Japanese)
Waning Moon
Moon phase: New Moon 8:29 am
Color: Yellow

Moon sign: Aries
Moon enters Taurus 6:55 pm
Incense: Lavender

April

15 **Thursday**
Plowing Festival (Chinese)
Waxing Moon
Moon phase: First Quarter
Color: Purple

Moon sign: Taurus
Incense: Clove

---

16 **Friday**
Zurich Spring Festival (Swiss)
Waxing Moon
Moon phase: First Quarter
Color: White

Moon sign: Taurus
Incense: Alder

---

17 **Saturday**
Yayoi Matsuri (Japanese)
Waxing Moon
Moon phase: First Quarter
Color: Blue

Moon sign: Taurus
Moon enters Gemini 2:08 am
Incense: Rue

---

18 **Sunday**
Flower Festival (Japanese)
Waxing Moon
Moon phase: First Quarter
Color: Gold

Moon sign: Gemini
Incense: Frankincense

---

19 **Monday**
Cerealia last day (Roman)
Waxing Moon
Moon phase: First Quarter
Color: Gray

Moon sign: Gemini
Moon enters Cancer 7:39 am
Incense: Rosemary

---

20 **Tuesday**
Drum Festival (Japanese)
Waxing Moon
Moon phase: First Quarter
Color: Scarlet

Moon sign: Cancer
Sun enters Taurus 12:20 am
Incense: Basil

◐ **Wednesday**
Tiradentes Day (Brazilian)
Waxing Moon
Moon phase: Second Quarter 2:20 pm
Color: Topaz

Moon sign: Cancer
Moon enters Leo 11:42 am
Incense: Marjoram

April

22 Thursday
Earth Day
Waxing Moon
Moon phase: Second Quarter
Color: White

Moon sign: Leo
Incense: Carnation

23 Friday
St. George's Day (English)
Waxing Moon
Moon phase: Second Quarter
Color: Rose

Moon sign: Leo
Moon enters Virgo 2:24 pm
Incense: Yarrow

24 Saturday
St. Mark's Eve
Waxing Moon
Moon phase: Second Quarter
Color: Brown

Moon sign: Virgo
Incense: Sandalwood

25 Sunday
Robigalia (Roman)
Waxing Moon
Moon phase: Second Quarter
Color: Amber

Moon sign: Virgo
Moon enters Libra 4:16 pm
Incense: Heliotrope

26 Monday
Arbor Day
Waxing Moon
Moon phase: Second Quarter
Color: Silver

Moon sign: Libra
Incense: Lily

27 Tuesday
Humabon's Conversion (Filipino)
Waxing Moon
Moon phase: Second Quarter
Color: White

Moon sign: Libra
Moon enters Scorpio 6:28 pm
Incense: Cinnamon

☺ Wednesday
Floralia (Roman)
Waxing Moon
Moon phase: Full Moon 8:19 am
Color: Yellow

Moon sign: Scorpio
Incense: Honeysuckle

29 Thursday
Green Day (Japanese)
Waning Moon
Moon phase: Third Quarter
Color: Turquoise

Moon sign: Scorpio
Moon enters Sagittarius 10:36 pm
Incense: Balsam

30 Friday
Walpurgis Night • May Eve
Waning Moon
Moon phase: Third Quarter
Color: Purple

Moon sign: Sagittarius
Incense: Mint

Beltane
Rue-Fulls (*the Fae*)

Fill a basket with bundles of fresh herbs. Rue, sage, sweet woodruff, early parsley, and mint are good choices. Put flowers in with the herbs. Set the basket out on Walpurgis (Beltane eve). Retrieve the basket at sunrise, while the dew is still on the herbs. The herbs are faerie-blessed and are perfect for using in spells and incenses throughout the year. Those who wish to do love spells should include a few red roses; for money and wealth spells, include some stalks of lunaria (a.k.a. money plant).

–Elizabeth Hazel

May

1 **Saturday**
Beltane • May Day
Waning Moon
Moon phase: Third Quarter
Color: Blue

Moon sign: Sagittarius
Incense: Pine

---

2 **Sunday**
Big Kite Flying (Japanese)
Waning Moon
Moon phase: Third Quarter
Color: Gold

Moon sign: Sagittarius
Moon enters Capricorn 6:00 am
Incense: Almond

---

3 **Monday**
Holy Cross Day
Waning Moon
Moon phase: Third Quarter
Color: Gray

Moon sign: Capricorn
Incense: Hyssop

---

4 **Tuesday**
Bona Dea (Roman)
Waning Moon
Moon phase: Third Quarter
Color: Black

Moon sign: Capricorn
Moon enters Aquarius 4:52 pm
Incense: Cedar

---

5 **Wednesday**
Cinco de Mayo
Waning Moon
Moon phase: Third Quarter
Color: Brown

Moon sign: Aquarius
Incense: Lavender

○ **Thursday**
Martyrs' Day (Lebanese)
Waning Moon
Moon phase: Fourth Quarter 12:15 am
Color: Crimson

Moon sign: Aquarius
Incense: Myrrh

---

7 **Friday**
Pilgrimage of St. Nicholas (Italian)
Waning Moon
Moon phase: Fourth Quarter
Color: Purple

Moon sign: Aquarius
Moon enters Pisces 5:34 am
Incense: Violet

May

8 Saturday
Liberation Day (French)
Waning Moon
Moon phase: Fourth Quarter
Color: Brown

Moon sign: Pisces
Incense: Patchouli

---

9 Sunday
Mother's Day
Waning Moon
Moon phase: Fourth Quarter
Color: Gold

Moon sign: Pisces
Moon enters Aries 5:29 pm
Incense: Marigold

---

10 Monday
First Day of Bird Week (Japanese)
Waning Moon
Moon phase: Fourth Quarter
Color: Lavender

Moon sign: Aries
Incense: Rosemary

---

11 Tuesday
Ukai Season Opens (Japanese)
Waning Moon
Moon phase: Fourth Quarter
Color: Red

Moon sign: Aries
Incense: Geranium

---

12 Wednesday
Florence Nightingale's Birthday
Waning Moon
Moon phase: Fourth Quarter
Color: Topaz

Moon sign: Aries
Moon enters Taurus 2:48 am
Incense: Lilac

☽ Thursday
Pilgrimage to Fatima (Portuguese)
Waning Moon
Moon phase: New Moon 9:04 pm
Color: Purple

Moon sign: Taurus
Incense: Clove

---

14 Friday
Carabao Festival (Spanish)
Waxing Moon
Moon phase: First Quarter
Color: Rose

Moon sign: Taurus
Moon enters Gemini 9:18 am
Incense: Alder

15 Saturday
Festival of St. Dympna (Belgian)
Waxing Moon
Moon phase: First Quarter
Color: Gray

Moon sign: Gemini
Incense: Sandalwood

---

16 Sunday
St. Honoratus' Day
Waxing Moon
Moon phase: First Quarter
Color: Yellow

Moon sign: Gemini
Moon enters Cancer 1:46 pm
Incense: Juniper

---

17 Monday
Norwegian Independence Day
Waxing Moon
Moon phase: First Quarter
Color: White

Moon sign: Cancer
Incense: Lily

---

18 Tuesday
Las Piedras Day (Uraguayan)
Waxing Moon
Moon phase: First Quarter
Color: Gray

Moon sign: Cancer
Moon enters Leo 5:06 pm
Incense: Bayberry

---

19 Wednesday
Shavuot
Waxing Moon
Moon phase: First Quarter
Color: White

Moon sign: Leo
Incense: Marjoram

◖ Thursday
Pardon of the Singers (British)
Waxing Moon
Moon phase: Second Quarter 7:43 pm
Color: Crimson

Moon sign: Leo
Moon enters Virgo 7:58 pm
Sun enters Gemini 11:34 pm
Incense: Nutmeg

---

21 Friday
Victoria Day (Canadian)
Waxing Moon
Moon phase: Second Quarter
Color: Coral

Moon sign: Virgo
Incense: Rose

22 Saturday
Heroes' Day (Sri Lankan)
Waxing Moon
Moon phase: Second Quarter
Color: Blue

Moon sign: Virgo
Moon enters Libra 10:50 pm
Incense: Sage

23 Sunday
Tubilustrium (Roman)
Waxing Moon
Moon phase: Second Quarter
Color: Orange

Moon sign: Libra
Incense: Frankincense

24 Monday
Culture Day (Bulgarian)
Waxing Moon
Moon phase: Second Quarter
Color: Silver

Moon sign: Libra
Incense: Neroli

25 Tuesday
Urbanas Diena (Latvian)
Waxing Moon
Moon phase: Second Quarter
Color: White

Moon sign: Libra
Moon enters Scorpio 2:17 am
Incense: Cinnamon

26 Wednesday
Pepys' Commemoration (English)
Waxing Moon
Moon phase: Second Quarter
Color: Brown

Moon sign: Scorpio
Incense: Lilac

☺ Thursday
St. Augustine of Canterbury's Day
Waxing Moon
Moon phase: Full Moon 7:07 pm
Color: Turquoise

Moon sign: Scorpio
Moon enters Sagittarius 7:15 am
Incense: Carnation

28 Friday
St. Germain's Day
Waning Moon
Moon phase: Third Quarter
Color: White

Moon sign: Sagittarius
Incense: Orchid

May

♊

29 **Saturday**
Royal Oak Day (English)
Waning Moon
Moon phase: Third Quarter
Color: Brown

Moon sign: Sagittarius
Moon enters Capricorn 2:44 pm
Incense: Pine

30 **Sunday**
Memorial Day (actual)
Waning Moon
Moon phase: Third Quarter
Color: Yellow

Moon sign: Capricorn
Incense: Eucalyptus

31 **Monday**
Memorial Day (observed)
Waning Moon
Moon phase: Third Quarter
Color: Lavender

Moon sign: Capricorn
Incense: Clary sage

Ground Warts (*pixies*)

Paint a box of wooden golf tees gold. Glue a small piece of candy, such as Reese's Pieces or M&M's, to the top of each tee, and place them around an outdoor sacred circle or fire pit. Arrange at the base of an outdoor statue as a gift. Retrieve the tees when the candies are gone or before you mow the lawn.

–Elizabeth Hazel

June
♊

1 **Tuesday**
National Day (Tunisian)
Waning Moon
Moon phase: Third Quarter
Color: Black

Moon sign: Capricorn
Moon enters Aquarius 1:08 am
Incense: Bayberry

---

2 **Wednesday**
Rice Harvest Festival (Malaysian)
Waning Moon
Moon phase: Third Quarter
Color: Yellow

Moon sign: Aquarius
Incense: Bay laurel

---

3 **Thursday**
Memorial to Broken Dolls (Japanese)
Waning Moon
Moon phase: Third Quarter
Color: White

Moon sign: Aquarius
Moon enters Pisces 1:34 pm
Incense: Clove

◑ **Friday**
Full Moon Day (Burmese)
Waning Moon
Moon phase: Fourth Quarter 6:13 pm
Color: Coral

Moon sign: Pisces
Incense: Yarrow

---

5 **Saturday**
Constitution Day (Danish)
Waning Moon
Moon phase: Fourth Quarter
Color: Brown

Moon sign: Pisces
Incense: Pine

---

6 **Sunday**
Swedish Flag Day
Waning Moon
Moon phase: Fourth Quarter
Color: Amber

Moon sign: Pisces
Moon enters Aries 1:50 am
Incense: Hyacinth

---

7 **Monday**
St. Robert of Newminster's Day
Waning Moon
Moon phase: Fourth Quarter
Color: White

Moon sign: Aries
Incense: Hyssop

June ♊

8 Tuesday
St. Medard's Day (Belgian)
Waning Moon
Moon phase: Fourth Quarter
Color: Gray

Moon sign: Aries
Moon enters Taurus 11:41 am
Incense: Ginger

9 Wednesday
Vestalia (Roman)
Waning Moon
Moon phase: Fourth Quarter
Color: Brown

Moon sign: Taurus
Incense: Lilac

10 Thursday
Time-Observance Day (Chinese)
Waning Moon
Moon phase: Fourth Quarter
Color: Turquoise

Moon sign: Taurus
Moon enters Gemini 6:11 pm
Incense: Jasmine

11 Friday
Kamehameha Day (Hawaiian)
Waning Moon
Moon phase: Fourth Quarter
Color: Rose

Moon sign: Gemini
Incense: Thyme

☽ Saturday
Independence Day (Filipino)
Waning Moon
Moon phase: New Moon 7:15 am
Color: Blue

Moon sign: Gemini
Moon enters Cancer 9:50 pm
Incense: Patchouli

13 Sunday
St. Anthony of Padua's Day
Waxing Moon
Moon phase: First Quarter
Color: Orange

Moon sign: Cancer
Incense: Frankincense

14 Monday
Flag Day
Waxing Moon
Moon phase: First Quarter
Color: Lavender

Moon sign: Cancer
Moon enters Leo 11:54 pm
Incense: Clary sage

June

15 Tuesday
St. Vitus' Day Fires
Waxing Moon
Moon phase: First Quarter
Color: Black

Moon sign: Leo
Incense: Cedar

16 Wednesday
Bloomsday (Irish)
Waxing Moon
Moon phase: First Quarter
Color: Brown

Moon sign: Leo
Incense: Lavender

17 Thursday
Bunker Hill Day
Waxing Moon
Moon phase: First Quarter
Color: White

Moon sign: Leo
Moon enters Virgo 1:41 am
Incense: Nutmeg

18 Friday
Independence Day (Egyptian)
Waxing Moon
Moon phase: First Quarter
Color: Pink

Moon sign: Virgo
Incense: Rose

◑ Saturday
Juneteenth
Waxing Moon
Moon phase: Second Quarter 12:30 am
Color: Gray

Moon sign: Virgo
Moon enters Libra 4:13 am
Incense: Ivy

20 Sunday
Father's Day
Waxing Moon
Moon phase: Second Quarter
Color: Gold

Moon sign: Libra
Incense: Marigold

21 Monday
Litha • Summer Solstice
Waxing Moon
Moon phase: Second Quarter
Color: Silver

Moon sign: Libra
Sun enters Cancer 7:28 am
Moon enters Scorpio 8:14 am
Incense: Lily

June

22 Tuesday
Rose Festival (English)
Waxing Moon
Moon phase: Second Quarter
Color: White

Moon sign: Scorpio
Incense: Basil

23 Wednesday
St. John's Eve
Waxing Moon
Moon phase: Second Quarter
Color: Topaz

Moon sign: Scorpio
Moon enters Sagittarius 2:10 pm
Incense: Honeysuckle

24 Thursday
St. John's Day
Waxing Moon
Moon phase: Second Quarter
Color: Purple

Moon sign: Sagittarius
Incense: Apricot

25 Friday
Fiesta of Santa Orosia (Spanish)
Waxing Moon
Moon phase: Second Quarter
Color: Pink

Moon sign: Sagittarius
Moon enters Capricorn 10:21 pm
Incense: Cypress

Saturday
Pied Piper Day (German)
Waxing Moon
Moon phase: Full Moon 7:30 am
Color: Indigo

Moon sign: Capricorn
Incense: Rue

27 Sunday
Day of the Seven Sleepers (Islamic)
Waning Moon
Moon phase: Third Quarter
Color: Yellow

Moon sign: Capricorn
Incense: Almond

28 Monday
Paul Bunyan Day
Waning Moon
Moon phase: Third Quarter
Color: Gray

Moon sign: Capricorn
Moon enters Aquarius 8:52 am
Incense: Rosemary

29 **Tuesday**
Feast of Saints Peter and Paul
Waning Moon
Moon phase: Third Quarter
Color: Red

Moon sign: Aquarius
Incense: Cinnamon

---

30 **Wednesday**
The Burning of the Three Firs (French)
Waning Moon
Moon phase: Third Quarter
Color: White

Moon sign: Aquarius
Moon enters Pisces 9:10 pm
Incense: Bay laurel

Litha
Love Chimes (*cupids*)

Gather six cinnamon sticks and five bells. Use a wide-eyed needle to run red string through a cinnamon stick, leaving extra string at the top. Knot a bell at the bottom, and run the needle and string back up through the stick. Again, leave extra string at the top. Do five sticks and bells. Use the sixth cinnamon stick as a hanger. Tie the five bell-sticks to the hanger stick. Make a "V" with copper wire, and wrap the ends to suspend the hanger. Decorate with copper charms or rose quartz beads. Hang the chimes on your door or porch, or on the branch of a fruit-bearing or flowering tree. Tell the Love Goddess your wishes for love. The bells will remind her of your request.

–Elizabeth Hazel

July

1 **Thursday**
Climbing Mount Fuji (Japanese)
Waning Moon
Moon phase: Third Quarter
Color: Green

Moon sign: Pisces
Incense: Jasmine

---

2 **Friday**
Heroes' Day (Zambian)
Waning Moon
Moon phase: Third Quarter
Color: Coral

Moon sign: Pisces
Incense: Vanilla

---

3 **Saturday**
Indian Sun Dance (Native American)
Waning Moon
Moon phase: Third Quarter
Color: Blue

Moon sign: Pisces
Moon enters Aries 9:44 am
Incense: Pine

◑ **Sunday**
Independence Day
Waning Moon
Moon phase: Fourth Quarter 10:35 am
Color: Yellow

Moon sign: Aries
Incense: Juniper

---

5 **Monday**
Tynwald (Nordic)
Waning Moon
Moon phase: Fourth Quarter
Color: Ivory

Moon sign: Aries
Moon enters Taurus 8:29 pm
Incense: Rosemary

---

6 **Tuesday**
Khao Phansa Day (Thai)
Waning Moon
Moon phase: Fourth Quarter
Color: Maroon

Moon sign: Taurus
Incense: Ylang-ylang

---

7 **Wednesday**
Weaver's Festival (Japanese)
Waning Moon
Moon phase: Fourth Quarter
Color: White

Moon sign: Taurus
Incense: Lilac

8 **Thursday**
St. Elizabeth's Day (Portugeuse)
Waning Moon
Moon phase: Fourth Quarter
Color: Turquoise

Moon sign: Taurus
Moon enters Gemini 3:51 am
Incense: Nutmeg

---

9 **Friday**
Battle of Sempach Day (Swiss)
Waning Moon
Moon phase: Fourth Quarter
Color: Pink

Moon sign: Gemini
Incense: Cypress

---

10 **Saturday**
Lady Godiva Day (English)
Waning Moon
Moon phase: Fourth Quarter
Color: Indigo

Moon sign: Gemini
Moon enters Cancer 7:38 am
Incense: Rue

☽ **Sunday**
Revolution Day (Mongolian)
Waning Moon
Moon phase: New Moon 3:40 pm
Color: Gold

Moon sign: Cancer
Incense: Eucalyptus

---

12 **Monday**
Lobster Carnival (Nova Scotian)
Waxing Moon
Moon phase: First Quarter
Color: Lavender

Moon sign: Cancer
Moon enters Leo 8:53 am
Incense: Lily

---

13 **Tuesday**
Festival of the Three Cows (Spanish)
Waxing Moon
Moon phase: First Quarter
Color: Red

Moon sign: Leo
Incense: Ginger

---

14 **Wednesday**
Bastille Day (French)
Waxing Moon
Moon phase: First Quarter
Color: Yellow

Moon sign: Leo
Moon enters Virgo 9:15 am
Incense: Honeysuckle

July

15 Thursday
St. Swithin's Day
Waxing Moon
Moon phase: First Quarter
Color: Crimson

Moon sign: Virgo
Incense: Myrrh

---

16 Friday
Our Lady of Carmel
Waxing Moon
Moon phase: First Quarter
Color: White

Moon sign: Virgo
Moon enters Libra 10:24 am
Incense: Orchid

---

17 Saturday
Rivera Day (Puerto Rican)
Waxing Moon
Moon phase: First Quarter
Color: Black

Moon sign: Libra
Incense: Magnolia

☾ Sunday
Gion Matsuri Festival (Japanese)
Waxing Moon
Moon phase: Second Quarter 6:11 am
Color: Orange

Moon sign: Libra
Moon enters Scorpio 1:42 pm
Incense: Hyacinth

---

19 Monday
Flitch Day (English)
Waxing Moon
Moon phase: Second Quarter
Color: Gray

Moon sign: Scorpio
Incense: Hyssop

---

20 Tuesday
Binding of Wreaths (Lithuanian)
Waxing Moon
Moon phase: Second Quarter
Color: Scarlet

Moon sign: Scorpio
Moon enters Sagittarius 7:48 pm
Incense: Geranium

---

21 Wednesday
National Day (Belgian)
Waxing Moon
Moon phase: Second Quarter
Color: White

Moon sign: Sagittarius
Incense: Bay laurel

22 **Thursday**
St. Mary Magdalene's Day   Moon sign: Sagittarius
Waxing Moon   Sun enters Leo 6:21 pm
Moon phase: Second Quarter   Incense: Mulberry
Color: Green

---

23 **Friday**
Mysteries of Santa Cristina (Italian)   Moon sign: Sagittarius
Waxing Moon   Moon enters Capricorn 4:39 am
Moon phase: Second Quarter   Incense: Alder
Color: Rose

---

24 **Saturday**
Pioneer Day (Mormon)   Moon sign: Capricorn
Waxing Moon   Incense: Sandalwood
Moon phase: Second Quarter
Color: Brown

☺ **Sunday**
St. James' Day   Moon sign: Capricorn
Waxing Moon   Moon enters Aquarius 3:38 pm
Moon phase: Full Moon 9:37 pm   Incense: Almond
Color: Amber

---

26 **Monday**
St. Anne's Day   Moon sign: Aquarius
Waning Moon   Incense: Narcissus
Moon phase: Third Quarter
Color: Silver

---

27 **Tuesday**
Sleepyhead Day (Finnish)   Moon sign: Aquarius
Waning Moon   Incense: Cedar
Moon phase: Third Quarter
Color: Black

---

28 **Wednesday**
Independence Day (Peruvian)   Moon sign: Aquarius
Waning Moon   Moon enters Pisces 4:00 am
Moon phase: Third Quarter   Incense: Lavender
Color: Brown

29 **Thursday**
Pardon of the Birds (French)
Waning Moon
Moon phase: Third Quarter
Color: Purple

Moon sign: Pisces
Incense: Apricot

---

30 **Friday**
Micman Festival of St. Ann
Waning Moon
Moon phase: Third Quarter
Color: White

Moon sign: Pisces
Moon enters Aries 4:42 pm
Incense: Yarrow

---

31 **Saturday**
Weighing of the Aga Kahn
Waning Moon
Moon phase: Third Quarter
Color: Blue

Moon sign: Aries
Incense: Sage

Lammas
Pitty Patens (*wood elves*)

Draw or copy a star or pentagram onto a piece of poster board and cut out to use as a template. Put small rolls of tape on the back of the template, and stick it to a plate. Stars can be centered, or smaller stars can be placed around the plate in different designs. Brush tempera paint over the entire plate, or use a sponge to get a stipple effect. When the paint dries a bit, pull up the template(s), and use to make another paten. You can do a whole stack of paper plates this way. Let the paint fully dry, and use them for god gifts like bird seed or bread crumbs.

–Elizabeth Hazel

1 **Sunday**
Lammas
Waning Moon
Moon phase: Third Quarter
Color: Gold

Moon sign: Aries
Incense: Eucalyptus

2 **Monday**
Porcingula (Native American)
Waning Moon
Moon phase: Third Quarter
Color: Gray

Moon sign: Aries
Moon enters Taurus 4:13 am
Incense: Hyssop

○ **Tuesday**
Drimes (Greek)
Waning Moon
Moon phase: Fourth Quarter 12:59 am
Color: Red

Moon sign: Taurus
Incense: Bayberry

4 **Wednesday**
Cook Islands Constitution Celebration
Waning Moon
Moon phase: Fourth Quarter
Color: Topaz

Moon sign: Taurus
Moon enters Gemini 12:54 pm
Incense: Honeysuckle

5 **Thursday**
Benediction of the Sea (French)
Waning Moon
Moon phase: Fourth Quarter
Color: Crimson

Moon sign: Gemini
Incense: Balsam

6 **Friday**
Hiroshima Peace Ceremony
Waning Moon
Moon phase: Fourth Quarter
Color: Purple

Moon sign: Gemini
Moon enters Cancer 5:50 pm
Incense: Mint

7 **Saturday**
Republic Day (Ivory Coast)
Waning Moon
Moon phase: Fourth Quarter
Color: Brown

Moon sign: Cancer
Incense: Ivy

8 **Sunday**
Dog Days (Japanese)
Waning Moon
Moon phase: Fourth Quarter
Color: Gold

Moon sign: Cancer
Moon enters Leo 7:23 pm
Incense: Frankincense

Monday
Nagasaki Peace Ceremony
Waning Moon
Moon phase: New Moon 11:08 pm
Color: White

Moon sign: Leo
Incense: Neroli

10 **Tuesday**
St. Lawrence's Day
Waxing Moon
Moon phase: First Quarter
Color: Black

Moon sign: Leo
Moon enters Virgo 7:01 pm
Incense: Ylang-ylang

11 **Wednesday**
Ramadan begins
Waxing Moon
Moon phase: First Quarter
Color: Topaz

Moon sign: Virgo
Incense: Bay laurel

12 **Thursday**
Fiesta of Santa Clara
Waxing Moon
Moon phase: First Quarter
Color: Green

Moon sign: Virgo
Moon enters Libra 6:43 pm
Incense: Carnation

13 **Friday**
Women's Day (Tunisian)
Waxing Moon
Moon phase: First Quarter
Color: Pink

Moon sign: Libra
Incense: Rose

14 **Saturday**
Festival at Sassari
Waxing Moon
Moon phase: First Quarter
Color: Gray

Moon sign: Libra
Moon enters Scorpio 8:26 pm
Incense: Sage

15 Sunday
Assumption Day
Waxing Moon
Moon phase: First Quarter
Color: Yellow

Moon sign: Scorpio
Incense: Juniper

◖ Monday
Festival of Minstrels (European)
Waxing Moon
Moon phase: Second Quarter 2:14 pm
Color: Silver

Moon sign: Scorpio
Incense: Lily

17 Tuesday
Feast of the Hungry Ghosts (Chinese)
Waxing Moon
Moon phase: Second Quarter
Color: Gray

Moon sign: Scorpio
Moon enters Sagittarius 1:34 am
Incense: Ginger

18 Wednesday
St. Helen's Day
Waxing Moon
Moon phase: Second Quarter
Color: Brown

Moon sign: Sagittarius
Incense: Lilac

19 Thursday
Rustic Vinalia (Roman)
Waxing Moon
Moon phase: Second Quarter
Color: Purple

Moon sign: Sagittarius
Moon enters Capricorn 10:17 am
Incense: Clove

20 Friday
Constitution Day (Hungarian)
Waxing Moon
Moon phase: Second Quarter
Color: Coral

Moon sign: Capricorn
Incense: Thyme

21 Saturday
Consualia (Roman)
Waxing Moon
Moon phase: Second Quarter
Color: Indigo

Moon sign: Capricorn
Moon enters Aquarius 9:37 pm
Incense: Patchouli

22 Sunday
Feast of the Queenship of Mary (English)
Waxing Moon
Moon phase: Second Quarter
Color: Amber

Moon sign: Aquarius
Incense: Heliotrope

---

23 Monday
National Day (Romanian)
Waxing Moon
Moon phase: Second Quarter
Color: Ivory

Moon sign: Aquarius
Sun enters Virgo 1:27 am
Incense: Narcissus

☻ Tuesday
St. Bartholomew's Day
Waxing Moon
Moon phase: Full Moon 1:05 pm
Color: Red

Moon sign: Aquarius
Moon enters Pisces 10:11 am
Incense: Cinnamon

---

25 Wednesday
Feast of the Green Corn (Native American)
Waning Moon
Moon phase: Third Quarter
Color: Yellow

Moon sign: Pisces
Incense: Lavender

---

26 Thursday
Pardon of the Sea (French)
Waning Moon
Moon phase: Third Quarter
Color: White

Moon sign: Pisces
Moon enters Aries 10:49 pm
Incense: Jasmine

---

27 Friday
Summer Break (English)
Waning Moon
Moon phase: Third Quarter
Color: Purple

Moon sign: Aries
Incense: Vanilla

---

28 Saturday
St. Augustine's Day
Waning Moon
Moon phase: Third Quarter
Color: Black

Moon sign: Aries
Incense: Sage

August ♍

29 Sunday
St. John's Beheading
Waning Moon
Moon phase: Third Quarter
Color: Orange

Moon sign: Aries
Moon enters Taurus 10:35 am
Incense: Almond

---

30 Monday
St. Rose of Lima Day (Peruvian)
Waning Moon
Moon phase: Third Quarter
Color: Lavender

Moon sign: Taurus
Incense: Clary sage

---

31 Tuesday
Unto These Hills Pageant (Cherokee)
Waning Moon
Moon phase: Third Quarter
Color: White

Moon sign: Taurus
Moon enters Gemini 8:19 pm
Incense: Basil

Keys to Prosperity (*dwarves*)

Purchase gold-colored key blanks from a locksmith's shop or hardware store. When the Moon waxes in an earth or water sign, cast a circle and light a green candle. Sprinkle cedar, cinnamon, and patchouli powder on a tray; arrange the keys on the tray. Touch each key with a magnet or lodestone, saying, "This is the key to the golden door, from which good luck and wealth do pour." Work this charm for three nights. Tie green and gold ribbons to each key with this binding charm: "Unlock the door to prosperity; to this purpose you're bound, three times three; as I will and charge, so mote it be." Wear on a necklace, carry in a pocket, attach to a key ring, or place in a wallet or cash register for prosperity.

–Elizabeth Hazel

September

♍

❍ **Wednesday**
Greek New Year
Waning Moon
Moon phase: Fourth Quarter 1:22 pm
Color: Brown

Moon sign: Gemini
Incense: Bay laurel

---

2 **Thursday**
St. Mamas' Day
Waning Moon
Moon phase: Fourth Quarter
Color: Purple

Moon sign: Gemini
Incense: Apricot

---

3 **Friday**
Founder's Day (San Marino)
Waning Moon
Moon phase: Fourth Quarter
Color: White

Moon sign: Gemini
Moon enters Cancer 2:50 am
Incense: Rose

---

4 **Saturday**
Los Angeles' Birthday
Waning Moon
Moon phase: Fourth Quarter
Color: Blue

Moon sign: Cancer
Incense: Sandalwood

---

5 **Sunday**
Roman Circus • First Labor Day (1882)
Waning Moon
Moon phase: Fourth Quarter
Color: Amber

Moon sign: Cancer
Moon enters Leo 5:45 am
Incense: Frankincense

---

6 **Monday**
Labor Day
Waning Moon
Moon phase: Fourth Quarter
Color: Silver

Moon sign: Leo
Incense: Rosemary

---

7 **Tuesday**
Festival of the Durga (Hindu)
Waning Moon
Moon phase: Fourth Quarter
Color: Gray

Moon sign: Leo
Moon enters Virgo 5:53 am
Incense: Cedar

September ♍

☽ Wednesday
Birthday of the Virgin Mary
Waning Moon
Moon phase: New Moon 6:30 am
Color: Yellow

Moon sign: Virgo
Incense: Lavender

9 Thursday
Rosh Hashanah
Waxing Moon
Moon phase: First Quarter
Color: Green

Moon sign: Virgo
Moon enters Libra 5:01 am
Incense: Nutmeg

10 Friday
Ramadan ends
Waxing Moon
Moon phase: First Quarter
Color: Pink

Moon sign: Libra
Incense: Mint

11 Saturday
Coptic New Year
Waxing Moon
Moon phase: First Quarter
Color: Gray

Moon sign: Libra
Moon enters Scorpio 5:21 am
Incense: Ivy

12 Sunday
National Day (Ethiopian)
Waxing Moon
Moon phase: First Quarter
Color: Gold

Moon sign: Scorpio
Incense: Juniper

13 Monday
The Gods' Banquet (Roman)
Waxing Moon
Moon phase: First Quarter
Color: Lavender

Moon sign: Scorpio
Moon enters Sagittarius 8:52 am
Incense: Clary sage

14 Tuesday
Holy Cross Day
Waxing Moon
Moon phase: First Quarter
Color: Red

Moon sign: Sagittarius
Incense: Ginger

September

♍

○ **Wednesday**
Birthday of the Moon (Chinese)
Waxing Moon
Moon phase: Second Quarter 1:50 am
Color: Topaz

Moon sign: Sagittarius
Moon enters Capricorn 4:30 pm
Incense: Honeysuckle

16 **Thursday**
Mexican Independence Day
Waxing Moon
Moon phase: Second Quarter
Color: Green

Moon sign: Capricorn
Incense: Myrrh

17 **Friday**
Von Steuben's Day
Waxing Moon
Moon phase: Second Quarter
Color: Purple

Moon sign: Capricorn
Incense: Orchid

18 **Saturday**
Yom Kippur
Waxing Moon
Moon phase: Second Quarter
Color: Brown

Moon sign: Capricorn
Moon enters Aquarius 3:35 am
Incense: Rue

19 **Sunday**
St. Januarius' Day (Italian)
Waxing Moon
Moon phase: Second Quarter
Color: Orange

Moon sign: Aquarius
Incense: Eucalyptus

20 **Monday**
St. Eustace's Day
Waxing Moon
Moon phase: Second Quarter
Color: White

Moon sign: Aquarius
Moon enters Pisces 4:15 pm
Incense: Lily

21 **Tuesday**
UN International Day of Peace
Waxing Moon
Moon phase: Second Quarter
Color: White

Moon sign: Pisces
Incense: Bayberry

September

22 **Wednesday**
Mabon • Fall Equinox
Waxing Moon
Moon phase: Second Quarter
Color: Brown

Moon sign: Pisces
Sun enters Libra 11:09 pm
Incense: Lilac

Thursday
Sukkot begins
Waxing Moon
Moon phase: Full Moon 5:17 am
Color: Crimson

Moon sign: Pisces
Moon enters Aries 4:47 am
Incense: Carnation

---

24 **Friday**
Schwenkenfelder Thanksgiving (Germ.-Amer.)
Waning Moon
Moon phase: Third Quarter
Color: White

Moon sign: Aries
Incense: Yarrow

---

25 **Saturday**
Doll's Memorial Service (Japanese)
Waning Moon
Moon phase: Third Quarter
Color: Black

Moon sign: Aries
Moon enters Taurus 4:17 pm
Incense: Pine

---

26 **Sunday**
Feast of Santa Justina (Mexican)
Waning Moon
Moon phase: Third Quarter
Color: Yellow

Moon sign: Taurus
Incense: Marigold

---

27 **Monday**
Saints Cosmas and Damian's Day
Waning Moon
Moon phase: Third Quarter
Color: Gray

Moon sign: Taurus
Incense: Neroli

---

28 **Tuesday**
Confucius' Birthday
Waning Moon
Moon phase: Third Quarter
Color: Scarlet

Moon sign: Taurus
Moon enters Gemini 2:10 am
Incense: Cinnamon

29 Wednesday

Sukkot ends
Waning Moon
Moon phase: Third Quarter
Color: White

Moon sign: Gemini
Incense: Marjoram

☾ Thursday

St. Jerome's Day
Waning Moon
Moon phase: Fourth Quarter 11:52 pm
Color: Turquoise

Moon sign: Gemini
Moon enters Cancer 9:46 am
Incense: Jasmine

Mabon
God Dogs (*gnomes*)

Using a small ball of clay, form a god image. It can be a face or head, a phallic representation, or a small dog shape. It doesn't have to be a work of art, just make sure to focus intently on a masculine image while forming the fetish. Let it dry. When the clay is dry, dig a small hole in the earth at sunset, and say, "Bones of the God given into the arms of the Goddess, return with vigor into the spring." This assures fertility in the coming year. The dog is a symbol of the underworld gods.

–Elizabeth Hazel

October

1   Friday
Armed Forces Day (South Korean)   Moon sign: Cancer
Waning Moon   Incense: Alder
Moon phase: Fourth Quarter
Color: Pink

---

2   Saturday
Old Man's Day (Virgin Islands)   Moon sign: Cancer
Waning Moon   Moon enters Leo 2:21 pm
Moon phase: Fourth Quarter   Incense: Sage
Color: Blue

---

3   Sunday
Moroccan New Year's Day   Moon sign: Leo
Waning Moon   Incense: Hyacinth
Moon phase: Fourth Quarter
Color: Gold

---

4   Monday
St. Francis' Day   Moon sign: Leo
Waning Moon   Moon enters Virgo 4:00 pm
Moon phase: Fourth Quarter   Incense: Hyssop
Color: Ivory

---

5   Tuesday
Republic Day (Portugeuse)   Moon sign: Virgo
Waning Moon   Incense: Ginger
Moon phase: Fourth Quarter
Color: Maroon

---

6   Wednesday
Dedication of the Virgin's Crowns (English)   Moon sign: Virgo
Waning Moon   Moon enters Libra 3:52 pm
Moon phase: Fourth Quarter   Incense: Majoram
Color: Yellow

☽   Thursday
Kermesse (German)   Moon sign: Libra
Waning Moon   Incense: Jasmine
Moon phase: New Moon 2:45 pm
Color: Purple

October

8 Friday
Okunchi (Japanese)
Waxing Moon
Moon phase: First Quarter
Color: Coral

Moon sign: Libra
Moon enters Scorpio 3:52 pm
Incense: Cypress

9 Saturday
Alphabet Day (South Korean)
Waxing Moon
Moon phase: First Quarter
Color: Gray

Moon sign: Scorpio
Incense: Ivy

10 Sunday
Health Day (Japanese)
Waxing Moon
Moon phase: First Quarter
Color: Amber

Moon sign: Scorpio
Moon enters Sagittarius 6:09 pm
Incense: Heliotrope

11 Monday
Columbus Day (observed)
Waxing Moon
Moon phase: First Quarter
Color: Lavender

Moon sign: Sagittarius
Incense: Rosemary

12 Tuesday
National Day (Spanish)
Waxing Moon
Moon phase: First Quarter
Color: Black

Moon sign: Sagittarius
Incense: Geranium

13 Wednesday
Fontinalia (Roman)
Waxing Moon
Moon phase: First Quarter
Color: White

Moon sign: Sagittarius
Moon enters Capricorn 12:17 am
Incense: Lavender

◖ Thursday
Battle Festival (Japanese)
Waxing Moon
Moon phase: Second Quarter 5:27 pm
Color: White

Moon sign: Capricorn
Incense: Myrrh

15 Friday
The October Horse (Roman)
Waxing Moon
Moon phase: Second Quarter
Color: Purple

Moon sign: Capricorn
Moon enters Aquarius 10:24 am
Incense: Orchid

---

16 Saturday
The Lion Sermon (British)
Waxing Moon
Moon phase: Second Quarter
Color: Indigo

Moon sign: Aquarius
Incense: Pine

---

17 Sunday
Pilgrimage to Paray-le-Monial
Waxing Moon
Moon phase: Second Quarter
Color: Yellow

Moon sign: Aquarius
Moon enters Pisces 10:52 pm
Incense: Frankincense

---

18 Monday
Brooklyn Barbecue
Waxing Moon
Moon phase: Second Quarter
Color: Silver

Moon sign: Pisces
Incense: Clary sage

---

19 Tuesday
Our Lord of Miracles Procession (Peruvian)
Waxing Moon
Moon phase: Second Quarter
Color: Gray

Moon sign: Pisces
Incense: Basil

---

20 Wednesday
Colchester Oyster Feast
Waxing Moon
Moon phase: Second Quarter
Color: Brown

Moon sign: Pisces
Moon enters Aries 11:23 am
Incense: Bay laurel

---

21 Thursday
Feast of the Black Christ
Waxing Moon
Moon phase: Second Quarter
Color: Crimson

Moon sign: Aries
Incense: Nutmeg

October ♏

☺ **Friday**
Goddess of Mercy Day (Chinese)
Waxing Moon
Moon phase: Full Moon 9:37 pm
Color: Pink

Moon sign: Aries
Moon enters Taurus 10:30 pm
Incense: Thyme

---

23 Saturday
Revolution Day (Hungarian)
Waning Moon
Moon phase: Third Quarter
Color: Brown

Moon sign: Taurus
Sun enters Scorpio 8:35 am
Incense: Magnolia

---

24 Sunday
United Nations Day
Waning Moon
Moon phase: Third Quarter
Color: Orange

Moon sign: Taurus
Incense: Almond

---

25 Monday
St. Crispin's Day
Waning Moon
Moon phase: Third Quarter
Color: Ivory

Moon sign: Taurus
Moon enters Gemini 7:47 am
Incense: Lily

---

26 Tuesday
Quit Rent Ceremony (England)
Waning Moon
Moon phase: Third Quarter
Color: Black

Moon sign: Gemini
Incense: Ylang-ylang

---

27 Wednesday
Feast of the Holy Souls
Waning Moon
Moon phase: Third Quarter
Color: Topaz

Moon sign: Gemini
Moon enters Cancer 3:14 pm
Incense: Honeysuckle

---

28 Thursday
Ochi Day (Greek)
Waning Moon
Moon phase: Third Quarter
Color: Green

Moon sign: Cancer
Incense: Clove

29 Friday
Iroquois Feast of the Dead
Waning Moon
Moon phase: Third Quarter
Color: Coral

Moon sign: Cancer
Moon enters Leo 8:39 pm
Incense: Yarrow

◐ Saturday
Meiji Festival (Japanese)
Waning Moon
Moon phase: Fourth Quarter 8:46 am
Color: Gray

Moon sign: Leo
Incense: Sandalwood

---

31 Sunday
Halloween • Samhain
Waning Moon
Moon phase: Fourth Quarter
Color: Orange

Moon sign: Leo
Moon enters Virgo 11:51 pm
Incense: Heliotrope

Samhain
Yearnin' Urns (*harpies*)

Three days before Samhain, decorate an empty jar with pins, ribbons, feathers, confetti, tissue paper, etc. You may also glue a photo of a deceased loved one on the jar. Write a letter to this dead relative, telling him or her about something you yearn for. Choose a serious need rather than a frivolous wish. Burn the letter and put the ashes into the Yearnin' Urn. Light a candle next to the urn and let it (safely) burn for three days. After dark on Samhain, take the jar outdoors and release the ashes to the wind.

–Elizabeth Hazel

November

1 **Monday**
All Saints' Day
Waning Moon
Moon phase: Fourth Quarter
Color: Gray

Moon sign: Virgo
Incense: Clary sage

---

2 **Tuesday**
Election Day (general)
Waning Moon
Moon phase: Fourth Quarter
Color: Red

Moon sign: Virgo
Incense: Basil

---

3 **Wednesday**
Saint Hubert's Day (Belgian)
Waning Moon
Moon phase: Fourth Quarter
Color: Yellow

Moon sign: Virgo
Moon enters Libra 1:19 am
Incense: Honeysuckle

---

4 **Thursday**
Mischief Night (British)
Waning Moon
Moon phase: Fourth Quarter
Color: Turquoise

Moon sign: Libra
Incense: Carnation

---

5 **Friday**
Guy Fawkes Night (British)
Waning Moon
Moon phase: Fourth Quarter
Color: Coral

Moon sign: Libra
Moon enters Scorpio 2:16 am
Incense: Rose

☽ **Saturday**
Leonard's Ride (German)
Waning Moon
Moon phase: New Moon 12:52 am
Color: Blue

Moon sign: Scorpio
Incense: Rue

---

7 **Sunday**
Daylight Saving Time ends
Waxing Moon
Moon phase: First Quarter
Color: Amber

Moon sign: Scorpio
Moon enters Sagittarius 3:28 am
Incense: Eucalyptus

8 Monday
The Lord Mayor's Show (English)
Waxing Moon
Moon phase: First Quarter
Color: Silver

Moon sign: Sagittarius
Incense: Neroli

---

9 Tuesday
Lord Mayor's Day (British)
Waxing Moon
Moon phase: First Quarter
Color: Maroon

Moon sign: Sagittarius
Moon enters Capricorn 8:37 am
Incense: Bayberry

---

10 Wednesday
Martin Luther's Birthday
Waxing Moon
Moon phase: First Quarter
Color: Topaz

Moon sign: Capricorn
Incense: Marjoram

---

11 Thursday
Veterans Day
Waxing Moon
Moon phase: First Quarter
Color: Green

Moon sign: Capricorn
Moon enters Aquarius 5:32 pm
Incense: Jasmine

---

12 Friday
Tesuque Feast Day (Native American)
Waxing Moon
Moon phase: First Quarter
Color: Purple

Moon sign: Aquarius
Incense: Thyme

☾ Saturday
Festival of Jupiter
Waxing Moon
Moon phase: Second Quarter 11:39 am
Color: Gray

Moon sign: Aquarius
Incense: Ivy

---

14 Sunday
The Little Carnival (Greek)
Waxing Moon
Moon phase: Second Quarter
Color: Yellow

Moon sign: Aquarius
Moon enters Pisces 5:24 am
Incense: Hyacinth

November

15 Monday
St. Leopold's Day
Waxing Moon
Moon phase: Second Quarter
Color: Lavender

Moon sign: Pisces
Incense: Lily

---

16 Tuesday
St. Margaret of Scotland's Day
Waxing Moon
Moon phase: Second Quarter
Color: Black

Moon sign: Pisces
Moon enters Aries 5:59 pm
Incense: Ginger

---

17 Wednesday
Queen Elizabeth's Day
Waxing Moon
Moon phase: Second Quarter
Color: White

Moon sign: Aries
Incense: Lilac

---

18 Thursday
St. Plato's Day
Waxing Moon
Moon phase: Second Quarter
Color: Purple

Moon sign: Aries
Incense: Nutmeg

---

19 Friday
Garifuna Day (Belizian)
Waxing Moon
Moon phase: Second Quarter
Color: Rose

Moon sign: Aries
Moon enters Taurus 5:04 am
Incense: Yarrow

---

20 Saturday
Revolution Day (Mexican)
Waxing Moon
Moon phase: Second Quarter
Color: Brown

Moon sign: Taurus
Incense: Pine

☺ Sunday
Repentance Day (German)
Waxing Moon
Moon phase: Full Moon 12:27 pm
Color: Gold

Moon sign: Taurus
Moon enters Gemini 1:46 pm
Incense: Juniper

22 Monday

St. Cecilia's Day
Waning Moon
Moon phase: Third Quarter
Color: White

Moon sign: Gemini
Sun enters Sagittarius 5:15 am
Incense: Clary sage

---

23 Tuesday

St. Clement's Day
Waning Moon
Moon phase: Third Quarter
Color: Gray

Moon sign: Gemini
Moon enters Cancer 8:14 pm
Incense: Ylang-ylang

---

24 Wednesday

Feast of the Burning Lamps (Egyptian)
Waning Moon
Moon phase: Third Quarter
Color: Brown

Moon sign: Cancer
Incense: Bay laurel

---

25 Thursday

Thanksgiving Day
Waning Moon
Moon phase: Third Quarter
Color: Crimson

Moon sign: Cancer
Incense: Myrrh

---

26 Friday

Festival of Lights (Tibetan)
Waning Moon
Moon phase: Third Quarter
Color: Pink

Moon sign: Cancer
Moon enters Leo 1:01 am
Incense: Mint

---

27 Saturday

Saint Maximus' Day
Waning Moon
Moon phase: Third Quarter
Color: Gray

Moon sign: Leo
Incense: Patchouli

◖ Sunday

Day of the New Dance (Tibetan)
Waning Moon
Moon phase: Fourth Quarter 3:36 pm
Color: Amber

Moon sign: Leo
Moon enters Virgo 4:34 am
Incense: Almond

November

29 **Monday**
Tubman's Birthday (Liberian)
Waning Moon
Moon phase: Fourth Quarter
Color: Ivory

Moon sign: Virgo
Incense: Narcissus

30 **Tuesday**
St. Andrew's Day
Waning Moon
Moon phase: Fourth Quarter
Color: Black

Moon sign: Virgo
Moon enters Libra 7:15 am
Incense: Cedar

Girl-goyles (*imps*)

To fashion an imp, find a three-branched twig with side branches joined at the same spot. Use two pieces of fabric for a dress and cape. Cut slits for arm holes, and glue the dress in place. Gather the cape with a running stitch; use the ends of the thread to tie it above the arms. Draw a face on a rectangular piece of craft paper. Put glue on the back of the stick and attach both sides of the paper; leave the paper slack. When the paper dries, stuff in corn silk for hair. Make a mini-broom to hang on one arm and tie a pouch, a string of beads, or a small charm to the other arm. Ground your imp in a jar of sand, or plant her by your front door. She will encourage mischievous imps to go elsewhere.

–Elizabeth Hazel

December

1 Wednesday
Big Tea Party (Japanese)
Waning Moon
Moon phase: Fourth Quarter
Color: Yellow

Moon sign: Libra
Incense: Lilac

2 Thursday
Hanukkah begins
Waning Moon
Moon phase: Fourth Quarter
Color: Green

Moon sign: Libra
Moon enters Scorpio 9:44 am
Incense: Clove

3 Friday
St. Francis Xavier's Day
Waning Moon
Moon phase: Fourth Quarter
Color: White

Moon sign: Scorpio
Incense: Rose

4 Saturday
St. Barbara's Day
Waning Moon
Moon phase: Fourth Quarter
Color: Gray

Moon sign: Scorpio
Moon enters Sagittarius 12:59 pm
Incense: Magnolia

☽ Sunday
Eve of St. Nicholas' Day
Waning Moon
Moon phase: New Moon 12:36 pm
Color: Yellow

Moon sign: Sagittarius
Incense: Hyacinth

6 Monday
St. Nicholas' Day
Waxing Moon
Moon phase: First Quarter
Color: White

Moon sign: Sagittarius
Moon enters Capricorn 6:16 pm
Incense: Clary sage

7 Tuesday
Islamic New Year
Waxing Moon
Moon phase: First Quarter
Color: Gray

Moon sign: Capricorn
Incense: Ylang-ylang

8 Wednesday
Feast of the Immaculate Conception   Moon sign: Capricorn
Waxing Moon   Incense: Lavender
Moon phase: First Quarter
Color: Brown

---

9 Thursday
Hanukkah ends   Moon sign: Capricorn
Waxing Moon   Moon enters Aquarius 2:30 am
Moon phase: First Quarter   Incense: Apricot
Color: Crimson

---

10 Friday
Nobel Day   Moon sign: Aquarius
Waxing Moon   Incense: Cypress
Moon phase: First Quarter
Color: White

---

11 Saturday
Pilgrimage at Tortugas   Moon sign: Aquarius
Waxing Moon   Moon enters Pisces 1:41 pm
Moon phase: First Quarter   Incense: Sage
Color: Indigo

---

12 Sunday
Fiesta of Our Lady of Guadalupe   Moon sign: Pisces
Waxing Moon   Incense: Marigold
Moon phase: First Quarter
Color: Orange

☽ Monday
St. Lucy's Day (Swedish)   Moon sign: Pisces
Waxing Moon   Incense: Hyssop
Moon phase: Second Quarter 8:59 am
Color: Gray

---

14 Tuesday
Warriors' Memorial (Japanese)   Moon sign: Pisces
Waxing Moon   Moon enters Aries 2:15 am
Moon phase: Second Quarter   Incense: Geranium
Color: Black

December

15 **Wednesday**
Consualia (Roman)
Waxing Moon
Moon phase: Second Quarter
Color: Topaz

Moon sign: Aries
Incense: Honeysuckle

---

16 **Thursday**
Posadas (Mexican)
Waxing Moon
Moon phase: Second Quarter
Color: Purple

Moon sign: Aries
Moon enters Taurus 1:49 pm
Incense: Jasmine

---

17 **Friday**
Saturnalia (Roman)
Waxing Moon
Moon phase: Second Quarter
Color: Pink

Moon sign: Taurus
Incense: Alder

---

18 **Saturday**
Feast of Virgin Solitude
Waxing Moon
Moon phase: Second Quarter
Color: Blue

Moon sign: Taurus
Moon enters Gemini 10:37 pm
Incense: Patchouli

---

19 **Sunday**
Opalia (Roman)
Waxing Moon
Moon phase: Second Quarter
Color: Gold

Moon sign: Gemini
Incense: Frankincense

---

20 **Monday**
Commerce God Festival (Japanese)
Waxing Moon
Moon phase: Second Quarter
Color: Lavender

Moon sign: Gemini
. Incense: Narcissus

☺ **Tuesday**
Yule • Winter Solstice
Waxing Moon
Moon phase: Full Moon 3:13 am
Color: White

Moon sign: Gemini
Moon enters Cancer 4:22 am
Sun enters Capricorn 6:38 pm
Incense: Cedar

December

22 Wednesday
Saints Chaeremon and Ischyrion's Day   Moon sign: Cancer
Waning Moon   Incense: Bay laurel
Moon phase: Third Quarter
Color: Brown

23 Thursday
Larentalia (Roman)   Moon sign: Cancer
Waning Moon   Moon enters Leo 7:51 am
Moon phase: Third Quarter   Incense: Balsam
Color: Turquoise

24 Friday
Christmas Eve   Moon sign: Leo
Waning Moon   Incense: Orchid
Moon phase: Third Quarter
Color: Rose

25 Saturday
Christmas Day   Moon sign: Leo
Waning Moon   Moon enters Virgo 10:14 am
Moon phase: Third Quarter   Incense: Sandalwood
Color: Black

26 Sunday
Kwanzaa begins   Moon sign: Virgo
Waning Moon   Incense: Heliotrope
Moon phase: Third Quarter
Color: Orange

◑ Monday
Boar's Head Supper (English)   Moon sign: Virgo
Waning Moon   Moon enters Libra 12:38 pm
Moon phase: Fourth Quarter 11:18 pm   Incense: Lily
Color: Silver

28 Tuesday
Holy Innocents' Day   Moon sign: Libra
Waning Moon   Incense: Bayberry
Moon phase: Fourth Quarter
Color: Scarlet

29 Wednesday

Feast of St. Thomas Becket
Waning Moon
Moon phase: Fourth Quarter
Color: Yellow

Moon sign: Libra
Moon enters Scorpio 3:49 pm
Incense: Marjoram

---

30 Thursday

Republic Day (Madagascar)
Waning Moon
Moon phase: Fourth Quarter
Color: White

Moon sign: Scorpio
Incense: Apricot

---

31 Friday

New Year's Eve
Waning Moon
Moon phase: Fourth Quarter
Color: Purple

Moon sign: Scorpio
Moon enters Sagittarius 8:21 pm
Incense: Vanilla

Yule Holly Mollies (*sprites*)

Pick enough leaves from a holly bush for each person in your family or coven and write each person's name on a leaf with a gold pen. Thread a wide-eyed needle with red string. One by one, thread each of the leaves onto the string. Think of a holiday wish for each person as you pull the thread through the leaf. When all the leaves are threaded together, tie a knot at the top of the thread so it makes a loop. Say, "May we be bound with love and good wishes, and prosper in the new year." Hang the Holly Molly on a Yule tree or on the branch of a tree near your house.

–Elizabeth Hazel

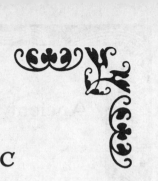

Fire Magic

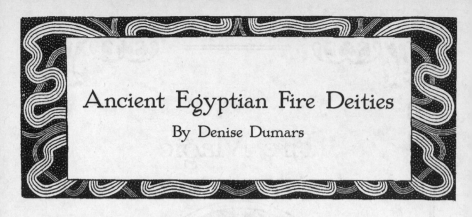

Ancient Egyptian Fire Deities

By Denise Dumars

With the exception of the gods of the night (such as moon and star gods) and the gods of the underworld, virtually all ancient Egyptian gods were solar deities, which makes them fire deities in one way or another. The reason is simple: the first and foremost influence on Egypt was the sun. Ra, the sun god, was seen by most ancient Egyptians as the supreme being. Ra (or Re) had many forms; depending upon which part of Egypt one was in, he might be known as Amun Ra or Ra Harakte, having taken on attributes of local solar deities. He was often portrayed as a man with a hawk's head wearing the solar disc and sacred uraeus.

A curious solar deity, possibly older than Ra, was Khepera. Often portrayed as a man with a scarab beetle's head, he was self-created and the sole parent of Tefnut and Shu, who in turn were the parents of Geb and Nut, who then produced Isis, Osiris, Set, Nephthys, and Horus the Elder. Khepera may have been the original sun god before the worship of Ra. Khepera was thought to be responsible for the rising of the sun, its ascension throughout the day, and its setting at night. Curiously enough, this metaphor comes from the observance of the scarab, which is a dung beetle, and which can often be seen rolling balls of dung across the landscape. Strange imagery for a sun god! In ancient Egypt it was believed that the scarab beetle spontaneously generated itself from dung.

But when we speak specifically of Egyptian gods of fire, the two that come to mind most often are Set and Sekhmet. First let's look at the myth of Sekhmet. In her creation story, Ra looked down upon the earth and what he had made and the way people were behaving, and he was unhappy. Old and senescent, he felt powerless to do anything about the degradation he saw being wrought on his beautiful planet. From his right eye he fashioned a goddess with the head of the lioness, a warrior goddess who would go down to the earth and slay anyone who was not righteous. This warrior goddess went about her duties quite effectively, but once all of the bad people were taken care of, like a true lioness, she had developed a thirst for blood and could not stop killing people. Ra found that he could not stop her, and he had to develop a plan quickly. So he tricked Sekhmet by pouring a great quantity of red beer into the Nile. Thinking it a river of blood, Sekhmet began to lap it up like a cat, becoming intoxicated and falling asleep, thus ending the carnage.

The priests and priestesses of Sekhmet used to offer red beer to the goddess every year at her festivals just to make sure that she never again went on a killing rampage. Sekhmet became a very powerful deity in her own right, and her magic was called red magic. As a goddess of menstruation, Sekhmet's magic was thought to be powerful women's magic. She was also a goddess of warriors and hunters, and great statues of Sekhmet—sentinels

made of black basalt, many of which can be seen in the Louvre Museum today—stood guard around some of Egypt's most important cities.

Red magic in ancient Egypt was akin to what we call black magic in our society today. To the ordinary person, it was frightening, and it was only employed by the priests and priestesses who knew best how to handle it. Not all red magic was bad, however; common prayers during magic spells, such as "Red magic flows through me like the blood of Isis," or "Red magic flows through me like the blood of Osiris," were and still are common for those who practice Egyptian magic—the imagery is synonymous with power, not evil.

Fire, frankly, is frightening, and so it is not surprising that fire deities are often frightening. The sun of Egypt, after all, could give life and it could also take life away. The god of the red desert, Set, was considered one of the most frightening gods of Egypt. He was called "the dry one," and his sun was not the life-giving sun of Ra; it was, in fact, the scorching desert sun that kills. Set had the body of a man and the head of some strange composite animal that looks like a combination of a donkey, an okapi, and the jackal. Whether one chooses to see Set as the

adversary in the Egyptian pantheon or in a more complex fashion, his function in ancient Egypt was quite clear: someone had to be responsible for all the negative aspects of nature.

However, this does not mean that the fire deities of ancient Egypt were all considered negative. Sekhmet, as we have seen, is considered a very powerful goddess of women's magic. She is also a healing goddess, for her knife not only slays, but it is also the knife of the surgeon who cuts away disease and heals the sick. In addition, Sekhmet also has a softer side, and her alter ego, Hathor, is yet another solar goddess. Hathor is often portrayed as a beautiful woman in a red or golden dress wearing a solar disc on her head and cow horns. She also sometimes has ears like a cow, and she is referred to as "the golden one." The cow was a very important symbol in ancient Egypt; it stood for fecundity, motherhood, and wealth, and even today one's wealth is measured in cattle in certain parts of Africa. Hathor was the goddess of passion. Parties were thrown and dancing was done in Hathor's name. The golden calf in the Bible was Hathor.

Hathor is thought to be the one who healed the eye of Horus after it was gouged out by Set, and so Hathor is also a healing goddess. In that particular myth, Hathor is the wife of Horus. However, Hathor is a much older goddess, predating the stories of Horus and the gods of Heliopolis, dating back to very early Egypt. Gold and red, the colors of the sun and of blood, had different connotations for both sides of the goddess Sekhmet/Hathor. You can imagine that much magic was done on both sides of that equation!

Fire has many connotations. Burning can consume or purify. Fire is a symbol of the passion of love. Fire was used in Egyptian magic for many purposes: to purify, to increase one's power, to find love or to make someone fall in love with you, to increase energy, or to act as a sacred flame in a temple. An eternal flame is a symbol of eternal life, an idea that the Egyptians were positively obsessed with.

Wax, especially red wax, was often used in Egyptian spells. The wax, melted by the flame, was seen as symbolically embodying and solidifying the fire. Red wax melted over a particular figurine or a particular written spell was meant to imbue that object or spell with the power of fire. In one story of the goddess Isis, fire was used in a spell to instill immortality. When Isis had fled Egypt, exiled with her son while Set ruled in Egypt after overthrowing and killing her husband Osiris, she visited the land ruled by the goddess Astarte. Astarte had a young son, and Isis grew very fond of him. She decided to bestow immortality upon Astarte's son, and so she held him over the fire while doing incantations. Astarte came into the room, and, misunderstanding the situation, snatched the child from Isis and from the fire, inadvertently ruining the immortality spell.

Incense was another important element of fire magic in Egypt, just as it is today. Burning cedar, frankincense, myrrh, or the Egyptian composite incense kyphi was a typical and important part of ritual, whether religious, magical, or both. Fire is said to be the active component of magic. In a recent report, an interesting result of burning frankincense was found—the fragrance from frankincense seemed to lift the spirits of people suffering from depression. Just as fire creates energy, so too can someone of low energy use fire as sympathetic magic to increase their energy.

There were other fire gods of Egypt, including Selket or Serket, the scorpion goddess. Selket was a protector who aided women in childbirth, and golden statues of her were found as guardians of the tomb of Tutankhamen. She is often shown as a woman with a scorpion as a headdress, or sometimes even as a scorpion with a woman's head! In some of the Egyptian papyri, Isis is depicted being attended by scorpion handmaidens. Neith, the old Egyptian war goddess and goddess of weavers, was a fire goddess as well, and her temples held lit oil lamps in every corner; Neith was self-created—like Ra and Khepera—and she shares some of their characteristics. Ami was a fire god, represented by a bird of prey. The Bennu bird (which we call the phoenix) was the symbol of immortality in Egypt, and as in similar myths in many cultures, this bird burned with holy fire and was reborn from its own ashes.

When referring to Egyptian fire deities in magical practice, remember to do so carefully and with respect. Accidents do happen when handling candles, oil lamps, and incense. Many people, when imploring the goddess Sekhmet, for example, kneel on one knee, place their right fist over their heart and bow in supplication to her. Many is the time I've heard of sudden blasts of hot air coming as if from nowhere during rituals involving Sekhmet and Set. The ancient Egyptians believed in fire demons and often asked deities of water and air for protection from them.

Fire can be a friend as well as a foe in magic. Just as the ancient Egyptians respected the power of the sun to both give life and take it away, so too their solar deities were imbued with the properties of fire magic and so to invoke them was to work with great power. Pursuing magic that invokes the positive side of the fire deities can have many dramatic results when used wisely.

For Further Study

Masters, Robert. *The Goddess Sekhmet*. St. Paul, MN: Llewellyn, 1991.

Reed, Ellen Cannon. *Circle of Isis*. Franklin Lakes, NJ: New Page Books, 2002.

Regula, deTraci. *The Mysteries of Isis*. St. Paul, MN: Llewellyn, 1995.

Roberts, Alison. *Hathor Rising*. Rochester, VT: Inner Traditions, 1997.

Cast Not Upon Me:
The Evil Eye in Myth
and Magic

by Nancy V. Bennett

For Witches, it seems that the eyes have it in for us. Either we are out of the eye of newts to put into some favorite recipe, or we are condemned for hexing someone with the evil eye. Where did this fixation start? Journey with me into the world of the evil eye.

The Desert Is Dry and Withering Is the Eye

In the desert regions of the world, especially in the Middle East, water was life. To have your well dry up could only mean one thing: someone had put a hex on you. It was not only wells that suffered from this drying demise. Women whose wombs had failed to produce or whose milk dried up were said to be under the spell. Animals that stopped feeding their young and even a man's ability to "rise to the occasion" were all caused by someone fixing the evil eye upon them.

To protect yourself from the evil eye, there was a wide variety of things to do or to have on your person. Amulets varied from culture to culture. For some, carrying gold coins or something containting the color blue was said to protect the owner from harm. Being careful how you ate, and who you ate with, was also recommended, for the soul is most vulnerable when your mouth is open. Perhaps this is why our mothers always drilled us to chew with our mouths closed!

Praise for the Baby,
and Spit in Your Eye

When someone says sweetly, "Oh, what a beautiful baby you have!" saying thank you comes to mind as an appropriate response. But only if you spit first. It is a common practice among Greeks to spit three times toward the person who has given you a compliment. This protects against the person laying a curse against you. According to custom, compliments could be envy in disguise and could make your baby sick, especially when given by a childless person.

To further protect a baby from the evil eye, or ayin ha'ra, as it is known, Jewish Christians often employ the use of a red thread tied to the left wrist of the baby. In Scotland a red cord was tied round the baby's neck, sometimes with a cross of rowan wood. Not only newborns are subject to this ritual for protection but elders as well. If you feel you are being hexed by someone, have a person you love and trust tie a red cord on your left wrist.

If red is not your color, why not try another Greek custom? Use a blue bead painted with an eye as a necklace or bracelet to "stare back" the evil eye. Unfortunately, if you are blue-eyed, you might find people on this island nation trying to avoid you. Blue-eyed people are supposed to be inherently gifted at laying curses with the evil eye.

Beads made from coral are favored for protection in Naples, and Arabs used salt thrown into a fire before starting out on a journey to market to keep anyone from cursing their wares. In the Middle Ages, an amulet or charm with the word *Abracadabra* was often employed.

The Eyes of Horus, Ra, and Kali

The god Horus had two eyes. One was the sun and one was the moon. His brother Set (or Seth) was the god of storms and sand and bringer of strange and dangerous weather.

He and Horus battled each other. In the epic fight, Set lost his testicles, while Horus had his eye plucked out.

The magic of Thoth restored the eye of Horus. Once the eye had been restored it became known as *Wadjet*, meaning "whole." In some telling of the myths it is the left eye that is plucked out, the moon eye. Like the moon, which disappears after its cycle until it is again restored to fullness, the eye is seen as magical.

Horus gave the eye to Osiris, who was dead. Osiris ate it and was restored to life. No mention is made of whether the eye returned to Horus in one form or another, but its reputation for healing powers have filtered down into our modern times.

The shape of the eye of Horus is often associated with the eye of a falcon. It also is a rather complex hieroglyphic. Within the hieroglyphic of the eye are six parts, representing thought, smell, sight, taste, touch, and hearing. Together they form a whole, healthy person.

Modern uses for the eye of Horus include the eye of Providence, which can be found on U.S. bills, the all-seeing, all-knowing eye. The "Rx" of prescriptions can also trace its origins to the eye of Horus.

In another myth, the eye takes on a more evil meaning. The Egyptian god Ra is upset because the people are not respecting him. He sends an aspect of his daughter (the eye of Ra) to earth in the form of a lion. His daughter wreaks havoc upon the land, killing and maiming. Ra is moved by the pleas of the remaining people and orders her back, but she is deep within her bloodlust, and the slaughter continues. It is only after she has been subdued by beer and pomegranate juice that she finally falls asleep and wakes up with a terrific hangover.

It is interesting how this myth is also mirrored by an Indian one, that of Kali. This goddess has three red eyes, representing the past, present, and future. Some believe

her third eye also represents wisdom. When she is in her loving mother form, she keeps her eyes shut so as not to frighten anyone. Like all great mothers, you may seek her wisdom but be prepared, for life is not always pretty, nor the future without its challenges when one looks deep into Kali's eyes.

Medusa's Stare

In the myth of Perseus, Medusa is a nasty piece of work. Her body is that of a serpent and her stare enough to turn a man into stone. Yet, her blood has healing aspects, depending on which side of the body it is drawn from.

Medusa's tale began with an ancient Lybian legend in which she was worshipped as a serpent goddess. Her dreadlocked hair showed her African origins, but these were later were corrupted into snakes. Medusa's name meant "wisdom" and her stare did not mean instantaneous death. Those who did lift her veil and look into her all-knowing eyes would see their own destiny, the time and place of their own demise. Few men and women would willingly search out this knowledge, and so Medusa's stare was avoided.

Perseus then entered Medusa's cavern, surrounded by men she'd turned to stone statues. He used a shield as a mirror to destroy her and took her head as a weapon. Despite being severed from her body, the head of Medusa still retains the ability to turn living things to stone.

The head was then returned to Athena, who uses it to keep her enemies at bay. Later, mortals would paint the face of Medusa upon their armor to protect them in battle. Like so many of the ancient goddesses, Medusa evolved with her people: once an all-knowing but mysterious seer, then a healer, and finally a warrior.

Balor and the Evil Eye

In Ireland long ago, a great war raged. The Fomorians, a gang of sea pirates, waged war against the ancient tribe in power, the Tuatha Dé Danann. The Fomorians had for a leader a cruel man named Balor. When he was a child, Balor had crept up to a house where a group of magicians had gathered. He peered in the window, which was open a crack, and as he did his eye was stung with smoke. Writhing on the ground, Balor realized he had been blinded. The magicians hurried outside to see what all the shouting was about.

"Boy," they said, "we were working a death spell when you spied upon us. From now on, the gaze from your blinded eye will have the power of death over all." From that day forward, Balor kept his eye shut when amongst his kin. But when he went to war, he had only to fix his powerful gaze upon the enemy and they would instantly be struck dead.

Years before, the Druids had told Balor that he would meet his death at the hands of his own grandchild. He had an only daughter, called Eithlinn, whom he locked up in a tower with twelve women to guard her so she would not have a child. Despite this, and with the aid of a female Druid named Birog, a man named Cian managed to get into the tower. Cian, disguised as a woman, entered the tower with Birog. Birog put all the guards to sleep and Cian and the beautiful Eithlinn lay together. A child was born nine months later.

Balor, upon hearing the news of his grandson, traveled to the tower and cast the infant into the sea. But the Druid Birog saw it all and used the wind to gather the child up from the waves and lead him to safety. Cian was delighted to have his son back, and he was raised to be a strong and intelligent man. He took the name Lugh of the Long Arm and made his way into the court of the king.

Lugh was determined to put an end to the rule of the pirates and his evil grandfather Balor. By this time, Balor had grow so big that his eyelid was droopy, and he had to use a special ring to open it. Ropes tied onto the ring raised the eyelid when he wished to cast his evil eye upon the enemy.

In a great war fought between the pirates and the Tuatha Dé Danann, Lugh and the king rode bravely into battle. Balor felled the king with one swipe of his sword. Lugh was determined to avenge him.

Taking out his slingshot and stone, Lugh began to taunt the evil Balor. "Let me feast my eye upon the loud-mouth who dares to speak to me!" shouted Balor and his men began to pull the ropes to release the gaze of death. When the eye was open but before it could fix on him, Lugh swung his slingshot and loosed a stone. It embedded deeply into the eye, so deep that it drove the eye through his head, and the eye now stared at his own people. Balor died, and many of his pirates with him. Those who survived ran quickly to their boats, never to return again.

Future Uses for the Evil Eye?

According to a BBC news report, residents of a South African town are using "the evil eye" in an attempt to clean up their neighborhood. Groups of concerned citizens flanked with yellow bibs stare down prostitutes and potential customers until they vacate the area. The staring eyes of the groups also help to discharge transients and drug dealers, who are unnerved by the piercing gaze. Perhaps the evil eye has a good side after all!

For Further Study

Rose, Carol. *Giants, Monsters and Dragons: An Encyclopedia of Folklore, Legend and Myth.* New York: W. Norton and Company, 2001.

Heaney, Marie. *The Names upon the Harp.* New York: Arthur A. Levine Books, 2000.

Websites

Holmes, Hannah. "The Skinny on: The Evil Eye." *Discovery.com* www.discovery.com/area/skinnyon/skinnyon970425/skinny1.html

Hefner, Alan G. and Demetrius Drystellas. "Evil Eye." *the Mystica.org* www.themystica.org/mystica/articles/e/evil_eye.html

Amvrazi, Alexia. "The Eyes Have It." *Athens Guide.com* www.athensguide.com/journalists/articles/evileye.htm

Hill, Jenny. "The Eye." *Ancient Egypt Online* www.ancientegyptonline.co.uk/eye.html

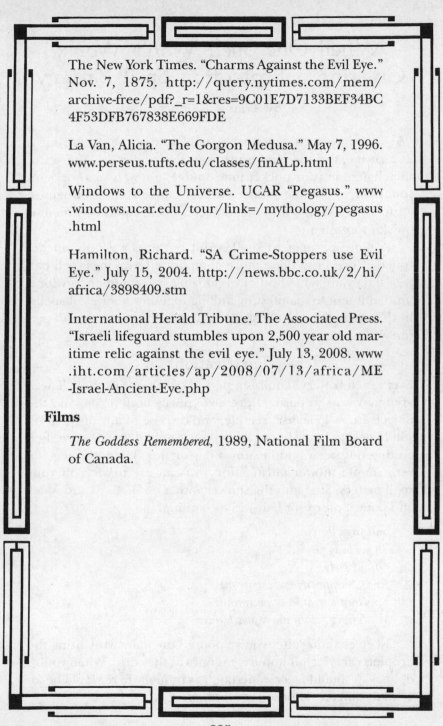

The New York Times. "Charms Against the Evil Eye." Nov. 7, 1875. http://query.nytimes.com/mem/archive-free/pdf?_r=1&res=9C01E7D7133BEF34BC4F53DFB767838E669FDE

La Van, Alicia. "The Gorgon Medusa." May 7, 1996. www.perseus.tufts.edu/classes/finALp.html

Windows to the Universe. UCAR "Pegasus." www.windows.ucar.edu/tour/link=/mythology/pegasus.html

Hamilton, Richard. "SA Crime-Stoppers use Evil Eye." July 15, 2004. http://news.bbc.co.uk/2/hi/africa/3898409.stm

International Herald Tribune. The Associated Press. "Israeli lifeguard stumbles upon 2,500 year old maritime relic against the evil eye." July 13, 2008. www.iht.com/articles/ap/2008/07/13/africa/ME-Israel-Ancient-Eye.php

Films

The Goddess Remembered, 1989, National Film Board of Canada.

When One Spell Won't Work: Creating a Protection Spell Battery

by Diana Rajchel

A one-time spell can work—stand under the moon, say a rhyme, feel the wind brush your skin, move on. Afterward, the change in your pocket may double, a new love knocks on your door, or nothing happens when nothing is exactly what you want. The result is quick, the impact is small, and the incident is quickly forgotten.

A more permanent spell result requires a more concentrated effort. I call these more complicated workings spell batteries: they are a method of organizing space and energy for a unified intent to manifest by linking together a series of spells. In the example here, the shared intent is the protection of person and property.

Purification

Every spell battery requires a period of self-purification. There are many ways to purify; I prefer to purify both myself and the objects I use. I cleanse, recycle, and dispose of any of the junk still lingering in my home and go on a mild detoxification diet, cutting out sugar and fats for a day or two. The following is a very simple shower purification you can use to kick off your spell battery. Step into the shower with a bowl of salt and water and pour it over your hair while chanting:

Salt from the sea
To my body
Off my body
Purify me, purify me, purify me
Sins that are mine, other iniquity
Wash away, wash away, wash away

Keep chanting after you've poured the water, visualizing the droplets carrying off impure energies as they drip. When you're done, you should feel cleaned out, as though there would be an echo if someone knocked on your chest.

Banishing

Once you have purified yourself, the next step is to banish. Banishing is the phase where you get rid of internal and external energies that may cling despite purification.

To banish, try writing what you want gone on a piece of paper, setting the paper on fire, and (after it has burned down in a heatproof container) allowing the wind to take the ash. Phrase your request carefully—being too specific or too general may end in unexpected or undesired results. "I banish what needs to be banished" is a safe and workable phrase. While the paper burns, pantomime an X in the smoke with your finger and push the X westward, visualizing it disappearing against a sunset.

Uncrossing

Uncrossings are intended to remove the effects of "the evil eye." When people look at you with a specific emotion, especially a negative one, that emotional energy builds up. It is typically not the result of a concentrated magical attack; it's more like the eventual karmic result after cutting off way too many people in traffic. All those emotional hits attach themselves and slowly make life more uncomfortable, so an uncrossing is a way above and beyond purification and banishing to settle that energy sent our way, intentionally or otherwise, by others. When you're attempting difficult spell batteries, any lingering negativity will hinder you.

For a simple uncrossing, burn some lemongrass herb on a charcoal disk and chant:

I uncross this little jinx
You angry, vexing little minx
And burn this cursing by and by
I am clean now in my god's eye

If you prefer a different route than a candle-burning or bath-based uncrossing, you can do a variation by writing your name on a piece of paper and anointing it with a seal of Saturn drawn in oil. As you burn the paper, do a chant similar to the one above.

House Blessing

Because this is a deep protection battery, you will also need to charm your home. Ultimately, there are only two things you really need to do: get out bad/stagnant energy and seal in or attract positive/protective energy. The household cleanup at the beginning of the battery completes a vital part of this process. Follow this with a household banishing: take a broom and "sweep out" stagnant energy, spirits, and entities that might linger in doorways, cupboards, or odd little nooks of your home. After the sweep, ward doors and windows with a symbol or seal and smudge the space with sage, juniper, or cedar. (If you live in a nonsmoking area, use a salt water spritz.) Your home will be safer both physically and metaphysically when you are done.

Protection of the Aura and Body

Now that you are purified and your home is protected, you can add layers of protection to your person. While doing these workings, don't seal yourself too tightly: if you shut off your psychic faculties, you will shut down your sixth-sense alarm system. You need that alarm system, because without it, all the protection energy in the world would be useless.

Shielding

First, create an extra aura or "shield" around your natural aura that is flexible like a tensile fabric woven from aluminum. You can do this by visualizing yourself surrounded with white or blue light, then adding details to that light. It will take a long time to truly master an auric shield; Witches dedicate years to building and readjusting their shields.

Anchoring

Anchors can assist shields when you're not able to feed and reinforce them daily. My favorite anchor uses charged and blessed temporary tattoos placed at key chakras. Affix one at major energy points: over the heart, at the small of the back, over the solar plexus, on the inside of the wrists, on the back of the hands, and at the top of the feet. As I apply each tattoo, I speak a small protective chant and visualize each one glowing and connecting to each of the other tattoos like an electrical system.

Aftermath

With protection, the best way to know that it worked is to shrug and say "nothing happened." While it's not glamorous, it's useful. I've enjoyed a rather banal life despite living in interesting neighborhoods for several years, and I attribute it to my magical efforts to keep things boring. Once in a while, the protection working will need some tweaking—shielding requires regular practice, and house blessings need repetition at least once a month because wear and tear happens just as much to wards as it does to carpeting. Once done, you'll have your magical security system down, and you can weave that right in around locking your doors and setting your alarm system.

~

Spell batteries can be incredibly effective in maintaining long-term results or major changes. The protection spell battery here is just an example of how a series of small spells can be combined to have a greater result. Experiment with combining related spells to achieve your own spell battery effect!

Magick on Campus

by Ellen Dugan

It's that time of year again, when my garage resembles a storage unit and my daughter is organizing, packing, and making lists as she prepares to head back to campus for the fall. There are boxes of school supplies and suitcases full of clothes, nonperishable food, and other assorted paraphernalia required for a college student stacked in Kat's bedroom and in my living room. Off she goes for another year at college.

So if you are a Pagan or Wiccan who lives on a college campus, how do you turn your dorm room into a magickal environment? Well that depends on you, and on your magickal personality. Do you want to go over the top and hang your Pagan pride flag over your bed and watch the conservative roommate squirm just for the hell of it? Or do you want to keep it subtle? There is no rule that says you can't keep a low profile. Nor do you have to hide your faith either. The bottom line is that religion is an intensely personal thing and how *you* choose to express your beliefs is completely up to *you*. Today many universities have Student Pagan Organizations. If you feel like being sociable with other Witches and Pagans on campus, these groups can be a great thing. However, there are many college-aged Pagans and Witches who are quietly going about their business on campus. Here are a few practical magick ideas to take with you when you return to campus this August.

Where There's a Witch, There's Always a Way

Setting up a subtle altar that has one of each of the four natural elements represented on it can be cleverly done. Reserve a little corner of your desk, the dresser, or even a bookshelf. Then arrange a small lava rock for fire, a feather for air, a seashell for water, and a crystal point for earth. To most folks this is just a clever arrangement of items from nature. With these small items you have a physical representation of each of the four elements. These items can easily be worked into any type of magick. You could even place them at the four quarters in place of burning candles to mark the cardinal points should you care to cast a circle in your dorm room.

How about making a clever bewitching collage to hang on those bland dorm room walls? There's plenty of attractive art that illustrates various gods and goddesses. Instant representation of the Lord and Lady. If anybody asks and you feel the need to keep a low profile, just tell them you are into world mythology. No one has ever even questioned my daughter's choice of artwork or knickknacks—why? Because she's an anthropology major. I suppose they imagine that she's just *really* into Egyptian stuff.

You could do the same artwork idea to represent the four elements as well. Scenes from gardens or the forest are lovely representations for earth. Birds in flight, a hawk or eagle, or clouds in the sky for air. A scenic photograph or poster of the ocean or a lake is a no-brainer to represent the element of water. Finally, for the element of fire, you can use a picture of the sunset, a volcano, or even an illustration of a dragon. Use your imagination.

Since most dorms have strict "no candles" and "no incense" rules, what's a magickal person to do if they want a little fire and air energy? For starters, you need to think outside the box a bit. As an alternative to candles, use those little battery-operated tealights that "flicker." These give you the look and feel of a candle without the flame. If you like, you can slip it inside of a colored glass votive cup and coordinate your "candle magick" to the color you need. Or do as I suggested in my book *Elements of Witchcraft,* and use a fresh flower in a vase instead of a candle for your various spellworkings. When the flower fades, return it to nature. Apply your knowledge of color magick to choose the appropriately colored flower.

Don't forget to avail yourself of crystal magick as well. A pretty ceramic or glass bowl full of various, tumbled, magickal crystals and stones looks attractive sitting out on your dresser.

Again no one but you has to know that they are indeed magickal tools. I would suggest using the various stones in your spellwork. Slip a few in your pocket and off you go. For good luck, work with the green, sparkly aventurine. Need mental clarity? Try green and purple fluorite. For protection, work with black tourmaline or jet. If you wish to draw new friends to you, work with the rose quartz crystal. You can also surround a battery-operated tealight with various stones that are harmonious to your spellwork. Casting spells with crystals is a time-onored and very practical form of the Craft.

For an alternative to burning incense, try those plug-in air fresheners. My daughter takes one to school that has a patchouli scent. That way she has a fresh-smelling room with a dose of witchy aromatherapy tossed in for protection. You could try a vanilla scent for comfort and love; a spicy apple scent for abundance, friendship, and happiness; or a citrus scent for energy and inspiration. Aroma travels on the air, whether it's smoke from traditional incense or from an electric fragrance diffuser. The bottom line here is that magick is what you make of it, and creativity is the key.

Calling on Artemis for Help with College Life

The first year my daughter lived in the dorms, she called me one December night very agitated because there was a major drama unfolding on her dormitory floor. It seemed that several girls were having an ongoing argument about roommates and room assignments, and the entire floor was affected by the battle. One of the girls in the thick of things was Kat's roommate, and my daughter was counting the days until the end of the semester when everyone switched roommates. With the pressure on for finals and no one getting any quiet for study time, she called and asked me for a spell idea to help things settle down on her floor. I thought about it a moment. I made up a quick rhyming spell, repeated it to her over the phone, and she carefully wrote it down. I then suggested that she turn on that patchouli-scented room freshener and get some magickal aromatherapy going. She also put a bit of water on her fingers to draw a banishing pentagram on the inside of her room's door in order to cleanse the dorm room and banish all the drama and loud voices.

I also recommended that she call on Artemis, the Greek goddess of the hunt. I figured if any deity was no-nonsense and tough enough to take on a bunch of arguing college girls, Artemis could handle the job nicely. While my daughter and I were talking, I could hear an argument in full swing outside her room and Kat muttered that she'd had enough and was going to fix this situation *right now*. She promised to call me in a few days and let me know how the spell had turned out. I had to smile at the thought of my low-profile daughter casting in her dorm room at college.

The next afternoon, Kat called back to let me know that not only had the spell worked for peace and quiet the night before, but that it had actually worked within minutes. It was finally calm and also, her troublesome diva of a roommate was in the process of moving completely out of the building and off campus altogether, that very day. So Kat had her week studying for finals in blissful solitude and peace. It seems like a few other of her friends also decided that Kat's room was the best place to study to get some quiet. How interesting. The next semester, she got a new roommate and they get along wonderfully. And yes, she still has that spell I gave her back in her freshman year. As she is a resident adviser now, she says it comes in darn handy when the various roommates in the dorm are squabbling!

So we have just a few days before she moves back onto campus for her junior year. As I walk down the hall to her room, I see her in deep concentration while she selects and carefully packs in bubble wrap a few special items to travel along to campus with her once more.

What are these items, you may wonder? Her two-foot-tall statute of the goddess Bast, her patchouli-scented air freshener, a couple of battery-operated tealights, Halloween decorations—as a residence adviser, she loves to and is encouraged to decorate her room for the holidays. I notice some artwork with an Egyptian theme, also being carefully packed. Oh and sure enough, there is a copy of that original spell that called on Artemis. Just a few essential Pagan goodies that she takes along every year to make her dorm room on campus feel more like magickal home.

As Above, So Below

by Mickie Mueller

Many of us have heard the term "As above, so below; as within, so without." This is one of the main principles of magic. This phrase offers part of the explanation of why and how magic works. Just from reading the words, you can glean a very basic understanding of the teaching, but if we explore the concept, we can gain a deeper understanding of not only how magic works, but how the universe works. While the idea is deep and far reaching, there are practical examples and exercises that you can do to illustrate the principle in action, and therefore make it a real part of yourself and your ever-growing magical practice.

As Above So Below, a.k.a. the Law of Correspondence, is one of the Hermetic principles. The Hermetic principles come from an enigmatic document known as The Emerald Tablet, which is sometimes attributed to the Egyptian god Thoth or the Greek Hermes. The truth is, no one knows for sure where it came from or who first wrote it. According to one legend, it was seen in the library at Alexandria and described as an unnatural-looking tablet made of emerald with characters carved in bas-relief. Today we have different interpretations of the document, but they are all pretty similar. As Above, So Below is only a small part of the Emerald Tablet and the interpretations of the phrase that have come down through the ages.

What Does It All Mean?

One important interpretation of As Above, So Below is that man is the microcosm to the universe. This means in part that we carry everything in us and are a part of everything that is. After all, astronomer and astrochemist Carl Sagan pointed out that we are made of the same stuff as the stars and the rest of the universe. But this interpretation also paints a picture of the interaction between the realms of reality. It is important to know that, according to this law, the physical realm is a mirror of the spiritual realm. This mirror means if you want to change something in your life, you must change things in the higher realm. You have to have a spiritual plan for the world to follow. The spiritual realm is at our disposal and open to our will, because we're part of it, and it's part of us. How do we as humans in the physical realm make a change within the spiritual realm? Some people use creative visualization, some pray, and some use magical techniques.

We can actually break down the Law of Correspondence to understand the methods of magic that we use and why the magical correspondences (colors, stones, herbs, etc.) we use in spellcasting actually work to effect change in the universe. When doing that prosperity spell, do you know why that green candle works? The color green has become associated with money because money is green in many countries, but we also know that green growth has also been a symbol of abundance going back to the beginnings of agriculture. Therefore these energies are associated with prosperity in the spiritual realm. When we *purposefully* burn that green candle, we are sending a message to the spiritual realm that we're looking for prosperity. The spiritual realm gets the message because it understands the request, and then answers you by sending you prosperity because the *material realm is a reflection of the spiritual realm.*

As you can see, this is a principle that magical practitioners use all the time; even if we don't realize it, we've been using the idea of correspondences for ages. Many nonmagical people have rediscovered this particular principle and are using it all over the place. There is a reason that motivational speakers, business leaders, life coaches, and best-selling mainstream books are using this principle as a basis for manifesting positive change—because it's a universal truth. Should this upset us as magical practitioners? Of course not. There is plenty of magic in the universe to go around,; it belongs to everyone. If some choose not to call it "magic," it still is what it is. After all, it's not new; it's been around for a very, very long time. There are numerous interpretations out there for this principle, from the simple to the metaphysical and esoteric. They all agree however, that correspondence is the principle where the spiritual, mental, and physical meet in order to make magic happen.

A Practical View

One of my favorite emblems of As Above, So Below is the symbol of the sacred tree, branches seen above, and roots seen below the trunk, mirroring the branches. This is a great illustration of the principle: if the roots are damaged, the tops of the tree will suffer, and if the tops of the tree are damaged, it will be reflected in the rest of the tree. If the roots receive lots of water and nutrients, the tops of the tree will thrive, and if the leaves are able to process lots of

energy, the roots will be strong and grow deep. Each mirrors the other; each is part of the other. In this example, the sacred tree can be an example of the upper or spiritual realm, and the roots are the lower or inner realm; the trunk is anchored in the physical realm . . . the trunk is you.

What this means in everyday life is that we (and everything else) exist within all planes, astral as well as physical. In order to manifest something, a circuit needs to be completed, as in the health of the tree. Let's go back to the prosperity candle spell, which begins in the physical realm, as do all spells. On a Thursday you get your green candle, patchouli oil, gold coins, etc. Now you are going to light that candle and do that spell. What happens? You are sending your intention (to attract prosperity) into the astral realm. The act of doing your spell is what convinces your mind that this will work; it will bring you money you need. Now the deity, spirits, or energies that you worked with sense your belief that the spell is already working. Your mind is now open to the idea of gaining prosperity. Since magic takes the path of least resistance, your energy in the astral realm inspires a buddy who owes you money to drop by, a side job comes your way, or you get an unexpected bonus at work. The circuit is complete. What has just happened? As Above, So Below! You've been doing it all along.

It's deceptively simple. Here is another example you might not have thought of. You are struggling to carry too many bags of groceries into the house and all you can think about is how much you don't want to drop the bags. You focus on it so much that you are in fact seeing the bags fall, and feeling how much that would upset you, when suddenly, you lose balance and there go the eggs and spaghetti sauce, everywhere! Guess what? You made that happen. You are a magical practitioner used to manifesting things with your mind. It's not what you wanted to happen, but it was all you could think about, so it happened, like a self-fulfilling prophecy. Try it again. This time, purposefully use your magical skills, visualize yourself setting the bags safely on the counter and all in one piece—you will be amazed by the results. Send that image above, and you'll get it manifesting below. We have often been pre-conditioned to expect the worse, and therefore we get it. As magical practitioners, we have control over our own minds, which is the strongest tool that we use to manifest, and we need to use that tool to bring about the things we want, not the things we don't want. As Above, So Below can work with you or against you; it's *you* that decides.

Here is a very simple experiment you can do to illustrate the effects of As Above, So Below, As Within, So Without. This illustrates how your will and focus make the circuit work. The next time you are having a low day, maybe feeling a bit under the weather or just have a case of the blues, instead of laying around in a sweat pants, force yourself to get all cleaned up, put on that outfit that looks really good, groom your hair, and run a couple of errands. When you look good and you know it, you send that message up to the higher realm, and then you start to feel it! Whatever takes place on the spiritual plane is reflected in the physical plane. Changing your appearance is the tool by which you send that change to the spiritual plane. You will notice that other people will see it too, and by the end of the day, you have changed your energy. By changing what is "without," you have changed what is "within," and vice versa.

Here's a personal example. I had a day off work and had been doing artwork all day in my classic "day off" ensemble: a baggy paint-spattered T-shirt, my oldest jeans, no makeup, and hair in a scraggly bun and secured with a pencil. Wow, cover of *Vogue*, not so much! I was picking up my husband from work that evening when he told me that a band I used to do artwork for years ago was playing in the bar next door and they really wanted me to come over and see them! I panicked! In my old rock 'n' roll days, I prided myself in dressing the part, and here I was, looking like a deranged refugee! In fact, I wouldn't be caught dead at the drugstore at 2 am like that, much less at my friends' gig. We lived too far away for me to go change, so I smoothed myself down the best I could and used the only glamour I had at my disposal, my magic! I sent the image in my head of how I wished to be perceived into the spirit realm and brought it back into my solar plexus, let it swirl around a bit, and then expanded it until it encircled me. I walked into that bar confident with my head held high. And you could tell, no one saw that I had spent a day hunched over my art table with pencils between my teeth, they just saw me as they remembered, as I wanted them to.

How did I do it? As Above, So Below, As Within, So Without! I sent my will into the higher realm, and instead of focusing on how unkempt I thought I looked, I focused on an image of confidence. Then I moved that thought inside of myself and manifested it over my physical appearance. Did I physically look different? No. But I used my will to complete the circuit in order to feel different and be perceived differently. We call it a glamoury spell, but it is also the

Law of Correspondence in action. One's outer self is a reflection of one's inner self. What is manifested is whatever corresponds with your dominant patterns of thinking, whatever those patterns may be.

The act of doing spellwork can be a powerful catalyst for manifesting change through the Law of As Above, So Below. There is nothing wrong with attempting to create that spiritual change without ritual, candles, runes, stones, and herbs. The technique of manifesting without any tools is one that we teach in the more advanced degrees within my coven, and it is just as magical as using all the bells and whistles. The act of doing spellwork, however, is very beneficial when trying to enact the principle of As Above, So Below, especially when we are seeking a big change, because ritual can create a very strong adjustment within ourselves and how we relate to the spiritual realm. Spellwork is a tool by which you can change what is in yourself and your thoughts about the world around you, therefore allowing you to send the right energies into the astral realm in order to complete the circuit of manifestation. Yes, basically, if you simply focus on what you want and refuse to give any energy to what you don't want, you can manifest good things in your life. You don't have to cast a spell to do that. But if you are in a place where you have spent a lot of years, for example, thinking that you will always be broke, one of the best ways to help you send the opposite message to the universe is to alter your own perception and the thoughts you are focusing on prosperity through spellwork.

This is an important realization for us as magical practitioners. When we can see that this is how magic works, we can better create our spellwork around this concept and we can better bring about what we really want. The example of my old friend Jean comes to mind. Jean had been doing spellwork to open herself up to love. She didn't have anyone in mind, but she was looking for her perfect match. She had been working magic for several months and wasn't having any luck, so she asked me if I would look over her spells to see what she was doing wrong. As I read one of the spells she had written, it became glaringly obvious, she stated over and over within her spell, "I don't want to be alone anymore, I'm tired of feeling so alone, and I just need someone to fill this empty void," etc. Sheesh! I said, "Honey, these are the loneliest, most depressing spells I have ever read! This is what you are sending out there, so it's what you're getting back!" So we sat down and talked about what she *did* want as opposed to what she *didn't* want. We reworded what she had been doing with positives, "I want to spend time with someone I enjoy being with, I want to feel a sense of belonging. I am full of love that I wish to share with someone deserving of my generous heart." Guess what? Jean was dating a great guy within a month! All that time, she had been manifesting what she was focusing on, which was exactly what she didn't want! Once she focused on what she did want, she got it! The spellwork helped her consciously change her way of looking at love, and therefore she completed the circuit and activated the Law of Correspondence: As Above, So Below.

When you apply these concepts to your magic, you have the power to create change in your life, and you can do it every day. As Buddha said, "What you think, you become."

Cult of the Saints:
An Introduction to Santería

by Lily Gardner

Ever wonder why statues of Catholic saints are sold in the same shop next to mandrake roots and Eleggua candles? How the saints joined forces with the African pantheon that would become Santería or Voodoo is a story dating back to the late 1600s.

Huge populations of African prisoners of war, mainly from the kingdoms of Benin and Yoruba in western Africa, were enslaved and shipped to the Caribbean to work in mines and on cane plantations. The plantation owners baptized their slaves as Roman Catholics and prevented them from practicing their Pagan faith. But, recognizing similarities between the saints and their old gods, the slaves simply renamed their gods using the saints' names and continued with their old worship. The blending of these two religions became known as Voodoo in Haiti and the islands to the south and as Santería in Cuba and the islands to the north of Haiti.

Santería means "worship of the saints." Just as the saints serve as emissaries to the creator god in the Catholic religion, so Santería has a creator god and a huge number of lesser deities, or saints, known as orishas. The orishas rule over every aspect of nature and human endeavor. And like the saints, you can find an orisha for anything that ails you.

Santería is a decentralized religion with no template for ritual, symbol, or doctrine. The rituals and even the some of the saints will vary from house temple to house temple depending on the santeros or santeras (priests or priestesses). Worship takes place in a *casa de santos* (house of the saints). Central to the worship in Santería is dance, trance, and divination.

Worship of the orishas is pragmatic. When you have any sort of need, you entreat the orisha whose province fits your problem. You dress your altar much the same way we are familiar with, using the colors and symbols appropriate to the orisha. Be sure to use images of the saints on your altar. You can find statues and pictures of saints at Catholic stores or you can download images from the Web.

An important component is the sacrifice or offering made to the orisha. Sacrifice is the energy that fuels the magical working. Each individual orisha has his or her preferences for food, smoke, and drink. It is respectful to remember the orisha's feast day and to make an additional offering. It is said that the gods keep strict accounts of offerings made and favors granted.

Everyone is invited to worship the orishas, but it is strongly advised that the seeker enters into communication with gods with the utmost respect and care. Any sloppiness could result in your prayer being ignored.

Many people see Santería as the reconciliation between the Pagan African worship and Catholicism. Others feel the old Yoruba faith was maintained intact with only a superficial sheen of the saints overlaid to pacify the slave owners and later the Christian government and culture. Regardless of whether the devotee is in her heart praying to the saint and the deity, or only to the deity, images of the saints remain a vital part of the practice of Santería and Voodoo.

Yemaya/Mary, Star of the Sea

Yemaya is the African Mother Goddess, one aspect of the Divine Trinity. She rules over the oceans, the moon, women and children, fishermen and sailors, Witches, and secrets. All life comes from Yemaya the sea, and Yemaya never betrays her children. She is associated with the Virgin Mary in two of her aspects: Our Lady of Rule and Mary, Star of the Sea. Although little is known of Mary from the New Testament, early Christians recognized her as the Mother Goddess. They prayed to her, saw her in visions, and experienced miracles when they invoked her. Finally, the Catholic Church was forced to give her more prominence. Mary is known and worshipped under many titles and is the corresponding saint for a number of African gods.

Both Mary and Yemaya's colors are blue and white. Their day is Saturday. Pray to them for a safe journey on the sea, fertility issues, a healthy pregnancy, and healthy children.

If you wish Yemaya's protection, make a necklace with blue and crystal beads in the following pattern: seven crystal beads, seven blue beads, one crystal bead, and one blue bead. Repeat this pattern six times (for a total of seven sequences, 112 beads).

If you wish to ask a boon of Yemaya, leave her an assortment of grapes, pineapple, watermelon, and bananas in seashells or shell-shaped dishes at the edge of the sea or the banks of a river or lake. Make a circle around your offering with seven coins, a representation of the number of days between the phases of the moon. As you face the water, say a number of Pagan Hail Marys. A Pagan Hail Mary would go like this:

Hail Mary, full of grace,
Enlightenment is in thee
Blessed are thee among women and blessed is the fruit of thy womb.
Holy Mary, mother of us all, bless us mortals
Now and throughout our life.
Amen.

If you feel comfortable, you may wish to use rosary beads and say an entire rosary of Hail Marys. This form of prayer works in the same way a mantra works in meditation. When you're finished, tell the Goddess your problems and ask for her intercession.

Obatala/Our Lady of Mercy

Obatala is another aspect of the Divine Trinity. Like Yemaya, he is associated with the Virgin Mary, this time in the aspect of Mercy. As the first-born of the gods, Obatala is regal and wise. He blows away negative energies and resolves ethical issues. As Yemaya is the patron of mothers, Obatala is the patron of fathers. He has dominion over all white things, from bones to the clouds in the sky. Your offerings to Obatala must be white foods: white hens, rice, milk, etc. Unlike the other gods, Obatala abhors alcohol. Leave your offering to Obatala at the base of a tree.

To cleanse your aura, make a bath into which you have poured a cup of milk, seven white carnations, seven teaspoons of sugar, and seven drops of holy water. Light a white candle and slip into the bath. As you immerse yourself in this bath, say seven Our Fathers (The Lord's Prayer).

Chango/Saint Barbara

Chango is the third member of the Divine Trinity. He is the god of transformations, the god of thunder and lightning, and he should be prayed to when you need to strengthen your will. Perhaps the most startling pairing between saint and god is Saint Barbara with Chango. As a fire god, Chango is a passionate womanizer, whereas Saint Barbara was a chaste young woman. The connection becomes apparent when we discover that Chango is invoked when a person seeks revenge on his enemies, and Saint Barbara is patron of wrongful death. Barbara suffered death at her father's hands when he discovered she had converted to Christianity. At the moment her father beheaded her with his sword, he was struck down by lightning. Lightning is a potent symbol for both the Catholic saint and the Santería god, and both Chango and Saint Barbara are prayed to for protection in storms.

How does one reconcile revenge with Chango on the one hand and victimhood with Saint Barbara on the other? I would pair these two when seeking to reclaim one's own power. Because we are invoking fire gods, a candle spell would be most advantageous.

Make a ring of prayer beads to use in tandem with affirmations. The prayer beads should be red and white in this pattern: six red, six white, one red bead, and one white bead. The pattern should be repeated six times more for a total of ninety-eight beads. Say your affirmation once for each bead. The affirmations, however many you write, should be written as positive, present-tense statements of how you wish to see your life.

How you move from dream to plans to actuality is will, the special province of Chango and Barbara. Begin by decorating your altar using red and white cloths, symbols of machetes or swords, lightning bolts, towers, a cup, and images of Saint Barbara.

Burn a red candle beginning on a Friday night and say your affirmations using your special prayer beads. Repeat this ritual every night for a total of twenty-four nights. Each Friday during this period, leave an offering of dry red wine, apples, and bananas at the foot of a tree.

Eleggua/Saint Anthony

It was said that when Saint Anthony preached at a river, the fish stood on their tails so as not to miss a word. After hearing a sermon from Saint Anthony, people who hadn't spoken to each other in years became friends again and estranged family members were reunited. It probably is this eloquence that links Saint Anthony to Eleggua, the African Hermes, messenger to all the gods.

Eleggua is known as Legba in the Haitian faith, and sometimes as Eshu. He must be invoked before you can pray to any of the other gods. Say:

Eleggua, remove the barrier for me
Papa Legba, remove the barrier
So I may pass through
When I come back, I will salute the gods.

Eleggua is often portrayed as a large clay or cement head with cowrie shells positioned for eyes, nose, and mouth. As patron of doorways, Eleggua's place in the home is by the door to protect the home from any negativity. You could also string a special necklace to hang over the door: three red beads followed by three black beads, repeated until you have a necklace with twenty-one beads. Offer Eleggua rum and sweets on Mondays, his sacred day.

To protect yourself from violence, carry on your person a red-and-black bag. Into the bag, place coffee beans and a whistle. Purify the whistle with the four elements of fire, water, earth, and air and anoint it with coconut oil.

If you're in need of a miracle, light a brown candle before the likeness of Saint Anthony. Say:

Holy Saint Anthony, gentlest of saints. Miracles waited on your word, which you were ever ready to speak for those in trouble. I implore you to obtain for me [state your request]. The answer to my prayer may require a miracle. Even so, you are the saint of miracles. Please grant my miracle, Saint Anthony.

Imagine your prayers being lifted on the candle smoke up to Saint Anthony. Let the candle burn out. Then take a bag of canned food and bring it immediately to your local food bank as an offering.

Saint Anthony is most famous as the finder of lost things. Next time you can't locate something say:

Dear Saint Anthony, I pray
Bring it back without delay.

Osain/Saint Joseph

When the African slaves glimpsed depictions of Saint Joseph, an older man leaning on a crutch, they recognized their nature god, Osain. Saint Joseph as the husband of Mary, the Blessed Virgin, was known as "The Divine Cuckold" in the Middle Ages. According to the story, it was the Holy Ghost who impregnated Mary. In religious art, the crutch represented Joseph's alleged impotence. Despite the lack of respect paid to him, Saint Joseph is a powerful ally. It is said that he answers all prayers said from the heart. Saint Joseph is patron of fathers, foster parents, carpenters, laborers, houses, and a happy death.

Osain is the god of the forest. All wild plants are under his domain and he is the patron of all healers and herbalists. His creed is: *The woods have everything the santero needs to preserve his health and to defend himself from evil. But he must remember to ask the woods permission before removing a stone, or a leaf on a tree.* Osain oversees the safety of all sanctuaries. The protection of houses is where his domain intersects with Saint Joseph.

Go to any religious store and buy a statue of Saint Joseph. The clerk may ask you if you're selling a house—burying a statue of Saint Joseph is said to help bring a buyer to the home. This spell has worked for me and for several of my friends over the years!

Light a yellow candle and burn a stick of pine incense before your statue of Saint Joseph. Pass Saint Joseph through the incense smoke three times and say:

Smoke of pine and candle's fire
Bring to my house a qualified buyer.
Let the sale be quick and fair
Oh Saint Joseph, hear my prayer.

Visualize a "Sold" sign in your front yard. Your possessions are safely packed in a moving van. You're happy and the people moving into your house are happy.

Bury Saint Joseph on his head facing your house. Leave his statue in the ground after you move as a blessing for the new occupants.

Osain and Saint Joseph can also be invoked to protect your home. By the light of a yellow candle, string a necklace made with one white bead, followed with nine red beads, followed by eight yellow beads. Continue in this fashion until you've strung a necklace twenty-eight inches long. As you string the beads, pray to Osain:

Osain grows, grows,
All green things grow.
Osain heals, heals,
Osain's plants heal.
Osain guards, guards,
Osain, protect us.

Gather blackberry thorns, a piece of ash bark, cedar needles, eucalyptus leaves, and/or acorns. Any of these plants will do, so long as you find them in the forest and you humbly ask permission before gathering them. Tie a pouch full of these protective herbs with your necklace and complete this spell with a prayer to Saint Joseph to keep your house safe from theft and calamity:

> *My loving protector, Saint Joseph,*
> *That no one had recourse to your protection or asked your aid,*
> *Without obtaining relief.*
> *I come before you and humbly implore you,*
> *Protect this house from all evil.*

Leave an offering of tobacco at the base of a tree.

Oshun/Our Lady of la Caridad del Cobre (Our Lady of Charity)

Oshun is another goddess worshipped under the umbrella of the Virgin Mary—in this instance, Our Lady of la Caridad del Cobre, patroness of Cuba. As the love goddess, Oshun predictably rules pleasure and sexuality, marriage and the arts, but she also oversees all money matters. Oshun's famous generosity may be why she's paired with Our Lady of Charity. Her feast day is September 8.

As you would expect from a goddess who rules both love and money, Oshun is very popular with the other orishas and thus very spoiled. Though slow to anger, once Oshun loses her temper, she is extremely dangerous. She is often pictured dressed in gold or yellow, her arms encircled with many gold bracelets, her hair held back with tortoise-shell combs.

To attract love into your life, you must choose a gift for Oshun. If at all possible, give her a piece of gold jewelry. Place the jewelry in a dish of honey on a Friday night. Light a yellow or gold candle next to the honey and meditate on what you desire in a lover. Be as specific as possible.

The following morning, wrap the gold in a small square of yellow cloth and drive to the river. Throw your offering into the water with a prayer to Oshun. When you get back home, write all the traits you desire in a lover on a white sheet of paper with a pen that's never been used before. Fold the paper five times and tuck it beneath the yellow candle you used the night before in your meditation.

Light the candle and pray to Oshun. Tell her about your experiences; tell her why you want this lover. Tell her what you can offer such a lover. Continue this prayer as long as it feels right. When you're finished praying, snuff out the candle.

Repeat this prayer for a total of five days. At the end of that time, burn the paper containing your lover's traits in the candle's flame and bury the remains of the candle by your front door. Be sure to thank Oshun when your lover materializes. Make an offering of oranges and honey and leave it on the bank of the same river that you used for your first offering.

Oggun/Saint Peter

Perhaps it's because Oggun champions the working man that his saintly counterpart is Saint Peter. As the god of war, Oggun is belligerent and combative, but he also is hard-working and the patron of human effort. Likewise, Saint Peter, though not a warrior, has a reputation for being rough around the edges and is petitioned for success and employment.

To petition for a better job or for success in a new business venture, make your offering on a Tuesday. Construct an altar

using images of Saint Peter and an iron cauldron in which you've inserted two keys (emblems for both Oggun and Saint Peter) and seven other pieces of iron, such as nails or other tools. Use black and green altar cloths. Make a circlet of prayer beads using this pattern: seven green beads, seven black beads, one green bead, one black bead. Repeat this pattern six more times (112 beads). Your offering to Oggun should be a glass of rum, some smoked fish, and a cigar.

Write your request on a piece of paper and place it beneath a green candle. Light the candle and finger the prayer beads while visualizing your goal. Stay with this visualization as long as you can.

Oggun is an earth deity, so bury your offering at the end of the ritual.

~

There are hundreds of gods in the Santería pantheon to discover and possibly connect with. It's important to stress the respect and follow-through necessary when petitioning these gods. If working with the orishas resonates with you, you may wish to take the next step and approach a santeros or santeras. The closer you move toward the orishas, the more understanding you'll have of the deeper truths of Santería. May all your prayers be answered.

The Purpose of Magic:
A Neopagan Perspective

By Abel Gomez

The search for purpose is an integral part of our earthly existence, as old as humankind. Purpose informs our every action and without it, we are utterly lost. So great is our need for meaning that seekers, philosophers, and mystics throughout history have devoted their entire lives to its attainment. We all need an explanation for why we were put on this earth. For many of us, it was this very search for meaning and purpose that led us to Neopagan spirituality. But what is its purpose and how do we find personal meaning and fulfillment through magical spirituality?

No matter what path we choose (or which chooses us), we cannot walk the earth forever. Our days are numbered and finite, and thus, you must quickly decide how to best serve your purpose. Indeed, you may conclude that the search for purpose and meaning may be the root motivation for human existence on this planet. There is a common longing within each of our hearts that can only be fulfilled by living a life of purpose. Without a purpose, we cannot fully function in this world.

As Pagans, we believe our world's essential nature is beauty, wonder, and divinity. The earth itself is honored and worshipped as the living body of the Goddess. And yet, the grips of *Maya* (from the Eastern traditions, meaning "illusion") prevent us from fully experiencing this every moment. In some traditions, *Maya* refers to the condition of the world as essentially illusory, a world that we must transcend to experience the rapture of the Infinite. In Occult thought, however, it refers to the illusion of separateness from the divine, from other people, and from the world. Maya is that which prevents us from experiencing the fullness of our divine nature and discovering our purpose in this life. It is this illusion that we must transcend to truly achieve the Great Work.

This may be the cause of so-called evil and benevolence in the world. According to Hindu tradition, those who act in seemingly evil ways do so because they have lost touch with their God-selves. When we act purely from our instinctive, outer nature, we lose sense of divinity. Though we are inherently divine, it is easy to forget that, as we are constantly bombarded with tasks, deadlines, and bills. We find this reconnection through spiritual discipline.

For most of us, contemporary culture does not promote true spiritual practice. Every day we are assaulted with advertisements, shocking news stories, and highly sexualized images of anorexic models and plastic muscle men. It's hard for us to remember who we are, our place in the world, or our connection to the ever-present divine. This is where spiritual practice comes in. When we engage in spiritual practice, we are intentionally opening our awareness of our innate connection to the gods, re-acknowledging that we are sacred, existing in a sacred Universe.

Our practice is also what informs us of our true calling in the world. Perhaps it was the (in)famous occultist Aleister Crowley who said it best when he wrote, "Do What Thou Wilt shall be the whole of the Law." Though this statement is perhaps the most misunderstood and maligned statement in contemporary occultism, what Crowley was truly referring to was the spiritual practice that plunges us into direct contact with the Divine and one's God-self. It is here that we are able to understand our True Will—the work that is destined for our soul during this incarnation. The goal of spiritual practice is not

only to help us become more cognizant of the Divine in the world and in ourselves, but also to help us understand our purpose and place in the world. The more we practice and the deeper our practice becomes, the more tangible our earthly purpose becomes.

Spiritual discipline means different things to different people. For some people, this will involve simple devotional prayers; for others it involves elaborate daily rituals of alignment. What matters is the ability to tap into innate divinity and manifest that in the day-to-day world. When spiritual practices lead to a sense of presence, when every moment leads to deeper spiritual awareness, the practice is effective. As the Hindu god Krishna (often called the "Christ of the East") states in the *Bhagavad-Gita*, "If you focus your mind on me and revere me with all your heart, you will surely come to me; this I promise because I love you." When we engage in spiritual practice, we will experience the beauties and wonders of connection to the

Divine. This experience will ultimately lead to a conscious state of divine unity with all things.

We are all fated to experience this reconnection to the Divine. While some call it Moksha, the Great Work, Self-realization, Liberation, achieving one's True Will, or simply serving God, all these phrases are merely symbolic statements for the same essential state of being. Perhaps the term most Neopagans connect with is the Great Work, guiding and priestessing humanity to the next quantum leap of spiritual evolution. It is awakening and acknowledgement of our essential divine nature in all our parts, our connections to all things, and union with the Limitless. This is the enlightenment of the Eastern traditions, the awakening of the cosmic nature of one's own being during which one dissolves into the sublime bliss of divine unity. It is a quantum leap in the sense that we reach a higher level of cosmic awareness and acknowledge our role as a strand in the fabric of existence. This is the point at which we realize "we are in this together" and begin to think outside ourselves. For many people, the standard purpose of life is to "help people," and it is at this point that such a notion comes into play.

It is important to also stay grounded when seeking the Great Work. Though we may acknowledge a cosmic fate, our practice also reminds us that the Divine is manifest in all of nature. The purpose of the Great Work is not to disconnect from the material world, but to live more fully within it. There was no Fall of Man and all things are sacred, and thus there is no need to renounce the material plane in order to reach spiritual enlightenment. Quite the opposite. As Pagans, we believe nature is not only sacred, but it is literally the embodiment of divinity. Our gods are merely metaphoric forces; they are the living spirits of nature. By connecting to the natural world, we connect with gods. When we engage in this kind of spiritual practice, illusions dissolve and we are able to see the Great Mystery alive in all things.

The journey toward such a leap of consciousness may take many lives or reincarnations to achieve. As we continue on the path of spiritual evolution, fragments of our consciousness continue on after physical death. We are on a continual cycle of rebirths, each of which is meant to propel us toward deeper awareness. It is when one has truly achieved the Great Work that one's soul is released from the cycle of rebirth.

We are all seeking something. In our society it is typically temporal pleasure through unhealthy forms of sex, money, or power, none of which will last when one's life on earth ends. The realization through spiritual practice is that our true sense of meaning come from our connection to the Cosmic Intelligence. This is perhaps one of the most powerful lessons of the liturgical Wiccan ritual poem *The Charge of the Goddess,* in which the Goddess is channeled as saying, "For behold—I have been with thee from the beginning and I am that which is attained at the end of desire." When all cravings, longings, and wants fade away, it is our connection to the Divine that remains.

From a Neopagan and Occult standpoint, however, the Work does not simply end when one has experienced the sublime. Once one has touched the Great Mystery and discovered individual purpose, we are to bring that forth into the world. How does our path contribute to the healing of our planet? How does your individual Will guide the world into greater spiritual progression? It may be political activism, singing, writing, priestessing, or teaching to inspire the world to heal and discover the divinity that is everywhere. The specific method matters less than the intent and action.

Though our bodies will surely pass away, our souls will live forever. It's essential to maintain a healthy relationship with the body and the earth while acknowledging the time-less and cosmic nature of our God-selves. When we engage in personal spiritual practice, we are able to uncover our cosmic and individual fate and fulfill our purpose. We can then bring the wisdom and the power gained through practice out into the world and act as a conduit for true healing, compassion, and divinity. This will ultimately lead to greater wholeness and the healing of the world.

Playing It Safe: Everyday Protection Magick

by Deborah Blake

The world we live in can be a scary place. Not only are there the usual mundane dangers to worry about (accidents, muggers, and unexpected illnesses), but those of us who are aware of the invisible world must also be concerned with psychic attacks and other such unseen threats. What's a Witch to do?

Thankfully, there are many techniques to protect yourself and those you love. Protection magick is one of the oldest and most basic forms of magickal work and one of the simplest to master.

As with most forms of magick, it is up to each individual Witch to pick the tools and approaches that appeal to him or her most, and which seem to best suit the situation at hand. For instance, if you are trying to keep yourself safe while traveling, you will probably want something small and portable, like a charm bag. On the other hand, if your goal is to cast a spell of protection over your entire house, you might be better off using a combination of herbs, salt, and a Witch's bottle.

There are a number of the options available for use in physical, emotional, and psychic protection. Keep in mind that this type of magick is meant to be used for *defensive* purposes, not *offensive* ones. There may be times when your safety depends on more assertive measures, but in those cases I recommend turning to mundane solutions, rather than magickal ones.

Protection Basics

As with most types of magickal work, there are some generally accepted fundamentals for doing protection magick.

Keep in mind that these can differ from book to book and tradition to tradition, and that what is right for one Witch isn't necessarily right for another. I like to use these suggestions as a starting point and then follow my own intuition. Listen to your "inner voice" and it will guide you to the best possible tools to use and the most advantageous approach for any given situation.

There are a great many herbs with protective qualities. Some of my favorites include anise, basil, burdock, carnation (especially good for emotional protection), clove, dill, eucalyptus, frankincense, garlic, juniper (a good defense against thieves), lemon, lily, mistletoe, mustard, myrrh, nettle, onion, orange, parsley, pennyroyal, peppermint, rosemary, rue, sage, sandalwood, vervain, wormwood, and yarrow.

I think it is interesting that so many of the protective herbs are also medicinal herbs, like eucalyptus, which is a wonderful defense against colds. My particular favorites, and therefore the ones I use the most often in my own magickal work, are rosemary, parsley, peppermint, and sage. They are easy to find (both fresh and dried), easy to grow, and smell good together—always a bonus if you are making a protective mixture that will be hanging around your house or your person for a while!

If possible, try to grow some of these herbs yourself. As with all plants used for spellcasting, those you have grown with your own two hands have increased power and potential, because you are imbuing them with your will and intent from seed to harvest. If you don't have space for a garden, don't despair—herbs grown by someone else will still work. But you might try growing a few of your own herbs in a pot on a windowsill to use in especially important magickal workings.

For a simple way to protect your home and property, plant a few trees; those with unusually protective properties include ash, birch, hawthorn (because of its long thorns, no doubt), holly, juniper, oak, pine, rowan, willow, and yew.

There are also a number of gemstones that are particularly useful in protective magick. The simple agate is one of the best stones for defensive work, but there are many others that will work just as well, including amethyst, garnet, jasper, lapis, malachite, onyx, and tigerseye. I usually lean toward amethyst or clear quartz crystals (both of these are powerful, multipurpose stones that work for almost any magickal application), or a tumbled piece of black onyx or red jasper.

When burning candles or making cloth sachets, the customary protective colors to use are white, black, and red, although some folks are partial to blue for protective work as well. I also like to carve or draw a *thurisaz*, *eihwaz*, and *eolh* rune on any charms I make, since these runes signify protection—every little extra element you can add to a spell or charm will reinforce your intent.

Charms, Herbal Mixtures, and a Witch's Bottle

I practice three main types of protection magick, both for myself and (on request) for others. A charm can be hung up by the front door of a house or apartment, tucked into the glove compartment of a car, or carried somewhere on your body. Herbal mixtures are good for widespread use—for example, if you want to do some long-lasting protection work for your entire home. I have a mix that I make up once a year and sprinkle around the outside of my house and around the lines of my property. And a Witch's bottle is a traditional form of defense that is usually buried near the entrance to your home. (Mind you, some say that its original "traditional" use was as a defense against Witches . . . but, if it works, who cares?)

Charms come in various forms. One of the simplest is a symbol, such as one of the runes mentioned above, worn around the neck on a chain or cord. I prefer something a little more involved and usually make a charm using dried rosemary, basil, and parsley, to which I add a whole clove of garlic (it won't smell much as long as you don't peel it), a piece of agate, and a pin. The pin is said to catch and impale any negativity.

Wrap all the items in a square of white silk or cotton, tie it closed with a piece of red yarn, and say an appropriate charm blessing over it. For instance, if the charm is meant to keep a house safe, say something like, "I make this charm of power, to guard my home from this hour." Come up with words to fit whatever situation you are dealing with (e.g., travel protection), but they don't have to be very complicated. Then hang the charm up someplace unobtrusive or tuck it into a corner or a pocket.

The herbal mixture I mentioned is equally simple and very effective. I mix salt (which is also very protective) with dried peppermint, rosemary, sage, and basil. If possible, I use herbs that I have grown in my own garden and consecrated on my altar. I mix all the herbs together, place them in a pouch, and walk around the outside of my house and around my property boundaries saying, "This house is protected. This property is protected. All those who live here are safe from harm, intentional or accidental, from within or without. This house is protected." I repeat this over and over again as I sprinkle the herbal mixture, visualizing a protective light surrounding my home and the land it sits on.

This mixture can be used inside as well—simply sprinkle it around, let it sit for about twenty-four hours, then sweep or vacuum it up.

There are a number of different methods for creating a Witch's bottle. One way is to start with a small glass bottle or jar and place within it a few pins (to impale negativity), some dried rosemary (to send it far away), and a few stones or some salt to absorb anything nasty. If you want, you can even add some red wine, which is said to drown any negativity that makes it past the rest of the defenses. Then bury the bottle underneath a stone at the entrance to your home.

A Spell for Protection

If you feel as if you are under psychic attack or know that someone in particular is sending negative energy in your direction, try performing the following spell.

On the night of the New Moon (or whenever you need it, if you can't wait that long), gather together a black candle, a mirror, a long thin piece of white cloth, and a protection oil (this can be made from any of the herbs above, and while it is nice to have a "magickal" oil, any good essential oil will do).

Cast your circle and invoke the quarters, specifically asking them to guard you while you work the spell. Take a few moments to feel safe and protected within your sacred space, and visualize a golden light filling the circle. Then anoint the candle with protection oil (if you want, you can carve some rune symbols into the candle first, or even just the word "safe") and light it. Hold the piece of cloth in one hand, and the mirror—facing out away from you—in the other, and say this spell:

Harming none, I ask for safety
And protection from life's ills
Keep me free from dark intentions
Guard me from malicious wills
Bind the hands of those who'd harm me
Bind their eyes so they can't see
Reflecting back toward those who send it
Negative thoughts and energy
Surround me with a golden light
Send my heart serenity
Keep me safe and free from harm
As I will so mote it be

When you're done, tie the cloth into a knot, and leave it and the mirror—face down—in front of your candle for a bit. Make sure that the candle is in a fire-safe location, and don't leave it burning if you leave the room. Visualize yourself being surrounded by a golden protective light that will stay with you for as long as you need it. Thank the quarters and open your circle as you usually would.

⁓

The world is a scary place, it's true. But as Witches, we have a few extra tools available. Used properly, protection magick can help us to stay safe and feel secure. Don't use these techniques instead of the usual mundane approaches—it is still a good idea to lock your doors, drive carefully, and take care of your health. Rather, think of them as an extra layer of protection, like putting on a warm comfy jacket over your sweater when you venture out into a cold and uncertain world.

Aleister Crowley for Pagans

by Magenta Griffith

Aleister Crowley was perhaps the most influential occultist and magician of the twentieth century. His impact is still significant, six decades after his death. Many of the ideas that pervade modern Paganism, Witchcraft, and Ceremonial Magic originated with him or were inspired by him in some way.

Aleister Crowley was born Edward Alexander Crowley on October 12, 1875, in Warwickshire, England. (Aleister is the Gaelic spelling of Alexander. He never liked the name Edward, nor any of the nicknames for Alexander, and started using another name as soon as he could, probably while he was at Cambridge.) His parents were members of an extreme sect of the Plymouth Brethren. His father was a prosperous brewer who died when Crowley was ten. His mother chastised him, telling him he was sinful and evil, and saying he was the great Beast of Revelation. Crowley decided at a young age to live up to (or down to, as it were) his mother's description.

In 1895, Crowley went to Trinity College, Cambridge. His three years at Cambridge were happy ones, due in part to coming into the considerable fortune left by his father. He left Trinity College after three years without earning a degree.

Crowley was a man of many interests and talents. He was a chess prodigy but gave up playing in tournaments when he was twenty-two. He published his first book of poetry (*Aceldama*) when he was twenty-three.

Crowley was obsessed with mountain climbing, which he used as a tool to combat his chronic asthma. He taught himself to climb by scaling the Cumberland Fells and the chalk cliffs of Beachy Head, England, then he tackled the Alps. In March 1902, Oscar Eckenstein and Crowley undertook the first attempt to scale Chogo Ri, also known as K2, located in Pakistan. Two months into the expedition, they were forced to turn back due to poor weather conditions and the death of one member of the expedition. In the summer of 1905, Crowley was part of the first Western expedition to Kangchenjunga in

Nepal, the third largest mountain in the world. The assault was unsuccessful, and four members of that party were killed in an avalanche. Crowley's autobiography states they reached an altitude of about 25,000 feet.

When Crowley left Cambridge in 1897, he became acquainted with Julian Baker, who introduced him to George Jones, a member of the Hermetic Order of the Golden Dawn. Crowley had found what he had been seeking, and joined the Order.

The Hermetic Order of the Golden Dawn, often just called the Golden Dawn, was a quasi-Masonic magical order founded in 1888 by three men: William Robert Woodman, William Wynn Westcott, and Samuel Liddell Mathers. The Golden Dawn taught spiritual development, esoteric philosophy, Qabala, and Tarot. Many well-known people joined, including William Butler Yeats, Arthur Machen, and Evelyn Underhill. By 1897, one of the founders (Woodman) had died and another (Westcott) had left the Order, leaving Mathers in control. Toward the end of 1899, many of the members had become extremely dissatisfied with Mathers' leadership, as well as the growing influence of Crowley. In 1900, Mathers, then living in Paris, gave Crowley an initiation that had been refused by the London order. This contributed to a falling-out in the Order, which resulted in the formation of several other magical orders and several lawsuits about who had the right to the rites.

Through the Golden Dawn, Crowley became acquainted with Allan Bennett and asked him to move in as his roommate. Bennett became Crowley's teacher in both ceremonial magic and Buddhism. Bennett was the first Englishman to be ordained as a Buddhist monk of the Theravada tradition and was instrumental in introducing Buddhism in Great Britain. Crowley learned about Buddhism and other Eastern traditions from Bennett and eventually helped him move to Ceylon for his health. Crowley's association with Bennett enabled him to study yoga and other Eastern disciplines.

In 1899, Crowley decided to perform a ritual called the Abramelin working. This ritual involved extensive isolation and meditation over a period of weeks and was said to result in communication with one's Holy Guardian Angel, one's most divine self. He needed a site where he would have absolute privacy, and so bought an estate in Scotland called Boleskine House, which remained his home for a number of years.

In 1903 he married Rose Edith Kelly, sister of the famous portrait painter Gerald Kelly; the next year, he and his wife traveled to Cairo, Egypt. There, Rose started behaving oddly, which led Aleister to think that an entity had made contact with her. On March 20, 1904, he performed an invocation of the Egyptian god Horus. According to Crowley, the god told him that a new magical aeon had begun, and that Crowley would serve as its prophet. Rose continued to give information, telling Crowley in detailed terms to await a further revelation. On April 8, 9, and 10, at exactly noon, he heard a voice that dictated the words of the text, *Liber AL vel Legis*, or *The Book of the Law*. The voice said it was that of Aiwass (or Aiwaz) "the minister of Hoor-paar-kraat," another name for Horus, the god of force and fire, child of Isis and Osiris, and Lord of the New Aeon. This book dictated by a spirit was perhaps the most significant writing of Crowley's life; much of his later work sprang from it. The central doctrine of *The Book of the Law* is "Do What Thou Will shall be the Whole of the Law"; this doctrine is referred to as *Thelema*, the Greek word for "will."

In 1907, Crowley founded an occult group called the A.A. (*Astrum Argentum*), the "Silver Star." In 1910, Crowley performed with members of the A.A. his series of dramatic planetary rituals, the Rites of Eleusis. These rituals involved music and dance as well as words, designed to inspire religious ecstasy.

Crowley edited a publication called the *Equinox*, issued on the Spring and Autumnal Equinoxes of 1909 through 1913, ten volumes in all. The motto "The Method of Science, the Aim of Religion" guided these volumes. Crowley said he used the scientific method to study what were sometimes called spiritual experiences. By this he meant that mystical experiences should be critiqued and experimented with in order to arrive at their underlying religious, psychological, or neurological meaning. Crowley wrote a large part of the content of these volumes, with contributions by a number of other important occultists, magicians, and writers of the times, including Lord Dunsany and William Butler Yeats.

In 1910, Crowley was contacted by Theodore Reuss, leader of a German Masonic group called the Ordo Templi Orientis, often referred to by the initials OTO. They were deeply involved in magic, and Crowley joined them, contributing a great deal to both their struc-

ture and ritual. He eventually becoming the head of the OTO, and reorganized it to conform to his Thelemic principles. He also broke with the Masonic tradition of men-only lodges, and allowed women to join. He wrote the Gnostic Mass for the OTO in 1915; much of the text of that ritual comes from *The Book of the Law*. Crowley became the head of the OTO in 1922 and continued to serve in that capacity until his death.

The main principle of Thelema, "Do what thou wilt shall be the whole of the Law," comes from Crowley's *The Book of the Law*, as does much of the later OTO doctrine. Crowley's idea of *will* is not simply the individual's desires or whims, but the person's greater purpose or destiny, which is what Crowley termed "True Will." The second principle is "Love is the Law, Love Under Will." Both are repeated several times in the Gnostic Mass as well as other writings. By *love*, Crowley referred both to sexual union and the more general union of opposites. Another principle was "Every Man and Every Woman is a Star," emphasizing the importance and uniqueness of each individual.

Crowley founded the Abbey of Thelema in Cefalù, Sicily, in 1920. The Abbey's name is from Rabelais' book *Gargantua*, where the "Abbey of Theleme" is described as a sort of anti-monastery, where the lives of the residents were spent according to their own free will and pleasure rather than in accordance with rules of any sort. The program included daily adorations to the sun, a study of Crowley's writings, the practice of yoga, and daily ritual, which were to be recorded. The object was for students to devote themselves to the Great Work of discovering and manifesting their True Will. However, Mussolini's fascist government found their behavior too extreme and expelled Crowley from the country at the end of April 1923.

Crowley came up with the idea of spelling *magic* with a "k"— *magick*. This alternate spelling was used to differentiate it from other practices, such as stage magic. He defined magick as "the science and art of causing change to occur in conformity with the will." Again, he emphasizes the importance of the Will.

In 1900, Crowley traveled to the United States and Mexico, where he may have first come into contact with psychedelics, possibly peyote or psilocybin mushrooms. He experimented with laudanum, opium, cocaine, hashish, alcohol, ether, mescaline, and heroin, keeping a careful record for magical purposes. While in Paris during the 1920s, Crowley experimented with psychedelic substances, specifically peyote. In October 1930, Crowley dined with Aldous Huxley in Berlin, and rumor has it that he introduced Huxley to peyote on that occasion. Huxley's later use of peyote and mescaline (chronicled in his books *The Doors of Perception* and *Heaven and Hell*) were a major influence on the modern psychedelic movement.

Israel Regardie was Crowley's secretary from 1928 to 1932. In 1934, he joined the Stella Matutina, a successor organization to the Golden Dawn. When the group broke up, Regardie ended up with much of their papers, which he published, so that they would not be lost. The survival of much of the Golden Dawn material can be attributed to Crowley, and later to Regardie, publishing and publicizing their ideas.

In 1938, Crowley began to design a new tarot deck, the Thoth Tarot; Lady Frieda Harris would execute the art for the seventy-eight cards. It was a radical departure from traditional decks. Crowley used new symbolism throughout the deck and renamed some of the major arcana and the court cards. He also wrote a book describing and explaining the deck, *The Book of Thoth*, which was published in 1944. The deck was supposed to be finished in six months, but due to the painstaking nature of the task, Crowley's ill health, and the intervention of World War II, it required five years. The deck was never published in Crowley's lifetime, but today it is considered an original and major symbol system.

By the mid-1930s, Crowley was bankrupt. He survived by writing, and on gifts and loans from friends and associates. He lived the last years of his life in relative obscurity, plagued by ill health. He died of a respiratory infection in a Hastings boarding house on December 1, 1947, at the age of seventy-two. Readings at the cremation service in nearby Brighton included one of his own works, *Hymn to Pan*, and a memorial version of his Gnostic Mass. Local newspapers incorrectly referred to the service as a black mass.

OTO lodges were established in England, the United States, and Germany during Crowley's lifetime, but by 1945, only the Agapé Lodge in Pasadena, California, was still functioning. Following Crowley's death, Karl Germer became the head of the OTO but barely maintained the Order. Germer died in 1962. Grady McMurtry, who had been involved with the OTO for some time, became the new head in the late 1960s and built the OTO into the substantial international magical group that it is today. After McMurtry's death, his successor was chosen by a vote of the higher degree members.

In a poll conducted by the BBC in 2002 to find "the 100 Greatest Britons," Crowley was voted number 73. He is well known to the point of being a cultural icon. For example, his picture is one of the many on the cover of the Beatles album "Sgt. Pepper's Lonely Hearts Club Band." Jimmy Page, the Led Zeppelin guitarist and occultist, bought Crowley's mansion, Boleskine House, near Foyers, Scotland, and owns a large collection of Crowley memorabilia. Crowley influenced other musicians as well.

Crowley's writings have often been criticized for racism, sexism, and anti-Semitism. He was very much a product of his time and upbringing, an upper middle-class Englishman during the era of Queen Victoria. These prejudices have become far less common in the decades since his death, and so it is sometimes worthwhile to try to read beyond his bigotry and find the valuable parts of his writing.

Crowley was the first to talk and write freely about sex and sex magic, not to mention being more openly bisexual than was safe at the time. He had male lovers at the time Oscar Wilde was jailed for such practices. In some respects, Crowley was practicing what Freud was theorizing, rebelling against Victorian sexual repression.

Gerald Gardner, the founder of modern British Traditional Witchcraft, was an initiate of the OTO through Crowley. Gardner was given a charter to start an OTO lodge by Crowley, but there is no evidence he actually formed such a group. Crowley's writings heavily influenced Gardner. Sections of Gardner's rituals are derived from Crowley's Gnostic Mass. This is consistent with Gardner's statements that the rituals he had received were fragmentary, and that he had incorporated other material (without specifying what) to make a coherent system. However, despite rumor, there is no evidence that Crowley wrote the Book of Shadows that Gardner used.

Crowley helped foster many changes: magical groups allowing women to join, even permitting women to be officers and ritual leaders; the practice of sex magic, rejecting Victorian prudery and including the acceptance of homosexuality both as personal preference and for magickal reasons.

His label as The Wickedest Man in the World was mostly an epithet used by newspapers to sell copies. Much of Crowley's notoriety would be far less scandalous today—he had love affairs with other men as well as women, he took drugs, he said outrageous things . . . the sorts of behavior exhibited by many celebrities today.

Many of his books remain in print to this day. Major works include *Magick Without Tears, The Confessions of Aleister Crowley* (his autobiography), *Magick in Theory and Practice, The Book of Thoth,* his book on tarot, the Thoth Tarot deck, and of course, *The Book of the Law,* the seminal work from which many of the others derive.

Crowley was the domino that set into motion much of modern magic, paganism, and the counterculture. From his original rituals to his inventive symbolism, his sexual liberties to his use of drugs, Crowley was indeed one of the premier occultists of the twentieth century.

Tantra & Magic

by Chandra Alexandre

Witches the world over do magic—the mindful altering of consciousness—in order to affect the seen and/or unseen worlds. The ancient practices of Tantra similarly engage in transforming consciousness at will, usually for the sake of enhanced spiritual development. In this article, I offer an introduction to some Tantric practices that can greatly facilitate a Witch's ability to shape reality for the benefit of oneself and one's world.

Tantra is a complete spiritual system of thought and practice from India (one that goes beyond the sexually infused Neo-Tantra of the West). It is a profound and richly complex body of knowledge that offers great potential for psycho-spiritual growth. At its core, Tantra teaches the principles and dynamics of subtle energies, and it does so in a well-developed, pragmatic manner. Energy and consciousness are inextricably linked together in Tantra. Energy, called Shakti (shuhk'-tee), represents the activating female force. Consciousness, called Shiva (shih'-vuh), represents the potentiating male force. Together, they manifest all possibilities.

Tantric practice attempts to work the power of Shakti toward engagement with Shiva for the creation of specific outcomes on the spiritual journey. While, as in witchcraft, these outcomes are dependent upon the individual practitioner (and may be ego-driven or corrupt as much as beneficent), the heart of Tantra is life-affirming. The *sadhaka* (male spiritual seeker) or *sadhika* (female spiritual seeker) begins with a careful examination of her or his motivations. One then sets an intention for the sought-after outcomes to be in alignment with spiritual values and in accordance with the divine will. The practice of Tantra may yield unexpected and positive changes in the practitioner. One may even be surprised to gain *siddhis* (spiritual powers); but it is how one chooses to use these that makes all the difference on the Tantric path. If one is driven by power or vanity, for example, the true benefits will be short-lived.

Ultimately, Tantra is a deeply powerful tradition, with the dance of Shiva and Shakti itself creating magic. Tapping into the co-mingling of energy and consciousness through Tantric practice avails the sadhaka and sadhika of many spiritual tools. For any Witch looking to become proficient in magic, however, grounding and centering are where the work begins. These techniques are the fundamental prerequisites for doing spellwork. Within a Tantric framework, spells are simply the conscious movement of energy from one reality to another. A healing spell, for example, may help direct life-force energy toward a physical wound, or it might help guide emotional energy trapped in the body toward service in the natural world. Similarly, a protection spell may seek to gather the energies of nature around someone, or it may catalyze a person's internal fire for the purpose of deterring inimical spirits. With practice, the Witch gains not only desired outcomes such as health and the ability to help others, but also greater alignment of soul and divine purpose. Starting with these practices, Tantra can aid the Witch throughout all phases of the spiritual journey, from neophyte to adept.

The basics of grounding and centering in Tantra are done through breath and the activation of energy centers in the subtle body. Each energy center is called a chakra (chuh'-kruh). The Sanskrit word *chakra* means "disc" or "wheel," and each energy center resembles exactly that. Because the Tantric practices themselves are based on a belief in the connection of the body with the universe (one is understood to be a perfect reflection of the other), each chakra aligns not only with qualities of the physical, emotional, and psychic bodies, but also with astrological and cosmological realities. Through techniques such as pranayama and nyasa, discussed below, the Witch or spiritual aspirant can therefore become competent in the foundations of all magical work.

Pranayama

Pranayama, sometimes called breath work, activates shakti. *Prana* means "vital energy," and it is carried throughout the body on and with the breath. In this practice, energy is called prana-shakti to acknowledge the energy that is associated with our soul on one level and connected to the larger expanse of universal power and potential on another level. Conscious breathing through pranayama is what enables us to connect to static earth energy—the grounding force of nature. By breathing in an intentional way, one can balance and focus internal energies (centering), as well as gain greater access to the external energies needed to ground. Grounding is the ability to tap into the static force of nature, called tamas guna by Tantrics. Grounding helps stabilize energy flow, both internally and in concert with one's environment. To understand this idea, it is helpful to know that nature in this system is comprised of three fundamental energies or basic qualities, called gunas. They are: sattva guna, rajas guna, and tamas guna. Tamas, the quality of inertia, is prevalent in earth; rajas, the quality of activity, is prevalent in fire; and sattva, the quality of essence, is prevalent in ether.

To begin pranayama, sit comfortably and begin noticing your breath. Feel the breath as it moves within your body. Now, close your eyes and imagine the breath as vital, carrying shakti, the life force. Slowly deepen your breath, filling your lungs from the bottom of your belly to the top of your chest and throat. Your belly should expand like a balloon as it fills with air on your in-breath. When you exhale, flatten your belly completely as though laying it against your spine. Use your diaphragm and abdominal muscles to accomplish this. Your breath should progress in three parts like a wave, moving from the belly, drawing up the prana-shakti to the lungs, and completing the breath at the throat. The same process in reverse completes one cycle of breath.

Start this practice with a seven-minute sitting, then gradually progress to twenty-one minutes. Once proficient with it, do whatever length of time feels right to you. Let each session be meditative, and attempt to focus your mind only on your breathing. Should your mind wander, refocus and return your attention to your breath. You may wish to utilize an internal gaze at your ajna chakra (third eye) to help stabilize the practice. Do this again and again as you need, moving beyond judgment into pure acceptance. Over time, your focus will gain strength and clarity. At the end of your session, notice how you feel. Take stock of what, if anything, seems to be different inside. You may feel greater peacefulness or calm. You may experience the prana-shakti as heat or color. You may even be frustrated with the practice! Whatever your experience, the invitation is always to return.

As you begin to feel the positive effect the practice has on your well-being, you may wish to move to the deeper work of balancing solar and lunar internal channels. All energy in the body, according to Tantrics, moves along three main energy channels. These are the ida (lunar path), pingala (solar path), and sushumna. Sushumna is the main energy channel, a hair-width filament of the subtle body that runs alongside the spinal column and serves to calibrate and integrate all other energies. Begin by placing the thumb of your right hand on your right nostril. Breathe in through your left nostril for a count of four and hold the breath for a count of sixteen. Now, close the left nostril with the ring finger of this same hand and exhale for a count of eight through the right nostril. (Any ratio of 1:4:2 may be used for the practice, so feel free to modify according to your ability and inclination.) Remember that the three-part breath should be continued throughout the exercise. Stay relaxed, gradually deepening and slowing your breath. With this practice, you will cultivate internal balance (harmonizing Shiva and Shakti) as well as increased connection to the gunas—including, of course, earth's grounding energy. Other benefits of pranayama include more restful sleep, increased energy for work and play, a heightened sense of connection to the natural world, greater patience, and a more agile mind.

Nyasa

Once you have gained some degree of confidence with pranayama, you may wish to utilize it to begin the more advanced practice of activating the chakras. The practice of nyasa, meaning placement, is designed to further pranayama by bringing the external energies of the divine directly into the practitioner's body. This is initially done through touch and sound at the gateways of the chakras, awakening both physical and subtle bodies. The specific practice offered here (merely one of many forms of nyasa) accesses the elementals in order to broaden the energetic possibilities for spellwork and spiritual growth.

Again, backed by Tantra's understanding of the profound relationship between universal and individual realities, nyasa utilizes the chakras as the locus for increasing one's awareness of microcosmic/macrocosmic resonance. This awareness gives one greater facility with energy, the *prima materia* (first matter) of spellwork. Because the body contains seven main chakras (although Tantrics often work with many more), we must activate each one during nyasa. Doing so creates a more complete energetic spectrum within which and from which one can work magic.

To begin nyasa, make sure that each chakra has been readied through pranayama. Then, take your right hand and move it into tattva mudra—a hand gesture that welcomes the energy of the elementals—by putting the thumb between the base of the little finger and ring finger (all other fingers should remain outstretched and touching). In Tantra, the thumb represents the transformational power of fire, the ring finger represents earth, and the little finger represents the fluidity of water. Bringing these together creates a specific energetic template that unlocks the hand's own energy and allows nyasa to be effective.

Once you have established tattva mudra, place the center of your palm at the muladhara or root chakra. This energy center is located at the base of the spine, and you will have to tilt slightly to one side when in a seated position to find it. To locate the chakra, feel for energy at the center of your palm as you make several slow passes of your hand over the area. It may feel like heat or you may get a tingly sensation in your hand. Perhaps you will see a shift in light or feel texture as you pass over the chakra. If you experience nothing, just place your hand at your best approximation based on where you understand the energy center to be located.

Once you have the connection established, still your hand. Use light touch, but leave no more than an inch gap between your hand and the chakra. Now, utter the bija mantra LAM (luh'm) to invoke the presence of earth and place it into your body. A bija mantra is a single syllable, a "seed sound," that taps into the vibrational essence of the Divine in whatever form it is being called forth. Repeat the bija mantra as many times as you wish, starting slowly and then building speed. As you raise energy, visualize the chakra opening to receive the gifts of the elemental. Do so until you feel that you have established earth energy and this part of the practice is complete. The full list of chakras and correspondences can be found on the following page.

∽

When you have finished with the activation of all chakras following the same method as was done for the muladhara chakra, take some time to return to your breath. As you then begin spellcasting, you may be amazed at how much energy you have raised. When you finish your spiritual work, remember to ground and center again, returning to a round of pranayama to end. May your magic in this way always blessed be.

Chakras and Correspondences

Bija Mantra	Element or Spiritual Essence	Chakra Name (Sanskrit)	Approximate Location
LAM (luh'm)	Earth	Muladhara	Root chakra; base of spine
VAM (vuh'm)	Water	Svadishthana	Perineum; cervix in women
RAM (ruh'm)	Fire	Manipura	Below bellybutton
YAM (yuh'm)	Air	Anahata	Heart
HAM (huh'm)	Ether	Vishuddha	Throat
OM (Ah-oo-um)	Shiva/Shakti	Ajna	Third-eye
Silence (breath)	Pure consciousness	Sahasrara	Crown of the head

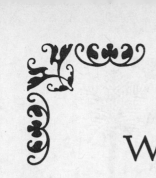
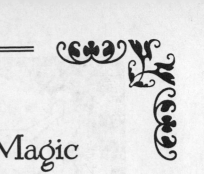

Water Magic

Ancient Egyptian Water Deities

by Denise Dumars

When working with elemental magic, the first patrons of the elements that come to mind for water are not usually Egyptian. However, there are several important Egyptian water deities that should not be excluded from elemental workings, nor from observances of Egyptian magical practices wherein water is a main theme.

Without the Nile River, life in Egypt would be impossible. All of the agriculture, trade, and most of the activity in Egypt takes place on and around the Nile River. So it is not surprising that two of its major deities, Osiris and Isis, both have strong connections to the Nile.

Usually portrayed as a mummy wearing a pharoah's crown, Osiris often has black skin. The color of his skin represents the rich, black silt that overflows the banks of the Nile every year during the inundation. It was the inundation of the Nile that fertilized the land, allowing agriculture to take place in Egypt, which was otherwise a barren desert. Osiris, in this way, symbolized the fertile soil itself, and therefore the basis for growing the food of Egypt. "Eat of my body," was said by Osiris, speaking of the food that was grown in the black silt.

Osiris is also portrayed as having green skin. The color "Nile green" in our palette comes from the shade of green that the waters of the Nile often present. Osiris' Nile-green skin was symbolic of the vegetation of the Nile and of the crops that were grown on and around its banks. Osiris is similar to other vegetation gods who are born, grow to adulthood, and then are sacrificed in order to make way for the new god—a cycle that is symbolic of the planting, growing, and harvesting of crops. Some in ancient Egypt believed that Osiris actually was the Nile River. Ancient Egyptian blessings included sayings such as "May Osiris bless you with cool water" and "May Isis bestow upon you the holy waters of Osiris, the Nile."

Isis, consort and sister of Osiris and mother of his son Horus, is often portrayed as a woman with a throne on her head or with the solar disc and cow horns. It may come as a surprise to some that she is also a water deity. The Isis Navigium, also known the Pliophasia, was a very important festival in the Greco-Roman era of the worship of Isis. The festival was a complex ceremony held during the Spring Equinox, when trading vessels began their yearly voyages. As part of the ceremony, prayers were made to Isis for prosperity and Isis' blessings were bestowed on the ships as they were about to sail. Accompanying this festival would be initiations to the goddess Isis as well. This tradition is also observed today by modern Isians at the seashore (whether literally or figuratively), where they launch symbolic boats asking for Isis' blessings.

When we think of most Egyptian deities, including Isis, we often think of their solar attributes. Yet Isis figures in many tales that revolve around water. After Isis' other brother Set slew her brother/husband Osiris and came after her, Isis hid from him in the marshy swamp lands around the Nile Delta. When Horus was born, she hid there as well in order to keep Set or anyone else from harming the baby. Similarly, when Set became enraged that his wife Nephthys had given birth to Anubis, a child who may not have been his, Isis saved the child and hid him in the bulrushes of the marshes, an earlier story similar to that of Moses.

While Osiris and Isis have many attributes outside of those of water, there are less famous Egyptian deities that have water as their main element. The most important one is probably Hapi. Hapi is depicted as a man with a big "beer" belly and pendulous breasts. The Egyptians were one of the first peoples of the ancient world to brew beer, so perhaps his belly is not so surprising! Hapi's breasts were symbols of fertility and the abundance of the Nile. His main purpose was to be a god of all of the abundance that came from the Nile, whether animal, plant, or goods from trading vessels. I consider Hapi to be the "party god," and perhaps the ancient Egyptians did as well!

Tefnut is a very ancient Egyptian deity who is "goddess of the moisture in the air." She is shown as a woman with a lioness's head or sometimes the head of a cobra. Her relationship to water is water in suspension in the air, whether as clouds, fog, mist, or just humidity. Her consort Shu is an earth deity, and the two of them are seen as creators of life through air, earth, and water.

There are many animals associated with the Nile, and some of the Egyptian gods were represented as aquatic animals. Taueret, the hippopotamus goddess, is one of the most common, and we are most familiar with her representation in blue faience statuettes of hippos. Perhaps because hippos have such large bellies, Taueret—who could be portrayed as either a woman with a hippo's head or as a hippopotamus itself—is the patron of pregnant women. She was both a protector of pregnant women, and also a goddess to petition if a woman wished to become pregnant. Hippopotami are, however, one of the most dangerous and feared aquatic mammals. Perhaps this is why in some myths, Taueret is believed to be one of powerful Set's mistresses.

The crocodile god, Sobek, is another Nile deity. Because crocodiles were greatly feared by the Egyptians, praying to him was believed to protect a person from crocodiles. Sobek, when portrayed as a ferocious crocodile, was taken as a patron of the army. Sometimes crocodiles were even kept in pools near temples to Sobek, where they were fed fresh meat and were even tamed to an extent. Many mummified crocodiles have been found in Egyptian tombs. Liked Taueret, Sobek sometimes has a dark side in which he is seen as a version of Set.

Although Set is the god of the red desert in Egyptian mythology, in the Greco-Roman worship of the Egyptian deities, Set was morphed into Typhon, instigator of "typhoons" and other storms at sea. Perhaps because the Greeks could not relate to a deity who was seen as the killing sun of the desert that the Egyptians feared (as opposed to the life-giving sun they experienced), his attributes were transferred to the natural phenomena that the Greeks feared: storms at sea. So the god the Egyptians called the "dry god," who was portrayed as a man with the head of a strange composite animal, was portrayed in Greek art as a sea monster! This transformation is curious, because one of Set's few positive portrayals is as the boatman who protects Ra's barque from his enemy Apep, the dreaded water monster of the Nile.

Another major deity related to the waters of the Nile, perhaps surprisingly, is Thoth. In magic, Thoth is usually seen as symbolic of the element of the air, because most of his attributes deal with the intellect and he is shown as a man with a bird's head. However, unlike most other Egyptian deities, Thoth is the god of the moon. The moon is always considered a strong influence on water—the tides of the seas and the tides within the human body and psyche. The ibis is an aquatic bird, closely related to herons, cranes, egrets, and other common water birds, and this is the bird that Thoth's head is based upon in artistic portrayals. Thoth is an extremely powerful and important deity, the patron of writers, doctors, and nearly all of the intellectual arts and sciences.

So while Thoth may have his "head in the clouds" like any good creative artist or inventor, his feet are firmly planted in the mud of the Nile, from whence creativity symbolically flows.

Many of the sacred Egyptian plants were water plants. The lotus, in particular, lives on the Nile and is probably the most widely depicted plant in sacred Egyptian art. Papyrus, a reed that was used to make paper, is sacred to deities of writing, such as Thoth and Seshat, and is also frequently depicted in Egyptian art. Lilies of the Nile are common flowers often seen in art on head-dresses or as decorations in portrayals of festivals.

In magic, when thinking of the Egyptian deities, the intent of a spell, ritual, or working must be considered. If Sobek relates to protection, Tefnut to air moisture, Osiris to the fertility of the land, Isis to the abundance of trade upon the sea, Hapi to commerce upon the Nile and goods from other ports, Taueret to fertility and pregnancy, and Thoth to creativity and new ideas (including inventions and medical advances), one can easily see that the element of water is well served by the Egyptian deities.

Among modern Isians or members of other neo-Egyptian traditions, Egyptian water deities have many purposes. For example, many pregnant women or women facing the challenges of infertility pray to Taueret. Men and women in the military ask for Sobek as their protector. Isian Priestess Ellen Cannon Reed, who died in 2003, tells of a time when she and other Witches in the dry foothills of Southern California prayed to Tefnut for the end of the fire season's wildfires. Shortly thereafter, the fires were contained, and a fire department spokesman mentioned the increase in "the moisture in the air" as an influence on the containment of the fires.

Modern Isians still enjoy the Navigium, in which Isis Pelagia (Isis of the Sea) is honored and petitions are sent by water at or around the Vernal Equinox. Indeed, among some of the Isian groups in Southern California, it is one of the major events of the year. Prayers to Osiris can accompany the planting of seeds and thanks to him can be given at harvest time. When boating, a prayer of protection from Set in the form of Typhon is certainly worth reciting. And those who are of a creative or inventive nature can pray for the intellectual fertility bestowed by Thoth and his ibises. Calling upon Egyptian deities when practicing elemental water magic is, therefore, highly recommended.

For Further Study

Harris, Eleanor L. *Ancient Egyptian Divination and Magic.* York Beach, ME: Weiser, 1998.

Reed, Ellen Cannon. *Circle of Isis: Ancient Eyptian Magick for Modern Witches.* Franklin Lakes, NJ: New Page, 2002.

Regula, deTraci. *The Mysteries of Isis: Her Worship & Magick.* St. Paul, MN: Llewellyn, 1995.

Witt, R. E. *Isis in the Ancient World.* Baltimore: Johns Hopkins UP,1974.

Magic and Subjectivity

by Elizabeth Barrette

*What was once called the objective world is a sort of Rorschach
inkblot, into which each culture, each system of science and
religion, each type of personality, reads a meaning only remotely
derived from the shape and color of the blot itself.*
—Lewis Mumford, *The Conduct of Life*

We live in a society that admires objectivity and mis-
trusts subjectivity. Yet objectivity, the perspective of
fact independent of opinion, proves elusive. Subjectivity
is the way we experience life—through the lens of our
own worldview and the beautiful clamor of our physical
and metaphysical senses, the interpretation our minds give
to the unorganized input that enters them. We constantly
create subjectivity out of objectivity so we can make sense
of things.

Magic has both objective and subjective aspects. Due
to magic's subtlety, people often doubt its existence. They
seek objective descriptions, perceptions, and processes of
magic. Yet magic most often reveals itself in subjective ways,
which can differ from one person to another. Instead of
dismissing magic as nonsense, or dismissing logic as irrel-
evant to magic, let's explore why magic refracts so oddly
across our perceptions, and how we can work with that
tendency instead of against it.

Subjectivity vs. Objectivity

Subjectivity and objectivity often coexist. To explore their
interactions, consider how they apply to the mundane
concept of temperature.

Temperature is both subjective and objective. Each person can perceive temperature, but not everyone responds
to it the same. One person in a room may feel too hot,

another comfortable, and a third too cold. So although the room's atmosphere has an objective temperature, that can be measured by a thermometer. Instead human senses create a subjective impression of temperature, measured not by degrees but by personal comfort (or lack thereof). People may argue about whether the room is too hot or too cold and what to do about it (open windows, put on a sweater, etc.).

To make things even more puzzling, try this exercise in relative perception. Fill one bowl with hot water (like a hot tub, not boiling hot), one with ice water, and one with tepid water. Put your left hand in the hot water and your right hand in the cold water, and wait about two minutes. Then put both hands in the tepid water. To your left hand, the tepid water will feel cold, because it is much cooler than the hot water; but to your right hand, the tepid water will feel hot, because it is much warmer than the ice water. The tepid water is still tepid; it has an objective temperature that could be measured in degrees, and even a subjective interpretation of "tepid" that under normal circumstances you would be able to feel. But right now, one hand insists that the water is cold while the other insists that it is hot. Your single brain is getting contradictory messages from your two different hands! Yet your mind recalls that the water in that bowl has an objectively tepid temperature.

All of the interpretations are equally valid; the truth of one does not reduce the truth of another. They are just true in different ways and situations.

In many regards, magic is the same way, except we don't have a thermometer. We don't yet have precise tools for measuring magical phenomena in consistent units to give an objective reading. We only have our subtle senses, which give subjective impressions that may vary from person to person. Some instruments can detect certain mystical phenomena where these spill over into the material realm, as with Kirlian photography capturing the aura's electromagnetic field. But that doesn't give us a precise measurement of the aura's mystical power in objective units, just a rough idea of where it is in relation to a plant or animal.

Sometimes people argue that magic is not "real," or that it cannot have objective aspects, just because we currently lack tools to measure it objectively and must rely on subjective interpretations. But it's like that room we discussed earlier: the fact that one person feels too hot and another too cold doesn't mean the room has no objective temperature, just that it isn't directly perceptible without a thermometer. Even with a thermometer, people may argue over whether 69 degrees Fahrenheit is "too hot" or "too cold" instead! Conversely the thermometer reading is unlikely to make anyone *feel* warmer or cooler.

So too, people may argue over different interpretations of the magical energy of a room. A high priestess who frequently handles large amounts of power may feel comfortable and refreshed by a level of energy that makes other people feel overloaded. The energy is what it is—even though we can't currently measure it precisely—but different people may interpret it in different ways. Furthermore, not everyone can perceive or work with every type of energy. To someone who can sense the available energy, the room may seem full; to someone attuned to some other type of energy, the room may seem empty. All of those factors affect what each individual could accomplish in that room, but the room and its contents remain the same.

The impression of a single person is pretty far toward the subjective end of the spectrum. But the subjective impressions of a group of people who agree can push the interpretation closer to the objective end of the spectrum. A room that everyone agrees is cold will almost certainly have a lower temperature than a room that everyone agrees is hot, even if there's no thermometer to check. "Haunted" buildings get a reputation as such because multiple people repeatedly experience weird effects there. Temples, henges, and other monuments may be placed at an energy vortex where many people have experienced strong positive forces. Subjective impressions leading toward consensus can produce useful and fairly consistent interpretations.

The world has both objective and subjective interpretations. Some are easier to obtain than others; some are more useful than others. All may be reassessed if we gain new tools that give us greater precision or if the context changes. As our grasp of magical theory grows, and technology evolves, we may discover how to build devices that objectively measure magical forces, much as our ancestors discovered how to build thermometers.

Binocular Vision and Magical Senses

Our perceptions, magical and mundane, are *influenced* by reality but they are not wholly *determined* by reality. Subjective impressions often outweigh objective information, even when we recognize both together. By changing the context—how we move our bodies or our minds—we may change what we perceive and how we interpret it. Consider this example by Suzette Haden Elgin in *Ozarque's Journal*, "Religious Language: Different Kinds of Truth," May 12, 2007, reprinted here with permission:

Suppose I cross my middle finger over my index finger and set my crossed fingertips down on the surface of a single marble. What I feel when I do that will be two separate marbles, each one fully realized and perceived, each one quite individual in its hardness and smoothness and roundness and all its other attributes. Both of those marbles will be absolutely real to me, and their realness will be supported by my sensory systems; I will be able to store my perceptions of those two marbles in my longterm memory, and I will be able to access those perceptions later if I choose to.

Now, I know the following things to be true:

1. If I look directly at the two marbles I feel with my fingertips, I will not see the second marble.

2. If someone else looks at the two marbles I feel with my fingertips, that person will not see the second marble.

3. It would be possible for any competent neurologist/neurolinguist/neurotheologian to explain to me the precise neurophysiological/neuropsychological mechanism(s) by which my brain and mind have created that second marble that no one else but me is able to perceive. That is: It can be scientifically demonstrated that the second marble isn't "real," and the mechanism(s) by which it appears to me to be real can be scientifically explained.

Well. Not one of those three facts makes the second marble any less vividly real to me, or makes it any less truly there in my universe. It is as real to me as the ground I feel beneath my feet and the tongue I feel inside my mouth. And the "facts" don't change that in even the smallest particular.

Try this exercise yourself. It demonstrates a common phenomenon based on the body's knowledge of where its parts belong. For most people changing the orientation of the fingers creates a tactile illusion. By experiencing the mundane, physical effect we can then apply a similar concept to mental and magical motions, which can explain certain differences in observations.

We don't always know the exact configuration of mind and magic. Suppose that two people examine an area, one reporting a single energy source while another reports two energy sources. Does the area contain one or two? It's possible that the first person has simply missed a source. It's

also possible that the second person has (perhaps unknow-ingly) done the magical equivalent of crossing their fin-gers, so that a single source appears—quite concretely—to be two separate sources.

Learning to shift the configuration of mind and magi-cal senses allows you to examine things in different ways. Sometimes that can give you more total information than examining something from a single perspective. For exam-ple, when I cross my fingers and touch a marble, I don't get an illusion of two marbles, but I do gain a much clearer perception of touching a *sphere*. Knowing that, if I'm unsure of the shape of an energy field I've touched, I can visualize crossing my fingers and touching it at two points. That gives me a clearer impression of a flat or curved sur-face. I can also combine unrelated magical senses the same way I combine mundane ones of touch and sight. Do some exploring and find out what effects you can discover.

There is value in approaching magic with precisely that type of composite observation. It's like binocular vision, but with more than eyesight. Magic is too vast and complex for us to comprehend fully, so all our observations of it are incomplete, like the blind men and the elephant. A group of blind men each touch an elephant in a different area (a leg, tusk, tail), then try to convince the rest that "elephant" is only what they experienced—round, pointed, smooth, rough, hairy, etc. Obviously, their ideas didn't match up! If the blind men had compiled their data instead of arguing over what an elephant was "really" like, however, they would've been able to assemble a pretty good model of the elephant. So by comparing different people's perceptions of magic instead of arguing over its "true nature," it is similarly possible to assemble a more thorough (though necessarily incomplete) concept of magic.

Handling Perceptions of Magic

Now that we have an idea of how objectivity and subjectivity interact, and how magical perceptions can vary, let's look at some ways of applying that knowledge to magical practice.

When someone expresses doubt about the validity of magic due to subjective variations in people's perception of it, use metaphors and exercises to explain how ordinary things behave similarly. This is most useful for helping new students of magic get past their initial skepticism to a more open-minded perspective that makes it possible for them to learn what they seek.

When an argument starts because people's perceptions of magic differ, remind them that magic has both subjective and objective aspects. It is possible for seemingly contradictory perceptions to be equally valid. Rather than arguing over which is "right," consider whether and how they are relevant to what you're doing.

Respect the subjective and seek the objective; each can lead to the other. When people respect each other's opinions, they share more, which can illuminate collective truths. The more people you have observing something, the more complete a picture of it you can assemble.

Practice using and interpreting your magical senses. You may do this alone or with a coven. Over time, patterns emerge. Perhaps you always sense energy before anyone else does: your range may be longer or your sensitivity greater. An intermittent tendency to interpret energy as negative may turn out to depend on how recently you've watched a horror movie.

Explore diverse sets of symbols. Your brain constantly interprets data based on established expectations, which create certain types of illusions that "fool the eye." Similarly, magical senses often use symbols to relay information. One person may perceive healing energy as green, while another person perceives it as white. Reading different lists of color correspondences can give you new ideas about what you're perceiving, especially if you see energy in a color that you don't recognize from your prior experience. What the heck is magenta energy? If you can find it listed somewhere, you can compare that answer to what you perceived and see if it makes sense. Dream dictionaries, herbals, magical writing systems, and other resources enrich your options.

Design rituals and spells with magical perceptions in mind. If you know that your covenmates focus on visual energy, make patterns with it; if they're more tactile, pass around objects to hold. Encourage and listen to feedback: the more you learn about people's perceptions of magic, the better you can craft activities that appeal to them. They also help improve your control, perhaps spotting thin spots in the energy flow the same way others notice you've left a button undone while you're clueless!

Subjectivity and objectivity are two sides of the same coin, like magical and mundane reality. As your understanding of them grows, so does your ability to use them to your advantage. And when you're manipulating the perception of reality itself, *that's* magic!

For Further Study

Belanger, Michelle. *The Psychic Energy Codex: A Manual for Developing Your Subtle Senses*. San Francisco, CA: Weiser Books, 2007.
   Discussion and instructions for magical perceptions.

Bonewits, Isaac. *Real Magic* (revised edition). San Francisco, CA: Red Wheel, 2001.
   Theory and philosophy on how magic works and how we perceive and manipulate it.

Daston, Lorraine, and Peter Galison. *Objectivity*. New York: Zone Books, 2007.
   History of scientific objectivity and the evolution of how we perceive and understand the world around us.

Hawkins, David R. *I: Reality and Subjectivity*. West Sedona, AZ: Veritas Publishing, 2003.
   A sophisticated examination of human consciousness and ego, and how they relate to outside reality.

Penczak, Christopher. *The Inner Temple of Witchcraft: Magick, Meditation, and Psychic Development*. St. Paul, MN: Llewellyn Publications, 2002.
   Philosophy and practices of magic.

Internet

Bradley, Cheryl Lynne. "Synaesthesia: The Crossing of the Senses." Real Magick: The Occult Library. www.realmagick.com/articles/10/2210.html
   A discussion of subjective mixing of objective sensory input.

de Sousa, Ronald. "Twelve Varieties of Subjectivity:

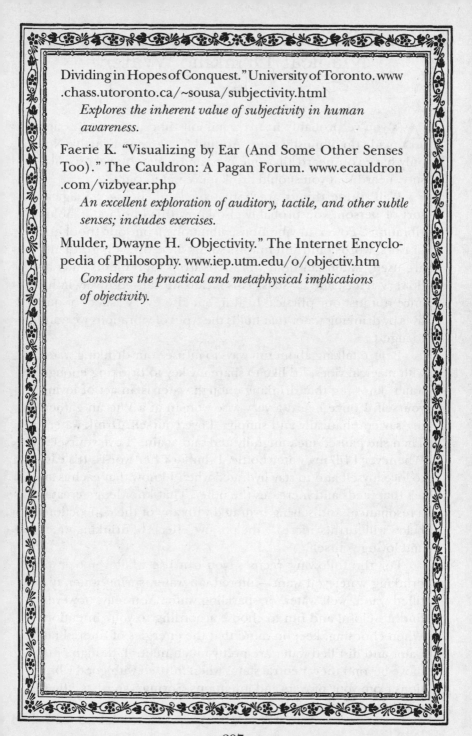

Dividing in Hopes of Conquest." University of Toronto. www
.chass.utoronto.ca/~sousa/subjectivity.html
*Explores the inherent value of subjectivity in human
awareness.*

Faerie K. "Visualizing by Ear (And Some Other Senses
Too)." The Cauldron: A Pagan Forum. www.ecauldron
.com/vizbyear.php
*An excellent exploration of auditory, tactile, and other subtle
senses; includes exercises.*

Mulder, Dwayne H. "Objectivity." The Internet Encyclopedia of Philosophy. www.iep.utm.edu/o/objectiv.htm
*Considers the practical and metaphysical implications
of objectivity.*

Magical Drinking Water

by Tess Whitehurst

As you've probably heard a million times, our bodies are made up of mostly water. Around 60 percent, actually. Not only have you heard that one over and over, you've also, I'm sure, heard that you should drink more water, right?

Well, these things are both true. And, being a magical sort of person, you probably also know this one: water holds vibrations. Powerful vibrations, vibrations from our thoughts, prayers, words, and intentions. And, when other ingredients are used, water can hold vibrations from ingredients such as flowers, fruits, and crystals. This means we can positively influence not just our physical health, but also every aspect of our lives by drinking water that holds the types of vibrations we want to ingest.

Before talking about fun ways to infuse your drinking water with magical vibes, I'd like to share my key to drinking enough water: knowing that drinking enough water is an act of loving yourself. I once heard a very wise woman at a Wiccan gathering say emphatically and simply: "Love yourself. Drink water." Then she paused meaningfully and said again, "Love yourself." Whenever I fill my water bottle, I think of her words. It's easy to love myself and to stay hydrated when I know that each is an act that feeds and increases the other. That knowledge creates a resonance. And staying hydrated with any of the concoctions below will further increase the positive effects of drinking water and loving yourself.

For the following recipes, you can use whatever type of drinking water you want—filtered tap water, spring water, distilled water, well water, or sparkling water. You may, however, find it helpful and fun to choose according to your intention. When choosing, keep in mind that the energies of filtered tap water and distilled water are pretty much neutral, though both move beyond their neutral status when infused with good vibrations from your prayers and intentions. Spring water has a flowing, buoyant, cheerful energy; well water has more of a deep, still, and centered energy; and sparkling water has an uplifting, giddy energy.

Many of these recipes contain one or more flower or gem essences. If you haven't heard of these before, they are the pure vibration of a blossom or crystal in water, preserved with brandy or glycerin. You can read about how to make flower and gem essences yourself, find them at some health food and metaphysical stores, or purchase them from numerous sources online.

Oh, one more note: I also find it easier to drink more water when I have an attractive water bottle or glass that I adore.

OK, on with the potions!

All-Purpose Drinking Water

I drink this water almost every day. It's perfect for any time, and you can even make it in a restaurant without anyone noticing. The only ingredient is water. It is inspired by the healing water at Lourdes, France, which is believed to be blessed and empowered by Mother Mary.

Hold the water in both hands and say, silently or aloud:

Mother Mary, Queen of the Angels, please infuse this water with vibrations of healing and love.

Visualize thousands of angels surrounding the water and filling it with very bright white light.

Drinking Water for Clarity and Focus

    One organic lemon
    Rose water
    Fluorite essence
    White quartz essence

Into your water, put one or more slices of lemon and a tiny bit of rose water to taste. Hold the water in both hands and say something like:

This water is now infused with the bright light of clarity.
This water is now infused with the bright light of focus.

Visualize the water filled with the white, clear light of a sunrise. Put three drops of fluorite essence and two drops of white quartz essence into the water. Drink generously and repeat as desired.

Drinking Water to Open the Heart

Opening your heart wakes you up to all the things that are wonderful about life, such as self-love, compassion, deep connections with others, appreciation of beauty, sharing and expressing your emotions, and romantic love. This is a great one to drink if you are feeling closed-off, untrusting, or emotionally numb. Like the rest of the water potions, you can make this water frequently and drink as much as you like.

> Rose water
> Holly essence
> Emerald essence
> Optional: a pink or green bottle

Put rose water in the water to taste. Hold the water in both hands and say:

I now call on the pure light of love.
Please enter this water and infuse it with your powerful,
heart-opening vibrations.

See the water swirling and sparkling with pink and/or green energy. Put in two drops each of holly and emerald essences.

Drinking Water to Soothe the Mind and Uplift the Spirit

We all have days when our minds and spirits need a little soothing. This water is great for moving you into a happier and clearer vibration when you feel stressed, heavy, or preoccupied.

> Organic crushed mint leaves
> Rose quartz essence
> White chestnut essence

Add mint leaves to taste. Hold the water in both hands and say:

This water is filled with fresh and peaceful vibrations.

Visualize the water filled with the clear, soothing energy of a waterfall deep in the mountains. Put in two drops each of rose quartz and white chestnut essences.

Drinking Water for Confidence and Courage

Going on a job interview? Meeting the new partner's parents? Bungee jumping? This water is for you!

> Organic orange slices

Hematite essence
Rock rose essence

Add one or more slices of orange to the water to taste. Hold the water in both hands and say:

> *Archangel Michael, I call on you.*
> *Please infuse this water with powerful vibrations of courage,*
> *confidence, and calm.*

Visualize the water bottle nestled within the center of a trunk of an ancient living tree, possibly a sequoia. See the roots of the tree going deep into the ground and the top of the tree reaching up into the sunlight. Know that the water now holds a very strong and centered energy. Put in two drops each of hematite and rock rose essences.

Drinking Water to Know Your Own Beauty

Seeing your own beauty allows other people the luxury of seeing your beauty, too. When consumed regularly, this water has the added benefit of clearing and beautifying your skin.

Organic cucumber slices
Crab apple essence
Fluorite essence

Put one or more cucumber slices in the water to taste. Hold the water in both hands and say:

> *Archangel Jophiel, I ask that you infuse this water with the light of*
> *inner recognition. I now choose to see and know my own beauty in*
> *all ways, and I generously share my beauty with the world.*

See the water filled with sparkly, lavender light. Put in two drops each of crab apple and fluorite essences.

Drinking Water for Pleasant Dreams and Restful Sleep

Blueberry juice or juice blend
White chestnut essence
Amethyst essence

Put a splash of blueberry juice in the water to taste. Hold the water in both hands and say:

> *Mother Mary, please infuse this water with vibrations of deep sleep*
> *and blissful dreams.*

Visualize powerful indigo and/or violet light filling the bottle. Put in two drops each of white chestnut and amethyst essences. This potion is most effective when consumed on a regular basis, during both day and night.

Drinking Water for Effervescent Energy

Drinking this water regularly will help restore excitement and joy. It is very highly charged.

    Slices of organic ruby red grapefruit
    Hornbeam essence
    Apophyllite essence

Put one or more slices of grapefruit in the water to taste. Hold the water in both hands and say:

> *Ten thousand angels and spirit of Hummingbird,*
> *Please infuse this water with vibrations of effervescent energy.*

Visualize and feel the water being charged with very bright light and very quick, humming vibrations, like the wings of a hummingbird. Put in two drops each of hornbeam and apophyllite essences.

Drinking Water to Aid Physical Healing

This water helps strengthen the natural healing powers of your body, mind, and spirit. Make this for yourself or for someone else, or have someone make it for you if you don't feel up to it.

Aloe juice
White quartz essence
Gardenia essence

Put a splash of aloe juice in the water to taste. Hold the bottle in both hands and say:

Archangel Raphael, please infuse this water with powerful vibrations of wholeness and health.

Visualize very bright, vibrant green light filling the bottle. Put in three drops of white quartz essence and two of gardenia essence. Drink often and generously during the healing process.

Drinking Water to Aid Creativity

Moonstone essence
Iris essence

Hold the water in both hands and say:

Great Goddess, please fill this water with a rainbow of pure creativity.

Visualize a very bright, sparkly, rainbow-colored light filling the water and swirling around in it. Put in two drops each of moonstone and iris essences.

Drinking Water for Abundance

Slices of organic orange
Gold essence

Put one or more slices of orange in the water to taste. Hold the water in both hands and say something like:

This water is filled with the golden, magnetic light of abundance.

Visualize sparkly golden light filling the bottle. Put in two drops of gold essence.

The Rites of Huna

by Estha McNevin

When I first heard of Huna, a wave of excitement washed over me. The mere thought of a preserved polytheistic tradition from Polynesia made me feel nothing less than giddy. It was as if the ancient myths of complex Neolithic civilizations were somehow validated by the potential of such an enduring shamanic tradition. I thought that Huna must be the shamanic echo of the lost Lumerian Tribe civilization and I was filled with excitement to explore this possible link. Like most overzealous seekers, however, my studies began and ended in the sad tale of misrepresentation and the well-woven fabrications of Max Freedom Long (1890–1971).

Huna History

From the distortion of the Hawaiian language to the adaptation of various New Age and Spiritualists techniques, Max Freedom Long dedicated his life to the creation of an eclectic neoshamanic tradition. He chose the word *Huna*, meaning "shadow" or "hidden path," to encapsulate his expression of Hawaiian shamanism. This and many of the other terms used in the tradition were taken from Lorrin Andrews' 1865 *A Dictionary of the Hawaiian Language*, a poorly assembled collection of various (oftentimes misrepresented) terms and dialects of the Polynesian tribes. The dictionary had been compiled by early European merchants and explorers; it was drawn up from their experiences with the native populations of the greater Polynesian islands, which made little distinction between the various tribes in the huge geographic region.

As a result of this misguided dictionary, many of the terms and rituals that Long used to define his system of Huna are not founded in the traditional language or necessarily representative of the shamanic practices of the Polynesian people. Long's love of Hawaiian culture was sparked in 1917 when he moved there to teach elementary school after graduating from UCLA. His intrigue with the indigenous peoples' use of magick, coupled with the profound levels of superstition he observed, piqued his interest in Hawaiian shamanism and led him to seek out the principles of the ancient culture.

Long published many texts on spirit and soul work, and he was heavily influenced by the New Age and theosophical movements in Europe. Many of these techniques were fused with native Hawaiian ideology or molded to fit within Long's structure for Huna. His esoteric life was full of gray areas and fishy information sources. The truth is that much of what is attributed to the Huna practice is New Age adaptation. Some even view Huna as a bastardization of native Polynesian shamanism. This conflict of origin casts a heavy cloud of disillusionment over those who seek to follow Huna.

There is much controversy surrounding the groups Long helped form during his life, such as the Huna Research Associates and the Huna Church. While many of the techniques he used are shamanic in nature, they remain modern in origin and leave many seekers torn between their desire to follow an ancient shamanic tradition and the very real benefits that many Huna practitioners find in Long's techniques.

Activities like cord-cutting, or Ho'oponopono Aka, involve letting go of the ties that bind us energetically to other people or

events and working toward a genuine state of forgiveness as a living vow of self-healing and awareness. Ha, or breath, exercises are also utilized in meditation, as in other traditions like Yoga. Many Huna practitioners use the rhythm of the breath as a focal point for the living breath of the cosmos, which is viewed within Huna as being shared by all living beings in unison. These widespread, eclectic principles of synchronicity, interconnectedness, and active mystical focus have provided a foundation of Huna based on the three layers of the self and the seven principles of life.

Below are tables of the separate levels of self and the seven principles of Huna. The Kanaloa is the symbolic representation of the physical body, which contains these aspects of the self and as such, represents their total balance and integration. These were all formulated by Max Freedom Long and show clear signs of eclectic and New Age influence that in no way mirror the Hawaiian shamanic rituals or the use of the animistic and transformative guides within that tradition. Whatever its source, this information has become a trusted framework for much of the work that is done within Huna. I highly encourage anyone interested in Huna to meditate on the varying systems of New Age thought and to include Huna among them, rather than to see it as a perfectly preserved native Hawaiian shamanic tradition.

As with all knowledge, the proof lies in the results of practice and many followers of Long continue to see results with Huna to this day, despite the system's obscure origins. There can be little doubt that Max Freedom Long was inspired by the potential of New Age ideas to invigorate the old shamanic traditions.

Many of the genuine tribal practices preserved through Huna and oral traditions are not eagerly shared with outsiders. Until the American Indian Religious Freedom Act was passed in 1978, many oral traditions were outlawed, including Huna. The traditional shamanic techniques and the subtle forces of nature are seen as separate entities, generating countless gods and goddesses. Authentic Huna poses a real difficulty to any outside seeker who attempts to practice the spirituality.

In some ways, the distortions of Huna's origins force seekers to base their practice on their own results rather than a storied history. Even native Hawaiians are of varying opinions when it comes to Huna. Many practice and teach Huna while others

306

outright condemn its principles and the adoption of the Hawaiian language for New Age use. Whatever the case, Huna has had a profoundly shamanic effect on the modern healing community and continues to incite debate over the creation of new systems of esoteric study. Huna is sure to continue evolving, just as it has since Max Freedom Long's time.

Ocean Bottle

Mana, the central divine force of life, is seen as electric in nature. The magnetic qualities of Mana cause this life force to move and flow seamlessly through time and space; this force is best symbolized by the element of water. When Mana is drawn together or pooled into something or someone with a specific regenerative intent, the potency of the current of energy becomes amplified.

Mana is the vital essence of everything, so it cannot be contained. Instead it must be stirred up or activated within a predetermined and well-defined space and then allowed to dissipate, carrying our prayers or intent along with it. The blessing for the following Ocean Bottle is meant to pool all the Mana of the ocean, which lies dormant in each water molecule and is invoked here and given its own element of rule. Mana is generated in the bottle when it is gently shaken during ritual or meditation.

Living in Montana has always made me crave the waters of life. As a child, there was no coaxing me out of a body of water once I had gotten in; as an adult, I find that the moving and vibrant energy of water cures all that ails me. In every way it has become a necessary rejuvenating force in my life. The spell for this bottle is eclectic and arose from my travels in England. It is based on the common Witches' bottle. It was originally used to carry back the essence of the Scottish Coast, a shoreline with more power and will than any I have ever experienced. It is a versatile spell that can be tailored to any body of water or scrap of ground, but as listed below, it is fittingly suited to the energies of the Pacific and to the ancient Polynesian civilization.

Once the Ocean Bottle is capped, it should not be reopened for any reason. The necessary elements of creation will remain vibrant and active within the bottle until it is carefully broken within a cotton bag or cheesecloth and its remains are given a respectful burial (made complete with earnest offerings of release,

The Three-Fold Aspects of the Self

Actual Hawaiian Meaning	Level of Self	Aspect	Role	Deity
Family or personal gods that are deified ancestors or clan heroes	Aumakua Higher Self	The Super Conscious which connects the higher realms, the perfection of the gods within each individual	All-knowing and perceptive part of our being that comprehends the simplicity and the interconnectedness of everything.	Kane: Creator god of the sky and of lightning and thunder. One of the original creators of the universe.
Soul, Spirit or Ghost	Uhane Conscious Mind	The Active Mind which invokes our choices and reacts to stimulus based on our free will	The judgmental aspect of the self that makes decisions based on logic and objective rationale.	Lono: God of fertility and rain. He is believed to descend the rainbows to bless the earth with the fertility and replenishment of the heavens.
Spirits of the Dead	Unihipili Subconscious Mind	The Base or Low Self which responds to symbolism and experiences reality	Stores and represses memories while determining reality based on sensory perceptions. Also rules automatic body function and raw instincts.	Ku: God of war and conflict, to whom the sick or dying were sacrificed to appease the gods.

Seven Principles of Huna

Principles	Meaning	Color	Animal
Ike	The world is what you think it is. When we change our thoughts, we change our perceptions of the things we choose to experience and therefore we affect our reality. Thoughts are bound to the inevitable nature of the manifest.	White	Dolphin/ sea mammal
Kala	There is no limit. Everything is possible. We are only limited by our ideas of restriction and inability. Anything is possible if one can figure out how to do it. Our connection to and quest for this knowledge defines our connectedness with everything in the universe.	Red	Birds
Makia	Energy flows where attention goes. Our physical, emotional, and mental focus can act as a channel for our intentions. This link allows us to tune in to others and helps us to attune and formulate our life paths.	Orange	Cat
Manawa	Now is the moment of power. All power exists in the present moment. The power of the past is carried forth only by our continued reactions to it. The power of the future cannot influence us until we experience it. The present is where we sow the seeds of the future or reap the harvest of our past.	Yellow	Ox
Aloha	To love is to be happy with (someone or something). The source of all energy is love because it is the vital essence of life and creation. It nourishes the soul, heals the body, and personifies the goodness of creation and of the gods.	Green	Horse
Mana	All power comes from within. The active force of Spirit, which resides within us, is the vital source of our power and essence. It is the vibrant spirit of life that animates all beings and transmutes itself at the moment of death.	Blue	Bear
Pono	Effectiveness is the measure of the truth. All paths of wisdom and methods of action that work are valid. There is no singular truth or way, all systems contain certain keys of enlightenment because it is human nature to progress toward our own consciousness of the universe. Use what works!	Violet	Wolf

like flowers, liquor, or fruit). Ocean Bottles are best utilized when kept on west-facing water altars or in bathrooms. They are a magnificent bath toy when used with caution and provide a wonderful blue ball of etheric waves when left in the sunlight. The activated Mana from the Ocean Bottle can empower and balance emotions as well as promote energy flow and healing. It will give a noticeable charge to any body of water in which it is shaken and can profoundly enhance any water-based meditation. Enjoy!

1 large blue glass bottle
24 cowry shells (preferably from the Pacific Coast)
½ c. white sand
½ c. black sand
1 pinch kelp granules
½ c. Pacific Coast sea salt

Cup the blue bottle in your hands. Take a moment to connect with the base substance of the bottle. Feel the glass react to your own warmth. Tap into the transformation of the sand that formed the glass, seeing the bottle as the will of man. Visualize the manifested heat as it persuaded the granules of earth into a molten form that air whispered into the solid bottle now in your hands. Feel all of the memories of the empty bottle and imagine its journey to you. When you have connected yourself to the bottle, call out to it:

O' Vessel of Earth! Your form is made here for my intent; I call out to you in humble thanks. Swallow this universe and be honored thus as the body of the God. Be that manifest cell of life which regenerates all Mana to its highest form and activates all life in the current of the One Great Essence. Flow freely as an ever-replenished tide upon the shoreline of my soul and awaken the forces of creation, which I shall assemble here within you.

Pour the salt into your right hand, cover with your left hand, and chant the following three times:

Salt of life,
Blood, body, and sea,
Purify the forces of life within me.
Essence of earth,
Crystalline and pure,
Dissolve and coagulate creation here.

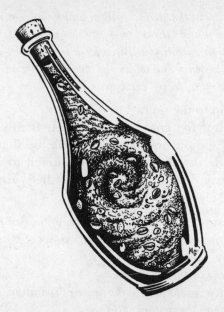

Put the salt in the bottle. Next, pour the black and white sand into bowls. Hold the bowl of black sand in your left hand, and the bowl of white sand in your right. Feel the difference in energy and essence between the two types of sand. Recognize their similarities and polarities and contemplate their origins. Where did each particle of sand begin its journey? Do you hold in your hand all that is left of some great and long lost mountain or cliff or monument of earth? Tap into the essence of earth as the crystalline reality of sand. Call out to it:

> *O' Vital substance of earth! You are weathered and whittled and worn down for me. I call out to you in gratitude for your journey and for the wisdom of all creation, which you bring into this space with you. Oh sweet dust of the stars, fill this place with the perfect balance of that which is and that which is not. Settle into that solid form and be the bed of foundation upon which all creation must be conceived.*

Add the sand to the bottle.

Place the pinch of kelp granules in your hand and feel the vibrant energy of life within them. Visualize the journey of the seaweed as it grew to maturity in water and was dried down and packaged for you to use here in this ritual. Call out to the plant:

O' Vigorous life of the ocean, awaken and know again the breath of animation as you are thrust now into this vessel of life and carry the force of creation within you. Burst forth that essence which is bound up in all of existence and weave the threads of life once more, ever more, further more, let life persist everywhere.

Add the kelp to the bottle.

Finally, gather the cowry shells in your hands and tap into the energy of their journey to you. Feel the life that once sought protection inside the shells and allow yourself to draw out that energy of home and protection. Move the shells around between your hands and chant:

O' Vibrant essence of progression and life, of the sun and security.
I honor your journey to me, I honor the rhythm of the sea.
Here and now I weave the waters of life,
In a vow to the rhythm of the sea.
I pour my prayers into you, in the name of evolution;
I cast them upon the rhythm of the sea.
Awaken here, all the vibrations of the living,
Evolve and quicken the rhythm of the sea.
Tumble in tune, sweet bells of the ocean,
Chiming out the rhythm of the sea.
Roll and journey as the stars in space,
Ringing out the rhythm of the sea.
In your every wave, carry these words of my will,
Upon the rhythm of the sea.
Rise up the life and ring out these prayers,
Be as the tide and the rhythm of the sea.
Life, let the rain of blessings fall,
Swell these waves, both great and small,
Pulsing out the rhythm of the sea.

Place the shells into the bottle. Fill the bottle with water and activate it by shaking it for five or ten minutes. Remember to shake the bottle gently and to treat it always as if it were a tiny, self-contained universe, and thus, a living entity of truly cosmic proportions!

Water-Pouring Rituals for Magic and Therapy

by Janina Renée

There is something meditative about the sight of flowing water and the act of pouring water. Think about this the next time you pour a bath: relax, and gaze at the water cascading out of the faucet (take in the sound, too), and notice what sort of effect that has on you. When you are entranced by the action of streaming water, it is natural to contemplate the purification of mind and body. Water is, of course, one of the great elemental forces, so the act of pouring water is used throughout the world in ceremonies of blessing, healing, purifying, fertility, and nourishing. The archetypal magic of water pouring is even represented in tarot: in the Star card, a maiden's act of pouring water onto the land as well as into a pool suggests revitalizing the energies of nature; and in Temperance, an angel mixes water by pouring it back and forth between two pitchers, again suggesting an energy stream and the need for the right blend of healing energies in our lives.

Libations

One of the most common ritual actions is libation pouring. When using water, "living water" from pure, running streams is preferred. Libations can also be of milk, wine, beer, or any other favored beverage. When it is not convenient to pour the fluid directly on the ground, it is poured into another

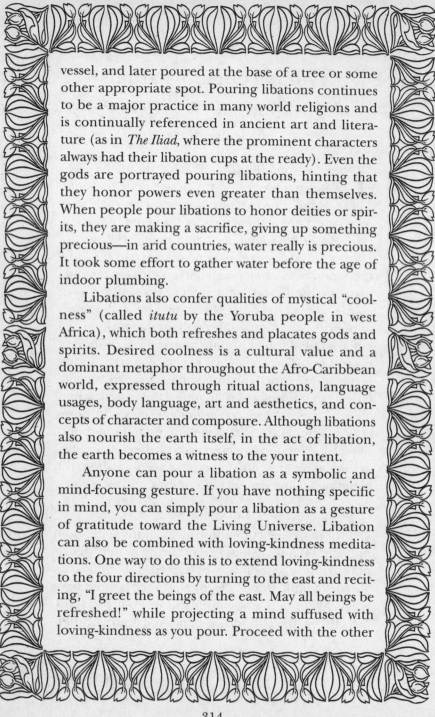

vessel, and later poured at the base of a tree or some other appropriate spot. Pouring libations continues to be a major practice in many world religions and is continually referenced in ancient art and literature (as in *The Iliad*, where the prominent characters always had their libation cups at the ready). Even the gods are portrayed pouring libations, hinting that they honor powers even greater than themselves. When people pour libations to honor deities or spirits, they are making a sacrifice, giving up something precious—in arid countries, water really is precious. It took some effort to gather water before the age of indoor plumbing.

Libations also confer qualities of mystical "coolness" (called *itutu* by the Yoruba people in west Africa), which both refreshes and placates gods and spirits. Desired coolness is a cultural value and a dominant metaphor throughout the Afro-Caribbean world, expressed through ritual actions, language usages, body language, art and aesthetics, and concepts of character and composure. Although libations also nourish the earth itself, in the act of libation, the earth becomes a witness to the your intent.

Anyone can pour a libation as a symbolic and mind-focusing gesture. If you have nothing specific in mind, you can simply pour a libation as a gesture of gratitude toward the Living Universe. Libation can also be combined with loving-kindness meditations. One way to do this is to extend loving-kindness to the four directions by turning to the east and reciting, "I greet the beings of the east. May all beings be refreshed!" while projecting a mind suffused with loving-kindness as you pour. Proceed with the other three directions. In Asia, this would be a form of "making merit" (generating good karma).

Blessings and Healing

In other Asian ceremonies, people may pour water from an ewer into a bowl while listening to monks chanting, or while thinking about one's desire to extend merit to loved ones who have passed away. Indeed, whenever we are engaged in some kind of water pouring, we might remember what Buddha said: even when pouring out the water you use to wash your bowl, if you do it with the wish that it will be of benefit to other beings, you will make merit. Other Asian rituals include gently pouring water over the hands of elders and others to show them respect and wish them good luck, or pouring water over sacred statues. In some Thai marriage rites, water is poured from a conch over the newlyweds' hands to symbolize a harmonious union, or the couple will pour water together. In Japan, water pouring can be part of the rites of grieving.

When used in healing rites, water pouring symbolically washes away disease. For example, the Sumerians poured enchanted water over the head of a person afflicted by headaches, and over other body parts or the whole body for other ailments. In fact, the Sumerian term for doctor was *A-Su* or *asu*, meaning "one who knows water." Because Babylonian magic was big on the use of figurines, it is possible that they may have poured water over figurines as proxy when a sick person couldn't be present. (Conversely, some black magic involved pouring dirty water or other fluids over figurines of the cursed persons.)

Rain Magic

Water-pouring ceremonies are often practiced in the dry season, when water is most scarce, and they have been extensively used in rainmaking magic. The custom of pouring water over special stones, often those with natural indentations, is widespread throughout the world. (One of my uncles had an ancient "rain stone" on his ranch near the Klamath tribe in Oregon.) In India, some villagers sprinkle water over frogs or effigies of frogs as a plea for rain, and some even hold frog weddings in which water sprinkling plays a role. When my area has been having a bit of drought, I have induced rain by setting a malachite frog on a stone by a sprinkler. A ritual gesture for rain can also be a way of inviting revivifying moisture into your personal life when you have been suffering from a dry spell, whether that be in the areas of love, work, creativity, or matters of personal vitality.

Blessing the Earth

Today, many people are participating in earth-honoring rituals, including water-blessing ceremonies inspired by Professor Masuru Emoto's discovery that the inner structure of water droplets responds to our thoughts and words, and that polluted and distressed waters can be revitalized through prayer and ritual action. Thus, in coordinated ceremonies including those by Lake Kiwa in Japan, the Sea of Galilee, the Rhine River, and Onondaga Lake in New York state, people have prayed over water containers, voiced expressions of love and gratitude, and mixed their prayer water into bowls, which were then poured into the larger bodies of water. If you have the opportunity to visit a local body of water, you could scoop some water and bless it by intoning words like, "Waters of [name], you have my love and gratitude. May you have peace and healing." Voice your words vibrantly, and then gently return the blessed water to its source.

Abundance

In addition to the focusing and purifying effect of water pouring, water symbolizes abundance. Think of all of the drops of rain that fall to the ground, and all of the drops of water in the ocean. If you feel you aren't deserving of more good things or other spiritual graces in your life, or if you are held back by a belief in "limited good," a water-pouring action can

also be helpful. Reminiscent of the Star woman's act of drawing and pouring water, and of Louise Hay's well-known suggestion of visualizing yourself by the ocean filling buckets of water in the knowledge that there is more than enough for everybody, you could go down to the shore to scoop and pour water. While so doing, recite affirmations about the give and take in the flow of cosmic energy, such as "All the world's abundance is here for me. There is more than enough for everybody." Scoop and pour until your body/mind tells you the message has been absorbed.

Devising Water-Pouring Rituals

Because water-pouring actions have so many therapeutic possibilities, you might want to devise some water rituals of your own. If you would like to acquire some special vessels for use, you could take inspiration from the older French tarot designs of the Temperance and Star cards, and get one red pitcher and one blue to represent the hot and cold, yin and yang principles. To engage solar and lunar symbolism, use gold and silver vessels. Alternatively, scoops fashioned out of gourds are extensively used in folkways the world over (and gourds are especially suggestive of the fertile female body). There's a lot to choose from, because vessels of different shapes and materials dominate the material culture of magic. As you experiment with water-pouring actions and accessories, you'll find that the creative possibilities are truly inspiring.

Magickal Arts . . .
Not Just for Ritual Anymore!

by Paniteowl

Darkness enfolds our path through the forest as we come together to celebrate another Full Moon ritual. Each of us, in our own way, has prepared for this event. We've brushed out our cloaks, we've polished our circlets, we've taken a ritual bath, and now, as we join our covenmates, we are looking forward to a magickal experience. We know some of our covenmates have been to the ritual site earlier to prepare for this night. The ground is swept, the altar set with candles and flowers, and a side table will soon hold the cakes and ale. All is in readiness as the High Priest and High Priestess take their place in the center of the circle, welcoming all. People clasp hands, and the physical circle is formed. Smiles and glances go around the circle as we renew our friendships and share the strength of our gathering. Softly, our Priestess reminds us to gather our focus by grounding and centering. Each of us feels our connection with the earth as we envision our roots spreading deeply into the soil. We breathe deeply, three cleansing breaths, and take into our bodies the scents of nature. We feel the energy welling up in ourselves, and pass it along to those who stand with us, hands joined, hearts ready to experience the joy of life. As we bring ourselves into spiritual focus, our eyes rise to the shining orb above us, the Full Moon, and she bathes our faces in her light. The circle is ready to enfold us. We are enraptured.

For those who have stood in such a circle, you know my words can't do justice to the euphoria of truly being there. For those who have not yet had the opportunity, please know that as much as you can imagine, the actuality of the circle experience will go far beyond your expectations.

There is so much we learn in circle that it is truly hard to share the experience, yet I feel that this is something we all must do. Why? Well, because I've found so many people who have kept the secrets of the circle locked up within their memories as a separate thing from their everyday lives. At one time, perhaps, it was imperative to keep our rites secret and our teachings locked away from prying eyes. However, in today's world, Witches, Pagans, Wiccans, Heathens, etc., have all begun to open their ranks to those who are truly seeking a new way of connecting with our old gods and goddesses. Even those who don't follow our paths have at least begun to show more than just a tolerance, there is even a respect for our ways. This is a good thing! But it brings its own problems as people become more aware of the practices without realizing the depth of the teaching that goes on in circle. This is not something we do each month, just to get together and run around in the woods. (Though that can be fun!) This is something that influences every facet of our lives. What works so beautifully in circle can also work in our day-to-day lives. Approaching the daily grind with the same attitude we use to approach ritual can greatly benefit our overall spirituality and practice.

Let's go through a few of the ritual preparation basics and apply them to our mundane lives. Let's start with "grounding and centering," and what that does on a spiritual, physical, and emotional level. The first cleansing breath sets you up to experience the future positively. Your expectations are heightened, and physically, you are opening yourself to your surroundings and the possibilities of magickal things. The second breath brings the physical you to a deeper awareness of your environment. Physically, you are trying to sense the earth, above and below. You are truly stepping out of yourself in order to have a different perspective. The third breath triggers the calming sense of being both within and without, and emotionally you are focused on the *now*. This exercise, in preparation for a spiritual experience, brings your physical and emotional realities into a common focus. As the spiritual experience weaves your physical and emotional levels together, you feel whole. You feel prepared. You feel acceptance, and you accept. This is a wonderful state in which to be! Why would we not want to feel "totally together" all of the time? Well, because we forget that we can! We get caught up in the everyday, mundane tasks of living. We let ourselves get scattered while trying to cope with the stresses of our lives. And sometimes, it's simply that we, the teachers, forget to tell you that these bits of ritual are not to be hidden away and only taken out for special occasions—they are methods you can use whenever and wherever you feel the need!

Are magickal practitioners the only ones who know this secret? Of course not! Books have been written, courses developed, and people have made a lot of money teaching others how to relax and become calm. Ever heard of biofeedback? Remember the transcendental meditation fad that swept the nation during the sixties and seventies? Machines have been developed to help people control their breathing, their heart rate, their nerves, their pain tolerance, and a host of other physical and emotional responses. These are simply different techniques or ways of saying, "ground and center!" Self-hypnosis is another method of relieving your stress as you change patterns in your life, such as weight loss or breaking the smoking habit. The next time you get stressed at home, at work, or even while driving, remember to ground and center just as you do when you begin your circle. You'll be surprised how easy it is to capture that feeling of peace and awareness in your regular life.

Now let's look at the practice of preparing ourselves for ritual, and preparing for the ritual itself. We take a ritual bath. We use scents that are pleasing to us and to our deities. We light candles and wash our bodies, but we also wash away the cares of the day, so that we can be truly involved in our circle. We don the appropriate clothing, and we wear jewelry that has significance to us. We prepare to be magickal.

Meanwhile, some of the members are setting up the altar. Paying attention to the placement in relation to the planned circle, the candles and seasonal flowers are arranged in a pleasing way. Tools of the Craft are polished or dusted and placed so that they will be readily available during the ritual. A fire pit may be readied by positioning seasoned wood along with starter scraps of dried leaves and twigs. Yes, it's important to remember to have matches! I know most of us have been in rituals that are not well planned and not well executed. Thank the God and Goddess that the Pagan community has a great sense of humor at these times. We can and do laugh at ourselves, and with others.

But once again, what does the preparation for a ritual teach you about mundane life? Simply that if you live every day as though you were preparing for something magickal to happen, then whatever your day brings will be good for you!

321

As a writer, I have my own ritual before I begin an article. I *think* about what I want to say. This could take me a day or two, or I could struggle with a concept for months. There will come a point when I have to get my notes together and put my ideas on paper (or, these days, on screen). Before I begin to seriously write, I clean off my desk. This is no little task. Everything accumulates on my desk, for I am the financial officer, insurance expert, time-management executive, management coordinator, and head of the mail room. In other words, I'm the Mom! I post reminders for everyone to keep track of their appointments. I know when premiums are due, and bills have to be paid. I also track cash flow and do the taxes for four other family members. All these records and receipts come across my desk. Sometimes they get lost there for a while, but eventually I do file them in their appropriate folders. These things must all be cleared away in order for me to write. So I practice my Craft by incorporating the same attention to preparation as I would use when getting ready for a Full Moon ritual. I get prepared for something magickal to happen when I begin to write. I want that feeling of being focused and grounded in my project. I want this ritual of writing to be a joy for me and not a chore. I want my thoughts to be clear and my words to be strong enough to strike a chord with my readers, but not be so pounding that they don't allow others to take the ideas and work them into their own lifestyles.

It would be wonderful if every day of our lives were as smooth as a well-planned ritual, but that's not the way life works. When we are as prepared as we can be to face the day, we are in a better place to deal with those events of chaos that are beyond our control. Our Craft and our ritual practices are methods of encouraging spirituality, but they also nurture our physical and emotional states of being. Why would we not want to bring our lives into the same balance that we strive for in rituals?

In our rituals, we have wonderful scents surrounding us. We chant, sing, and dance in a celebration of life. We are taught to enter into the circle with a feeling of perfect love and perfect trust. We are taught to participate in the circle with a focus of being in the "here and now, above as below, within as without." These practices should not be limited to the time spent gathered for formal ritual. Although that is wonderful, we truly should be using these teachings every day as we work, play, take care of our family and friends, and live our lives as part of the larger community.

I'm sure each person could think of ways to use other lessons of our Craft to improve the way they deal with their mundane lives. Wouldn't it be wonderful if there were no "mundane" lives? Wouldn't it be great to feel "magickal" all the time? Let's try to remember to ground and center as we greet each day. Let's try to be magickal every day as a way to integrate our spiritual, physical, and emotional aspects into our daily lives. Let us all remember who we are: the people who believe and know for sure that magick is afoot!

Blessed be.

Magickal Jewelry

By Raven Digitalis

Jewelry has long been used in magick. Its most common historical use in magick is protective: to guard against demons, malicious creatures, and adversaries' attacks. With the rise of metallurgy, specifically designed pieces came to be used as magickal amulets. These uses are prevalent in many societies, both magickal and superstitious.

Jewelry is relevant to any genre of magick—from shamanism to ceremonial magick—because many practitioners prefer wearing ritual jewelry in the form of charms, amulets, and talismans. Each piece is a significant reflection of a practitioner's individual callings. Many practitioners go skyclad during rituals, wearing only metal. Metal shimmers and reflects light, becoming important pieces of focus in ritual, especially those held under the shroud of night.

Jewelry can be a stylistic way to display your beliefs and alignments either inside or outside of the ritual circle. Some magickal practitioners choose to eliminate all decorative wear from the body prior to ritual, including jewelry. They believe the pieces detract from the energies raised, inhibiting the natural flow. On the other hand, most occultists feel that if the piece is properly charged, the magickal act is actually emphasized and the raising of energy can be better directed for a specific purpose. This debate goes hand in hand with the ideas of body piercing being either beneficial or detrimental to magickal work. Some believe that when used in ritual, metal is conductive to spiritual vibrations and that simply wearing it presents a suitable image of oneself to the gods and spirits, filled to the brim with sacred symbolism. This is especially beneficial when each piece has been previously charged with magickal intent.

This article examines metal jewelry and the metaphysical associations of metal in particular.

Bigghes

Jewelry reserved solely for ritual and ceremonial purposes are called *bigghes*. This separates ordinary jewelry from sacred jewelry. The term originally referred to a High Priestess' ceremonial jewelry but is now used to refer to any Witch's jewels.

Some choose to hide and physically protect their bigghes outside of the circle in order to ensure that no external energies become attached to the piece. A popular method is to wrap the ornament in cloth, specifically black for protection, or keep it locked up safe and sound. Some people choose to reserve certain jewelry for nocturnal rites and other pieces for diurnal, keeping the jewelry attuned to specific ritualistic energies.

Chinese Mysticism, Taoism & Metal

Spirit is commonly referred to as an individual element in Paganism and Wicca. This recognition places an emphasis on the Divine as the most important aspect of reality. On the Pagan/Wiccan pentacle or pentagram, Spirit is placed at the highest point, understood as supreme because it unifies the elements and seals them all together. Though Paganism recognizes Spirit individually, no separation is seen in the Chinese system between Spirit and the other elements. All intertwine and interconnect perfectly, forming the universe. The existence of Chi is understood as connecting the concept of the physical elements. The recognition of the five Chinese elements came about before humankind drew a strict separation between reality and spirituality. Therefore, it was unnecessary at the time to consider Spirit individually. Some Pagans use the Chinese elements instead of the traditional Pagan ones.

In Paganism, metals first and foremost correspond to the element of earth. In Chinese spiritual systems, the element metal is said to encompass all forms of rock and mineral life. In the Chinese Taoist practice feng shui, metal represents inner strength, determination, and receptivity. Physically, metal expands when heated. This expansion reiterates the energetic receptivity of metal, that is, if one understands physical reality (the metal itself) as a reflection of the spiritual. Within Chinese spiritual systems, metal's energy also dominates the autumnal season and draws energy inward for personal reflection and centering on the sub-conscious mind. In Chinese astrology, metal rules the birth signs Monkey and Rooster as their fixed element. In more detailed Chinese astrology, the element ruling each animal rotates continuously while certain attributions remain fixed, so that each birth year has an additional correspondence. Those ruled by metal tend to be confident, aggressive, and assertive in nature. Metal is said to correspond to the physical body's lungs, which hold the sacred breath of life. This is recognized in Buddhist *vipassana* (breathing or "insight") meditation which, though having originated with early Theravada Buddhism (which is a school of Hinayana or Early Conservative Buddhism), is common in the Chinese Chan (Zen) Buddhist tradition as well. The skin also breathes and is therefore also ruled by metal. The nose and mouth are also included, as they are gateways of the breath. Finally, the large intestine corresponds to metal, as oxygen in the diaphragm regulates abdominal pressure. Deep breathing is essential to keep the blood flowing and the body moving.

In the Chinese alchemical system (akin to Taoism), seven metals are specifically emphasized: iron, copper, silver, tin, gold, mercury, and lead. Each represents a particular stage in the development of humanity. Each corresponds to a planet, having specific astrological correspondences. Planetary associations to metals came about entirely as a result of the development of alchemical sciences. The symbolism of "seven" is reflected in the Western seven-point star called the septagram, and in the traditional Hermetic hexagram, wherein six planets represent each point of the symbol, with the sun resting in the center. The number seven is also significant in the Hindu chakra system as the body contains seven main energetic vortexes.

More Pointers on Magickal Jewelry

When searching for jewelry, or crafting it oneself, one must be mindful of the piece both in a magickal sense and physical sense. Magickal jewelry should be an extension of the practitioner's

internal spiritual being. Not only is a piece's symbolism significant, but its physical origin and placement on the body are of additional importance.

Sadly, the majority of today's jewelry is mass-produced overseas. Most of these pieces are made of tin, pewter, or reconstituted silver. These kinds of metals hold a low concentration of energy, in turn causing them to be more difficult to enchant or imbue with magickal properties. Though the price of "real" metal may be considerably higher than the mass-produced, it is magickally worth it in the long run, not to mention the aesthetic beauty it holds. Naturally handmade pieces hold more sentimental and actual value, even if the wearer does not personally know the creator. Each handmade piece is unique and can both conduct and hold a greater capacity of personal energy.

I strongly believe that jewelry should not be worn nonchalantly. I believe the wearers should have a good amount of knowledge about the symbol they bear and should carry personal sentiments for the piece. Far too many people walk around with flashy symbols completely unaware of their meaning—occult bling, basically.

In addition to having a personal connection to the symbolism of the jewelry, one should always be aware of the reaction it evokes from onlookers. How does the symbol affect other people? What emotions does it have the potential of bringing about in the viewer based on what it might represent to them? Perhaps a Seal of Saturn or Baphomet pendant isn't the best piece to wear to the dentist's office or to a parent-teacher conference. They would, however, be perfect for a Pagan festival or industrial club!

Any item added to the body naturally influences the body's energetic flow. Metals have specific properties that can either inhibit or increase the energetic flow in the area in which it is worn. If a piece is worn near a chakra or bodily energy vortex, effects are sure to follow. The placement of magickal jewelry is definitely of utmost importance.

Rings

Fashioned as a perfect circle, the ring represents eternity, reincarnation, and the cycles of the universe. It acts as a smaller representation of the magician or Witches' sacred circle. Because of the ring's shape, magickal energy flows very well through it when charged. Its smoothness symbolizes the smoothness of dancing life and all its cycles.

The ring has long been associated with love. It is a symbol of unity in modern marriage and handfasting ceremonies, solidifying the connection between two people and the influence of the divine in the ritual. The ring is placed on the third finger of the left hand, which was once believed to have a vein or nerve in it

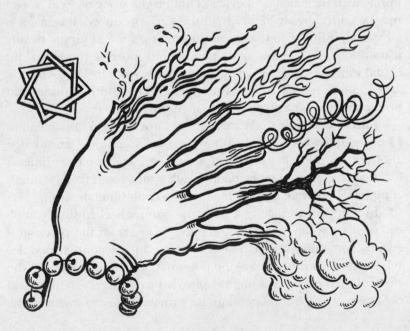

connecting to the heart. This fallacy was believed to be true by the Egyptians, later adopted by the Greeks, and finally by Europeans.

Magickal folk have long worn rings. The famous Babylonian magician King Solomon had a ring called Solomon's Seal, which mythically allowed him to accomplish any task he wished, including controlling demons, genies, and other spirits.

Rings can be magickally imbued with any purpose the wearer desires. Because they sit directly on the flesh, the energy of the charged ring has a constant connection with the body. Rings worn on the projecting hand (the hand you write with) should be imbued with properties you wish to project to others, such as healing, awareness, peace, and so forth. Rings worn on the receiving hand should be imbued with properties you wish to invite into yourself.

For some wearers, the finger on which the ring is worn is of extreme importance. Traditional Hermetic elemental attributions are as such:

Thumb: Water
Pointer: Fire
Middle: Spirit
Ring: Earth
Pinky: Air

Magickal practitioners and Witches can also channel the elements through the fingers when inviting them into ritual space. In some modern traditions, the associations between the ring finger and the thumb are switched. This second configuration actually makes more sense to me, considering that the thumb is more solid or earthy, and the ring finger is more undulant or watery. I do believe that the finger best associated with Spirit is the middle because it's the longest of the five. Think twice before flipping someone off . . . your spirit may be open for anyone to grab!

Necklaces

Necklaces are a part of every culture and are even included in popular myths. A necklace called the *brisingamen* was worn by the goddess Freyja in Norse mythology. The necklace was made of gold, created by dwarfs, and was associated with the magickal ability to bring out the beauty of the wearer. The enchanted necklace was later stolen by the trickster deity Loki—go figure!

Necklaces absolutely surround the wearer with the energies of the piece, melding its energy with that of the wearer constantly throughout the day; this is one reason the jewelry worn should be chosen with care! Necklaces can hang at the throat or heart chakra area. Therefore, the piece works with energies of each: The heart chakra is green in ethereal color and contains the vibratory qualities of love, compassion, empathy, and understanding. The throat chakra is blue, connected to energies of communication and self-worth. The jewelry worn on each chakra point can be attuned directly to these associations or can simply carry its own magickal charge, using these chakra points as an entryway into the energy body.

Bracelets

Fashioned in a circular form, bracelets hold similar properties to rings. Wearing empowered bracelets on each wrist is extremely effective for imbuing the wearer with particular vibrations, either balancing one's energy or attuning it to an intended purpose. For this reason, bracelets are especially good for magick of a self-transformative nature. Bracelets made of stone or of a series of threaded stones can be highly charged with magickal associations that are appropriate to the chosen stone. Metal bracelets carry associations (see the list of metals on pages 332–333), while magnetic bracelets are reserved for a specific energy healing practice called magnotherapy.

Earrings

Ear piercings were once thought to guard against disease, head pain, and "sinful words." This is more in the realm of superstition than magick, but earrings can still carry magickal associations. Because earrings in pairs are oftentimes worn on opposite sides of the head, they may be empowered with balance and equilibrium. Throughout the day, energies bounce from one earring to the other and thus through your head. If enchanted as magickal polarities, earrings can lend an extreme amount of power to the wearer, especially if the symbolism, structure, or content of the pieces are considered.

Crowns

Ceremonial crowns are absolutely gorgeous. They are most common with females because of their historic usage. Women tend to prefer crescent moons on their crown while men tend to prefer pentacles and God-horns in ritual. In traditional Wicca, a coven's Priest and Priestess wear crowns, symbolizing a connection to the gods. Most crowns are made of sterling silver and the well-made ones tend to be fairly pricy. If the Lady chooses to wear her ceremonial crown outside of circle, she best be prepared to live in magickal consciousness the whole day through, standing strong and spiritually aware as a Priestess of the Goddess. Some people wear tiaras and crowns non-ceremonially, for fashion's sake. This is simply for decoration, but as with all jewelry, it may be used to top off a magickal, enchanting outfit.

What Kind of Metal Is It?

I have always seen molded metal (such as jewelry) as corresponding to both the elements earth and fire, regardless of the type of metal. Metal is a natural substance of the earth, which is melted, molded, and formed in a process involving extreme heat from fire in order to take on a shape. The element earth represents strength, grounding, and Gaia-connection. It is the rational and logical portion of the human psyche. Fire represents passion, motivation, and strength. Its flame is a guiding light to spiritual awakening. Beyond the concept of earth-fire connectedness, the various metals also correspond to different elemental properties that distinguish their unique energetic vibrations. Metal jewelry may be worn to draw upon earth and fire alone, or magickally worked upon to fine-tune the specific qualities of the individual metal.

The Witches' athame and sword are metal tools, used to pierce between the worlds and serve as strong energy conduits. Though I may draw earth-fire correlations with physical metal, the magickal blades are ruled under the element air in traditional ceremonial magick, Hermeticism, and Wicca. This association makes sense, as blades are used in ritual to project intention, command forces, and direct energies; the force of will behind it can easily align with the element air.

The following is a list of generally recognized associations with various types of metals. I invite readers to reference this list when purchasing or creating magickal metallic jewelry.

Brass: Deflecting harm, fire magick, healing, love, luck, mental powers, money, protection. See also Copper.

Bronze: See Copper and Tin.

Copper: Amplifying energy, balance, beauty, calming, clarity, compassion, conducting energy, confidence, cooperation, creativity, divination, emotions, empathy, fire magick, friendship, harmony, healing, intuition, love, luck, lust, money, motivation, newness, passion, physical health, pleasure, preventing illness, prosperity, psychic development, sexuality, sociability, strengthening spells, sustenance, unity.

Gold: Acceptance, affirmation, art, assertion, balance, calming, courage, creativity, dedication, direction, energy, esteem, god invocation, guidance, happiness, healing, health, individuality, inspiration, life choices, male mysteries, mental powers, money, power, prosperity, protection, purification, realization, rebirth, satisfaction, seasonal connectedness, self-awareness, spiritual direction, strength, study, success, wisdom.

Iron: Action, aggression, balance, change, chaos, courage, cursing, deflecting harm, determination, emotional control, extraterrestrial communication, faerie magick, facing challenges, grounding, healing, instincts, justice, motivation, physical health, protection, pursuance, releasing anger, sexuality, strength, success, wealth, willpower.

Lead: Ambition, banishing, binding, boundaries, business, change, chaos, cleansing, cursing, death magick, deflecting harm, discipline, divination, exorcism, fear-based issues, freedom, grounding, habit breaking, healing, introspection, introversion, laws, magickal petitions, materialism, meditation, necromancy, new beginnings, past-life regression, protection, receiving, recurring cycles, releasing, restrictions and freedoms, self-control, stability, strengthening spells, thaumaturgy, transformation, wishes.

Pewter: See Copper and Tin.

Platinum: Abundance, balance, channeling, communication, friendship, growth, health, hope, intuition, love, materialism, memory, mental powers, money, optimism, psychic powers, sustenance, transformation, upperworld communication. See also Iron.

Silver: Acceptance, alignment, art, astral projection, balance, beauty, care, communication, dance, divination, dreaming, eloquence, empathy, female mysteries, fertility, gardening, goddess invocation, guidance, healing, hope, inspiration, intuition, love, lunar attunement, meditation, menstrual attunement, money, night magick, nourishment, nurturing, optimism, peace, personality, prosperity, protection, psychic powers, purity, self-reflection, sensitivity, study, travel, wealth.

Steel: Deflecting harm, divination, dream protection, grounding, healing, protection, stability. See also Iron.

Tin: Abundance, balance, creativity, divination, expansiveness, generosity, growth, healing, health, hope, ideas, intuition, justice, learning, love, luck, mental powers, money, opportunities, philosophy, prosperity, spiritual awareness, success, travel, wisdom.

The Weavers of Destiny

by Nancy V. Bennett

Many people believe that our fate is in our own hands, that we can control our final destiny. But what if it was really woven by a power greater than our own? Throughout time, and in different cultures, these weavers of destiny went by many names. So can we change the fabric of our own history? Or are the threads of our lives already intertwined too tightly? Oh what a tangled web we weave!

The Three Sisters of Fate

There once lived three sisters who had the upper hand on the future. Clotho spun the thread of life, Lachesis measured the thread, and Atropos cut the thread, deciding when a life would end.

The Three Sisters of Fate were said to be the children of Erebus and Nyx, though some believe their parents were Zeus and Themis. Still others claimed their parents were Kronus and Nyx, or even Oceanus and Gaia. Perhaps this last ancient set of parents would be the most likely, as the three sisters held the ultimate power not only over mortal lives, but over those of the gods as well.

The sisters were often pictured as old and lame hags dressed all in white. In their home were the deeds and life spans of all people, carved on tablets of brass and iron. It was from this information that they decided who should die, and when. Though they held the ultimate power, the sisters could be tricked.

When Prince Mealeger was born, he was visited by the three sisters. They told his mother that his life would be over once the log on the fire has been burned to ash. Hearing the news, the mother waited until they left, then snatched up the log and hid it in a chest. Her son lived, but later became a heartache to his mother. After he murdered his uncles, the mother retrieved the log and burned it, allowing his fate to finally be realized.

Apollo also wanted to ensure the survival of his good friend and shepherd, Admetus, so he got the Sisters of Fate drunk. While under the effects of wine, the sisters agreed that at the hour of his death, he would be spared if a family member agreed to die in his place. When the time came for his death, both his parents refused to take his place, and so his wife nobly gave up her life.

When Admetus' friend Hercules found out about her sacrifice, he journeyed to Hades to have her released. As she had not been a blood relation of Admetus, she was allowed to leave. The three sisters never again allowed themselves to be swayed by a handsome god bearing drink.

Grandmother Spider and Mokosh

How old is your grandmother? How wise and resourceful is she? Grandmother Spider of the First Nations people is an ageless entity who existed at the beginning of time, waiting for the universe to waken. When the people emerged, she attached a cord of her silk to each one, so that they would know her love and her protection. She is not only a weaver of life, but also a great teacher.

The Choctaw people also credit her with bringing fire to the earth. Many years ago, it was cold and dark, and the animals gathered together to see who could steal fire from the home of Tawa, the sun god. Many animals tried, including the buzzard, and the possum. They both failed, and finally Grandmother Spider was allowed to try.

She was so small and insignificant that Tawa did not see her as a threat. She spun a web up to the heavens to catch the fire and snatched it from under his nose, hiding it away in her cooking pot. Quickly she climbed back down with her pot. When the animals did not see the fire, they thought she had failed too, and they chided her. She then opened her pot and the fire arose from it.

Despite her age, she accomplished what other larger (and self-absorbed) entities had failed to do. In the Cherokee version of the story, Grandmother Spider brings the sun to earth.

In an interesting parallel to this First Nations myth, another goddess emerged for the people of Russia. She was known as Mokosh, one of the few goddesses in that part of the world to still be remembered. Mokosh spun the threads of a person's life and also affected the cycle of crops, health, and livestock. Later she became "Christianized" into St. Parasceve.

I am often puzzled by the way that many older people are disregarded in society. I am reminded of Grandmother Spider and Mokosh when I look back at the craft women who have taught me many things: my grandmother, who taught me sewing; my mother, who taught me to knit; and finally my sister, who taught me intricate bead work. Myth and legend shows us that these venerated women are often in control of our destiny and should be honored!

Hecate of the Crossroads

And finally we look at a rather dark weaver, Hecate. One of the oldest goddesses, Hecate was attuned to night and to the things that lay beyond the dark fold. Women who ventured out into the unknown would say a prayer to this ancient one.

The meeting of three roads were sometimes marked with masks in Hecate's honor, and offerings were left there for her counsel and to feed the newly departed.

Seek her counsel, but be forewarned: Like an all-knowing mother, Hecate will not coddle you. If you've brought about your own problems, expect no mercy from her. Still, Hecate can and will help you find a solution if you look deep into yourself and admit your wrongs.

Hecate is also a caring goddess who often took newly departed souls back to earth to visit when they were having trouble adjusting to the afterlife. She also helped Demeter to search for her daughter Persephone when Persephone was carried off by Hades. When Persephone had to spend half her year in the dark underworld, Hecate served as a surrogate mother and friend, consoling and advising her.

Hecate was often (and still is) invoked with the phrase "weaver of life." Though no actual weaving is attributed to her, she holds the secrets of our destiny, is with us when the final cord is cut, and takes us by the hand to lead us into the underworld. Without Hecate along on this new thread of our lives, it would a lonely and troubling journey.

For Further Study

Farrar, Janet and Stewart Farrar. *The Witches' Goddess.* Washington, DC: Phoenix Publishing, 1987

Conway, D. J. *Maiden, Mother, Crone: The Myth and Reality of the Triple Goddess.* St. Paul, MN: Llewellyn, 1996.

Internet

Hunter, James. "Mealeager." Encyclopedia Mythica. http://www.pantheon.org/articles/m/meleager.html

Lady Hecate. "Invocations to Hecate." Hecate's Cauldron. www.hecatescauldron.org/Invocation%20to %20Hecate.htm

StonE Productions "Native Lore: Grandmother Spider Steals the Fire." www.ilhawaii.net/~stony/lore120.html

Ti, Taino. "Grandmother Spider and the Web of Life." Weed Wanderings with Susun Weed. www.susunweed .com/herbal_ezine/September05/goddess.htm

Turnbull, Sharon, and Liz and Sarah Turnbull. "Hecate, Greek Goddess of The Crossroads." Goddess Gift. www.goddessgift.com/goddess-myths/greek_goddess_ hecate.htm

Wilcox, S. Lynne. "Grandmother Spider, Connecting all Things."*Preventing Chronic Disease.* www.pubmed central.nih.gov/articlerender.fcgi?artid=1832128

Mermaids: Swimming in the Realms of Wonder

by Gail Wood

What is it about the Mermaid that enchants us so? She calls to us and we long to see her and hear her beautiful song. The waves of the ocean pull at us, moving us to seek the strange creatures that dwell there. We see glimpses of mysterious play in splashes, in the foam, and in the whirlpools. We feel her and catch glimpses of her out of the corner of our eye as she teases us to find her and play with her.

Many of the world's cultures, tribes, clans, and people have stories of mermaids; various peoples of the world told many stories about the women who live in the sea. The stories continue into our twenty-first-century psyche and we find mermaids in our cartoons, movies, coloring books, television, and novels. The stories show the infinite variety of women living in water from the smallest gossamer drop of rain to the huge vastness of the oceans. These women of the sea are strong, beautiful, mysterious, beguiling, and as unknowable as the sea herself. The stories tell us she is independent, self-contained, and able to determine her own fate. She can fulfill dreams, break hearts, and bring mystery and magic to earthbound and landlocked humans. The mermaid on land is filled with an unspoken underlying sadness; she possesses a longing and sense that something dear is missing or lost.

The first ancestor of the mermaid is male, a story from a Babylonian fragment written by Berosus the Chaldean, a priest and astronomer. He told the story of Oannes, the Babylonian fish god, with the body of an animal and the reasoning power of a human. Oannes rose each day from the waves and journeyed across the sky, settling at the end of the day back into the ocean. Female mermaid ancestry has been traced to the Semitic moon goddess, Atergatis or Dirceto. She was depicted with fish extremities as she arose from the sea each night and journeyed across the night sky, returning at dawn to the waves. Mermaids have a long association with the sun and the moon.

The Greeks wrote of mermaids and told stories of the sirens, the alluring and dangerous water women whose song lured sailors to their deaths upon the rocky shores. The Roman writer and naturalist, Pliny the Elder, reported mermaids in his *Natural History* and through the ages, mermaids were analyzed in bestiaries and natural histories. The medieval folk called her "mer-mayde," literally, "the maid of the sea." During the Middle Ages, the mermaid was displayed in churches as a way to bring an illiterate, Pagan community into the church.

Even with the growing evidence of scientific inquiry, belief in mermaids persisted into modern times. Enterprising carnival and circus showmen displayed stuffed mermaids in their sideshows and told stories of sightings. For nineteenth-century folk, the mermaid tapped into their obsession with the princess of medieval chivalry and their fear of the modern temptress. In a century of sexual repression, frustration was expressed in a fixation on the sexuality of the mermaid. With her foreign and animal nether body submerged in the flowing, magical waters of the sea, the mermaid was a figure of sexuality and desire, unattainable, carnal, and tempting. She was alluring, mysterious, sensual, beautiful, and enticing. She beckoned, she called, she sang, asking men to act on their longings and desires.

It is only in the recent century that our belief in the existence of the mermaid has faltered. Even so, she still is alive in our imaginations and in our souls. She connects us to the life force of water and the regenerative powers of our psyche; for we are water just as surely as the mermaid lives in water. Our bodies are 60 percent water, having been carried for nine months in a world of 90 percent water. As we age, we lose the water in our bodies and by old age we are less than 50 percent water. Perhaps that is why we often lose our sense of wonder and belief as we age. Water is the transporter of magic, so when we lose water, we lose our sense of the possibility of wonder.

Water connects us to our subconscious, to our dreams, and to our souls. Water transports and transforms emotions. Water can engulf us and drown us; water can cleanse us of those things that keep us from knowing out truest, highest, most magical selves. Of all the elements, water has a unique ability to express our sorrows through our tears and to soothe us in its buoyant transformative waves. Water is duality and contradiction. Duality because it can heal and cleanse; contradictory because it both sustains life and destroys life.

The mermaid lives in the vastness of the oceans, something that is still unconquered to this day. There are dark and deep caverns that remain unexplored by humans, and our imaginations tell us that the mermaid has visited and lived everywhere under the sea. She is at home in the mysterious depths and survives every horrendous storm. Her ability to navigate the worlds of water and storms are supernatural and superb, all the while she is beautiful and alluring.

Mermaids are often depicted combing their hair and most often the stories tell of a beautiful young female. She's beautiful to those who behold her and she's lovely in her own eyes. In our society, with its mixed messages about definitions of beauty, a mermaid who accepts and celebrates her own beauty is a potent image both to those who desire her and to those who emulate her.

Another legend surrounding mermaids, sirens, and other sea creatures involves treasure. As they lure sailors and ships to the shore with their alluring and powerful song, sirens cause ships to wreck upon the rocks along the shores. The humans may lose their lives, but more assuredly, they lose the riches carried in their vessels. This loot slowly sinks in the water and is gathered up by the mermaids and stored in mysterious treasure chests beneath the sea. Pearls, diamonds, and coins, as well as silver and gold objects, are taken as prizes by these sea-folk. To what end is not clear. Stories abound of mermaids adorned with the jewels of lost ships, and sometimes enterprising men are rewarded with the restoration of these riches.

So what does the mermaid mean to the modern-day Pagan, Witch, and magical worker? What is her magic for us? Mermaids move between the worlds of water and land and they are shape shifters. Mermaids are a call to transformation, to exploration, and to moving with ease in all the worlds. She calls us to be at home in our own world, the worlds of shifting tides and storms, and the worlds of wonder. She teaches us to marvel at everything we know and see, and to be in awe of everything. She calls us to beauty and power, and she teaches us to sing our songs.

She speaks to us through the goddesses and we find her in several goddesses across cultures, and there are even more goddesses associated all the waters of the world. The ancient Greeks classified some of the sea maidens as Nereids, the fifty daughters of the Titans, Nereus and Doris. The Nereids lived in the inland seas of the Mediterranean and the Aegean while the Oceanids lived in the worldwide seas. Yemaya is an African mother goddess of the Yoruba people of Nigeria. She traveled to the Americas during the African diaspora and is still venerated in many of the Africana traditions as a sea goddess and patroness of people surviving a shipwreck. Mami Wata is an African water-spirit or goddess who is often invoked for beauty and wealth. The Roman goddess Venus and her Greek counterpart, Aphrodite, are also associated with the seas and oceans, since she was born fully grown, emerging beautifully from the waves. The mermaid is as alive and well as the Goddess. Like the mermaid who calls us to beauty and the embodiment of our physical selves, the Goddess calls us to meet her in her mermaid form.

Mermaid Meditation

We can meet Mermaid in sacred space and travel with her into her realms. We do this through meditation, journeywork, and ritual. In preparation, you may want to bathe in warm water while contemplating the magical powers of water and understanding how much of you already is water. Eat lightly, perhaps some seafood, so you are not distracted by hunger, but not overfed and lethargic.

Cleanse your space as you usually do. Create an altar in honor of the seas and the ocean. Use altar clothes of blues, greens, and grays, topped with a lacy white cloth reminiscent of the foam on the waters' surface. Use shells and sand to represent the ocean.

You may want to use seawater in your chalice. You can create seawater by combining sea salt with warm water. Soothe your soul with music that has the sounds of the sea.

Center and ground yourself in the rhythms of the waves hitting the shore. Feel the rhythm as part of your being. Then cast the circle, call in the directions, and call in deity as is your practice.

Once your sacred space is prepared and your circle is cast in the way you want, you are ready for the meditation. Take a deep breath and feel the pull of the ocean's tides in your body. Breathe deeply and feel the rhythm of the waves as they hit the shore. Hear the waves and smell the salt-tinged ocean breezes. Breathe deeply and feel the deep, eternal connection of land and sea. Breathe deeply and feel the ebb and flow of the sea.

Find yourself standing on a beach in the middle of the night. The Full Moon hangs above the world, illuminating the shore and the water. Breathe deeply and look around to notice all you can about the land behind you and to your left and your right. As you are looking and discovering, you hear musical notes of a song float on the air. You are beguiled and delighted and you look

around for the source of the music. Out across the water, you see rocks and notice there are women sitting on the rocks. No, wait, they are mermaids. They are singing and splashing in the water.

One of them notices you, and she calls to you. She calls you a special name known only to her and to you. She reaches out her hand and calls you to come to her. You wade into the water, drawing in your breath at its coolness and reveling in its refreshing feel on your skin as you immerse yourself. You feel the water move silkily over your body and you smell the wonderful scent of saltwater. You taste a little in your mouth as you easily swim out to the rocks. With each stroke, you get closer and the song gets lovelier and more personal. You reach the rocks and you are greeted by all the mermaids there.

As you reach the rocks, the mermaid who called you reaches down and pulls you up on the rocks. She tells you her name and teaches you a song. As you learn this song, she starts to comb your hair. All the other mermaids are laughing and telling you their secrets. Wisdom is eagerly given and gladly received. You happily learn from them.

When you have learned the song, the mermaid asks you to sing it to her, as she shows you your own image in her mirror. As you sing, she tells you about your personal beauty and your glorious being. She speaks of the wisdom of body, water, and loveliness. You find yourself shedding all your inhibitions and self-criticisms as you listen. When she is done, she places her hands on your shoulders and looks deep into your eyes. She speaks a final few words of wisdom and then uses her hand to push the words of beauty, power, and strength into your being. "You are beauty," she says to you. "Remember this mantra, 'I am beauty.'" Then she takes your hand and asks, "Are you ready to answer the call to transformation?"

When you nod yes, she splashes into the water and pulls you along with her. You feel the exhilarating freshness of the water against your skin and, as you continue to breathe, you realize you are changing. Your body is shifting into the shape of the mermaid. You feel your legs fuse together and become unified. You feel your body freed from the restrictions of clothes and foundation garments as the water swirls sensually around all your skin. You notice that your lower body is covered with beautiful scales that shine and flash as the water moves.

Your hair flows freely around you and it is the beautiful adornment you always craved. Your mermaid companion urges you to move downward into the water. You glory in the strong movement of your body as you swim, down, down, and downward still. You find yourself exploring the wonders of the sea. You see fantastic creatures and colors even as the sunlight completely disappears and you are in the deep, dark sea.

The darkness does not scare you as it envelops you completely. Your companion is near and you sense her compassion and support. You move forward in the darkness, guided by your inner intuitive sense. You finally come to the bottom of the sea, and you swim along this submerged place until you come to the opening of a cavern. You move toward it and know that you are meant to go inside. You stop there and wait for your companion. She says to you, "Farewell, my friend, from this point you journey alone. Be strong in your beauty and hold fast to your power. You will find what you seek."

You move into the cavern. You are again surrounded by many creatures of the deepest part of the ocean, some never recorded by people on the land. Some greet you and some ignore you. After moving through the caverns, you come to a large room within this cave beneath the surface. You are drawn to enter and you swim forward. Within the room, you see a woman seated on a couch of living coral before a low table. You move forward to sit across from her. She is a large woman, a mermaid of eternal age and wisdom. In her eyes, you see the wisdom of all the waters of the world, most especially of the seas. She captures the attention of all your senses as she looks deep into your eyes and speaks.

"I am the Ancient Mother of the Sea," she tells you, "and I am here to tell you of your life and of the treasures you hold inside you." She moves her hand across the table and it becomes a large scrying mirror. The mists swirl and then clarify as the mirror reflects the issues that occupy your mind and spirit at this time in your life. You look and listen as she tells you the information and wisdom you need to hear. You will remember as you listen with an open heart and soul. All your joys and sorrows are shown to you. The things that cause you happiness and the things that cause you to despair are revealed to you.

When you have looked your fill, she moves her hand across the mirror and the mists cover it again. "Look again," she says. "This time see what you need to know most at this time." She moves her hand across the mirror again and you look deeply into what is revealed there. You set aside any doubts you may have as you look once again in the mirror. Revealed there in the depths, you find that bit of wisdom you can most use right now.

At last, she calls you back and is now seated next to you. The Ancient Mother folds you into her embrace. You feel her strength, compassion, and mercy as you rest in her arms. She takes your hand and leads you to an enormous treasure chest. She opens it up and reveals many glorious treasures inside. She reaches in, pulls one out and hands it to you. You take it with thanks, as she says, "This is a talisman of your journey today. Keep it in your soul as a reminder of the work you have done and the work you must now do. Now go with my blessings. It is a joy, my child, and you may return to me again. You now know the way." You hold the treasure in your hand and take a deep breath as you find yourself back in this dimension of existence.

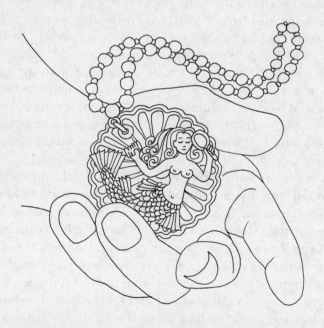

Take some time to ground and center. Be sure to record the wisdom of your journey by writing or drawing. You will find that your talisman will continue to manifest in your life as you seek the wisdom of the mermaid, she who continues to exist in the other worlds we explore as seekers of wonder. She connects us to the wild and the untamable. She reminds us that we are connected to the realms of mystery and power; she calls us to beauty and mystery. She swims into our soul bringing us wisdom and marvelous knowledge. Mermaid lives in water and because we are water, she lives in us. She reminds us that we are the mystery of the waters and the moon among the stars.

Making a Magical Healing Glove

by Suzanne Ress

One day, a few years ago, while carefully studying an antique cotton glove that had belonged to my great aunt, I had the sudden yearning to try making a glove myself. I kept this yearning secret for a few days, letting it mature into a complete idea. I realized what I wanted to make was a *magical* glove.

Because gloves are used to clothe, protect, or decorate the hands, they easily absorb whatever spiritual vibrations are passing through our hands. If made, charged, and applied correctly, gloves can become very powerful tools for magic.

Our hands are what make us human, and not only because we can fashion tools with them, but because we use them to communicate in many ways that we cannot with words. Our hands can convey negative emotion and negative spirit, as in a clenched fist, slap, or rude gesture, but these expressions represent a withdrawal of energy, rather than an expansion— think about how a clenched fist always feels cold.

Our true power, and hence, our true magic, comes from expanding our individual vital force. This is something that has been done via the hands for as long as we have been human. People still use the handshake—pressing their palms together to exchange life energy—to seal a deal or make an agreement. The first physical touch between lovers or would-be lovers is holding hands or placing a hand on the knee, hair, or face of one's partner, exchanging energy and signifying trust.

Traditionally, the energy flowing through the palms of our hands has been put to its greatest use in healing practices. The symbol of a human hand, palm forward, is universally recognized to mean peace and healing. One of the earliest known therapeutic systems to use the healing power of hands is the ancient Japanese Reiki technique. Reiki masters use the palms of their hands as conduits of the universal life force, which must flow easily and unhindered throughout and around each individual. Blockages in this life-force energy are what allegedly cause illness of any kind. A trained Reiki master uses hand movements above the patient's body, and sometimes light massage, to unblock the flow.

Some Christian spiritual traditions use the laying on of hands to heal a person who is unwell, with a remarkable rate of success. Instinctively, mothers place a healing palm upon their sick child's hurt or ill part, and everyone who recalls being a sick child can attest that Mother's (or Father's) hands do make everything feel better. The touch of human hands seems especially magical when used to heal animals, both domestic and wild.

Not only the palm of the hand, but the points of each finger can transmit powerful amounts of life energy as well. When the hand is put into a glove for reasons other than protection (from cold, harsh chemicals, thorns, germs, garden soil, etc.), the energy naturally flowing out of the palm and fingertips is filtered, according to the color, fabric, and intention of the glove.

For many years, up until the early 1960s, properly turned-out women and girls wore white or ivory cotton gloves to church. The idea was to prevent a lady's hands from coming into direct contact with impurities, but the white gloves also made a lady's touch seem to transmit goodness, peace, and serenity.

On the other hand, when a Hollywood starlet shows up to an award ceremony wearing full arm-length black satin gloves, the image she projects is one of sexual power, elegance, and perhaps a little bit of evil.

Gloves are often given as gifts signifying love or friendship, and wearing someone else's gloves gives one the feeling of "walking in that person's shoes," even more so than wearing their actual shoes!

Preparing for the Glove

When I visualized the magic glove I wanted to make, I saw it as a powerful tool for healing. At the time, I was head Witch in a small coven that met several times a month. Although there was no immediate known need for a powerful healing tool, I decided to go ahead and follow my intuitive idea to make a magic healing glove.

The idea behind making a magic healing glove is that, because it is handmade, custom-sized, consecrated, and super-infused with healing power during a group or solitary Full Moon rite, it will contain and transmit healing powers to a much greater degree than a bare hand.

The color of the glove is important, as is the material you select. The best colors for healing are in the blue to violet range, although there are people who feel strongly that green or white are the best healing colors. The color you use is really up to you, of course. What's important is that the color conveys a sense of peace and well-being. For my glove, I chose a pale, silvery shade of blue.

The type of material you select should have some stretch to it or the glove will be very difficult to put on and take off. Finely knit fabrics, especially those with a velvety finish, or woven fabrics with a touch of lycra will work well. You won't need much! Check your rag or scrap bag, consider recycling outdated or discarded clothing, or shop the remnants section of the fabric store. If you buy new fabric from a bolt, buy just one-quarter of a yard. There will still be a lot left over, but you will need this amount for the glove's width.

To make a pattern for your glove, simply trace your left hand on a piece of paper, making sure the lines do not come too close to your fingers. Keep the pencil vertical as you trace. Then redraw the line, adding about one-third inch all around—on both sides of each finger, thumb, and both sides of the palm.

You can make a short, hand-only glove; a glove that covers your wrist; or a "gauntlet" glove that goes about halfway to your elbow. Any longer than this and the glove becomes more difficult to don and remove without the benefit of buttons, hooks, or snaps. If you want your glove to extend halfway to your elbow, trace both sides of your arm on the paper to that length, and then add about an inch width on each side of the wrist and arm.

Sewing the Glove

Cut out the paper pattern of your hand (and arm, if needed). Fold your fabric, right sides facing together, and pin the paper pattern securely to both thicknesses of fabric. If you have pinking shears, use them to cut the fabric out along the lines of the pattern. Otherwise, use any good sharp pair of scissors.

Find thread that closely matches the color of the fabric. Keeping the right sides of the fabric together, hand sew the two sides together with small straight or running stitches, as close to the outer edge of the fabric as possible. Sew from one side of the wrist or arm; up the side of the hand; up, down, and between each finger; and down the other side of the hand to the other side of the wrist or arm. Remember to leave the wrist or arm opening unsewn! Once you have finished sewing, go back again, in the other direction, sewing over the previous stitches.

All the while you are handling and sewing the glove, you should be thinking positive, healing thoughts, and focusing on the ultimate purpose of the completed glove.

When you have finished sewing two times around the glove, sew it one more time, using whip stitches (also called a blanket stitch) to bind the raw edges of the fabric and add extra strength.

Now, using the eraser end of a pencil and a blunt-edged pair of tweezers, carefully turn the entire glove right-side out, and, very gently, try it on your left hand. Hopefully it will fit . . . like a glove!

Now, the glove may be decorated in any way that suits your desire, fancy or plain. Fringes on the inner side of the wrist, if you have made a gauntlet glove, are beautiful, and these can be made from dyed ostrich feathers, ready-made satin drapery fringe, yarn, embroidery floss, hair clippings, strips of fabric, or a series of tassels or braids. I used lavender-dyed ostrich plumes on my glove's wrist.

The back of the glove's hand, and the backs and points of the glove's fingers can also be decorated, but leave the palm and the fingertips plain.

Use your imagination when deciding how to decorate your glove. Just about anything you can think of will work—buttons, sequins, beads, feathers, ribbons, dried seeds, embroidery, hair, yarn, metallic threads or wires, tiny crystals, metal, wood or plastic charms, puffs of tulle, felt shapes, and on and on. Be certain that the colors and intent of the materials you use as decorations are all healthful and peace-inducing. Some excellent designs for healing are the counter-clockwise spiral, a miniature hand, five-pointed stars, heart shapes, oval or round shapes, running water and flame shapes, bees, harps, and unicorns. These are just suggestions; whatever feels right to you probably is, so go with it.

On the back of my glove, I sewed a large counterclockwise spiral in blue sequins. Onto each finger, where the tip of the fingernail would be, I sewed a tiny circle of silver beads. These decorations completed my glove, but I can easily visualize much more elaborate and much simpler gloves.

Once you are satisfied with your creation, find, sew, or buy a small black drawstring bag to hold your glove when you are not using it. It should be kept hidden somewhere it will not be disturbed, preferably with your other magical tools.

Consecrating and Charging

Consecrating and charging of the glove must be done on the night of a Full Moon, when the sky is clear and the moon's rays strong. If you are a member of a coven or magical or healing group, or if you have several or even a few or one sympathetic and like-minded friends, meet with them during the Full Moon to fix the powers of the magic healing glove. If you are a hedge Witch or a solitary worker, the glove can still be consecrated and charged, but may not, depending on many factors, make as powerful a tool. Still, it will generate more power for the healer than a simple bare hand.

You will need to prepare a small dish of saltwater, a small dish of sand, a white candle, and a branch of dried rosemary on a charcoal block or firebrick.

Find a clearing in the woods or in an open field where you are certain not to be seen, and where the moon is clearly visible as it rises, so that its cool and soothing white light will illuminate your ceremony and the glove. On the night of the Full Moon, cast a circle there. Enclose yourselves by moving counterclockwise, faster and faster, to raise up a protective wall of aura light. Everyone should then sit upon the ground, and the dishes of water and sand and the candle and herb should be placed in the center of the circle. Around these objects, trace a pentagram using a silver knife with a white handle. Light the candle and the rosemary branch, and place the glove, now taken out of its protective pouch, in the center of the pentagram, laying it spread out with the palm up.

Have everyone join hands, and with eyes on the glove, chant the following words in unison, as many times as is felt necessary:

A
AB
ABA
ABAN
ABANA
ABANAX
ABANAXO
ABANAXON

Visualize the light of the moon pouring increasing amounts of healing power into the glove as these words are chanted. You, the maker of the glove, will take the glove in your left hand and kiss each fingertip twice, the center of the palm once, and then carefully slip it onto your hand.

With each finger lightly touch the sand and just the surface of the saltwater, pass each fingertip and the palm through the rosemary smoke, and over the candle's light, being careful not to go too close to the flame. Speak these words:

Earth, sea, air, and fire, all
Work together in me to heal.

When this is done, you can remove the glove from your hand and pass it to the person on your right, who shall take the glove with their left hand and repeat the same ceremony. Each person in the circle should do the same, and if the glove does not fit someone, perform the ceremony by holding the glove to the left hand with the right hand. When the glove returns again to you, roll it up and place it back into its black pouch. The candle can be extinguished and the circle closed.

The powers of your magic healing glove will be at their peak when the moon is full. A simple laying on of the gloved hand or very gentle massage of afflicted areas proves most effective for healing. The glove can be used on oneself or other people or animals, at night or during daylight hours, but it must never be worn by anyone other than those who consecrated it.

Start New Holiday Traditions with Our *Sabbats Almanac!*

New this year is *Llewellyn's Sabbats Almanac*—an essential resource for celebrating the eight sacred Wiccan holidays. From rituals and rites to recipes and crafts, you'll discover unique and fresh ways to make the most of each Sabbat.

Silver RavenWolf, Ellen Dugan, Deborah Blake, and other popular authors offer their own spin on honoring the Wheel of the Year. Rediscover the fundamentals of each fesitval. Try new rituals and learn about historic folk rites. Transform these occasions into fun-filled family celebrations that also remind us of our indelible connection to the earth.

Also featured are astrological influences to help you plan Sabbat rituals and celebrations according to cosmic energies.

LLEWELLYN'S SABBATS ALMANAC
Samhain 2009 to Mabon 2010
312 pp. • 5¼ × 8
ISBN 978-0-7387-1496-7 • U.S. $12.99 Can. $14.95
To order call 1-877-NEW-WRLD

Get Your Daily Dose of Magical Spells

Give every day a magical lift with a spell from *Llewellyn's Witches' Spell-A-Day Almanac*. Elizabeth Barrette, Ellen Dugan, Raven Digitalis, and other Wiccan experts offer spells for every occasion—all easy to use with minimal supplies. Each spell is categorized by purpose: health, love, money, protection, and more. You'll also find recipes, rituals, and meditations to fortify your daily practice.

Perfect for beginning spellcaster, this annual spellbook gives advice on the best time, place, and implements for performing each spell. Astrological data is included for those who wish to boost their magic with planetary energy.

LLEWELLYN'S 2010
WITCHES' SPELL-A-DAY ALMANAC

264 pp. • 5¼ × 8

ISBN 978-0-7387-0696-2 • U.S. $9.99 Can. $11.50

To order call 1-877-NEW-WRLD